FROM THE BRINK

FROM THE BRINK

Experiences of the Void from a
Depth Psychology Perspective

Paul W. Ashton

KARNAC

First published in 2007 by
Karnac Books Ltd
118 Finchley Road
London NW3 5HT

British Library Cataloguing in Publication Data
A C.I.P. for this book is available from the British Library

ISBN-13: 978-1-85575-444-7

Edited, designed, and produced by Florence Production Ltd
www.florenceproduction.co.uk

Printed in Great Britain

www.karnacbooks.com

CONTENTS

ACKNOWLEDGEMENTS   xi
ABOUT THE AUTHOR   xiii

Introduction   1

THE TERRITORY   5

1   On the territory of the void   7
     In practice   13
     Void language   14
     Reactions to the void   16
     And experiences of it   17
     Some examples   19
     Alienation, fragmentation, and defence against dependence   20
     Some clinical material   22
     On having a skin   23
     An example   24
     Summary   25

2   A walk on the wild side: connecting "the void" with people   26
     Surrounding skins   31
     On metamorphoses   33
     The covering   36

3   Primary or secondary?   38
    Pulling the plug   39
    Won from the dark and formless infinite   40
    "Three colours blue"   42
    Boxed in by vision   45
    "Love is all you need"   47
    "Intimations of immortality"   48
    Conclusion   51

4   Psychotherapy and spirituality   52
    Exoteric or esoteric   52
    Form versus formless   53
    Wilber's levels   56
    The puer's *relation to the Self*   58
    The void in this process   61
    And the analyst in it   62

ORIGINS of the VOID EXPERIENCE   63

Introduction to ORIGINS of the VOID EXPERIENCE   65

5   Empty of oneself   72
    Amity   74
    Some difficulties   76
    And solutions?   77
    Whose cocoon?   78
    The replacement child   79
    Summary   80

6   The void in psychogenic autism   82
    Autistic objects   82
    Autistic shapes   83
    Origins of the black hole   84
    The nothing barrier   85
    Treatment   87
    Autistic objects and shapes vs. skin   88

7 Another "black hole"   89
   Eye/Witness   *90*
   Too light or too heavy   *92*
   Some thoughts about mirroring   *93*
   Explanatory doodles   *95*
   Summary   *100*

8 Memory within the Borderline condition   101
   Aloneness and memory   *102*
   Rage and the loss of memory   *103*
   Tolerance   *104*
   Clinical observation   *105*
   Summary   *106*

9 Trauma as a void experience   108
   The what and the why?   *112*
   Traumatic effects   *114*
   Conclusion   *117*

AMPLIFICATIONS   **119**
   Warning and encouragement   *119*

10 Myths and legends of the Creation   121
    None-ness or oneness   *121*
    From Egypt   *122*
    From Greece   *124*
    From the North   *125*
    In the Centre   *126*
    From the South   *126*
    Polynesia   *126*
    From the East   *127*
    In the modern West   *129*
    Together   *129*
    Conclusion   *132*

11 Dimitri's void   133
    Disconnection   *135*
    What to do   *137*
    On knowing what is   *138*

	By whom?	140
	A solid mandala	141
	Acceptance	142
	Conclusion	143
12	The King's sacrifice	145
	The first sacrifice	147
	The rejection	147
	The second sacrifice	148
	Submission or atonement	149
	Interconnections and submission	151
	Trauma and sacrifice	152
	Making sacred, giving up, and communion	153
	Mary's story	154
	Metabolism	158
	Conclusion	159
13	The "Birthday Present"	160
	Paradise?	160
	"The Great Mother"	162
	"There must be some way out of here" (Bob Dylan)	163
	Active or passive	164
	In the therapeutic vessel	165
	Real-life pathologies	166
	The fates	168
14	The dark night of the soul	171
	Eloi, Eloi, lema sabachthani?	171
	On being seen	173
	God and Job	174
	Kenosis	176
	Darkness and light	177
	Separation from (good) God	178
	Loss of the known	180
	Knowing and not-knowing, individuation and beyond	182
	Active imagination	185
	God and the void	186
	Consciousness or not	188
	Potjie-kos	189

TREATMENT   **191**

Introducing the management of void states   193

15 Aspects in the treatment of void states   197
        Connecting with emptiness   *197*
        Defining the lack   *199*
        On being known   *199*
        The covering of the pit   *200*
        What is there?   *202*
        Yearning, mourning, and acceptance   *203*
        Sage advice re: complexes and connections   *204*
        "Acceptance cannot reject"   *206*
        Witnessing   *206*
        Affective not effective   *208*
        Tolerating separation   *210*
        Denial or renunciation   *211*
        In summary   *213*

16 Connections, walls, and windows   214
        Contained by rhythm   *214*
        Rhythmicity that swings   *216*
        Some thoughts about music   *220*
        Connections without and within   *221*
        Metaphorical walls   *223*
        Aspects of linking   *224*
        Antinomies   *225*
        Summary   *226*

17 On active imagination   227
        The long fall   *227*
        Into the unknown   *229*
        Alchemical view   *230*
        The mortificatio   *233*
        And more   *234*
        The coniunctio in art   *237*
        Regression or transcendence   *238*
        Some examples   *240*
        Afterword   *244*

INDIVIDUAL EXPERIENCES   **245**

18 Void as a gender experience: Part I: Mostly masculine   247
        Gert   *251*
        Other formulations   *252*
        Vagina dentata   *253*
        Fear or desire re: the transformative feminine   *256*
        Gert again   *258*
        John   *260*
        Lysander   *261*
        Benny   *264*
        Clint   *268*
        Sammy   *271*
        Eric   *274*
        Behind the veil   *275*
        Timothy   *276*

19 Void as a gender experience: Part II: Female encounters   280
        Wilma   *280*
        Sarah   *283*
        Annette   *287*
        Sophia   *290*
        Mary   *291*
        Comparing the genders   *300*
        Summary   *302*

NOTES   303

BIBLIOGRAPHY   306

INDEX   312

ACKNOWLEDGEMENTS

My journey into the realm of the void started when I listened to Ricky Emanuel present his paper on void states in Cape Town in 2000. That was followed by the reading of a number of papers addressing void issues that were part of our reading list in the Cape Town Child Psychoanalytic Study Group. This group discussed the papers, and members presented material around the subject, which highlighted for me the ubiquity of the void in the experience of individuals.

As my interest burgeoned I became more alert to void language and my analysands and patients seemed to "bring" me void material. I would start to have a presentiment that the void was being described and adjure myself not to use the "V" word, and yet out it would come from a wide variety of mouths describing a wide variety of experiences. This made me realize that it is not just a pathological experience but is also fundamental to the human condition. I am enormously grateful for my clients' permissions to quote from their material.

Part of the difficulty in researching this area is the lack of references to it, especially in the Jungian literature. Even Hester Solomon's 2004 article, entitled *Self Creation and the Limitless Void of Dissociation: The "as if" Personality*, does not use "void" as one of its key words. I was very lucky to come across a paper by Marilyn Charles, which alerted me to the fact that she had written deeply on the subject. Through communication with her my understanding of the breadth of the subject widened as my reading list increased.

I have discussed the void with Art Therapists both in South Africa (Angela Rackstraw) and in the UK, a Music Therapist (Helen Anderson), Movement Therapists at the Barcelona Congress, and numerous colleagues at home and abroad. I would particularly like to thank colleagues who have read and commented on some of the chapters of this book: Carole, Rod, Tanya, and Ursula. Joy Jobson deserves special mention, and gratitude, for being the first person to read and comment on the whole manuscript. My friend Peter Hodson has been a constant source of comment, ideas, and support. The theologian Denise Ackermann gave me generous advice on one particular chapter, *The Dark Night of the Soul,* as did John Dourley; their astute reading necessitated a number of changes. From the Barcelona congress, Ladson Hinton, with whom I shared a platform and with whom I entered a fruitful correspondence, Melinda Haas, whose paper *The Third in Mahler's Ninth* I found mind and soul expanding, and John Dourley, *Jung and the Mystical Anamnesis of the Nothing,* were particularly inspiring.

My reading has been eclectic, not only in the domains of psychology but in those of art, music, and creative writing. Lyn Cowan's writing has been a source of inspiration and something to aspire to. Her wry humour and support of my endeavours has been enormously appreciated over the few years that I have known her. (However, she does not reference the void in her *Portrait of the Blue Lady,* the book's one lack.)

Charles Abbott, a friend in need and deed, has fielded innumerable phone calls about IT matters with calm good humour, guiding me through some of the intricacies of writing on a computer and at last gathering the disparate papers into a form that can be considered a book. I am immensely grateful to him for that.

My family has been particularly supportive during the long days of the writing and the many hours of obsession about this very difficult and often painful place. The insights of both my wife and daughters have been arresting and Frances' capacity to make jokes about this space of great use in helping me tolerate it. Without them it is doubtful whether I could ever have finished this book.

ABOUT THE AUTHOR

Paul Ashton is a Psychiatrist and Jungian Analyst living in Cape Town. He is a father of three daughters and has two granddaughters. Having completed a circumnavigation in a self-built yacht he has now developed a passion for the mountains and bush (flora and fauna) of Southern Africa; a passion he shares with his wife Helise. He has published review articles on books by Lyn Cowan and Rose-Emily Rothenberg and delivered lectures on *Medea and Filicide*, the sculptors Hepworth and Moore, and *The Art of the Void*. He has a deep interest in literature, art, and music.

*This book is dedicated to my wife Helise
and daughter Frances, with love and gratitude*

Introduction

A commonly encountered experience of both analyst and analysand is that of the void. It is spoken about at different stages of therapy and refers to experiences that have different origins. Sometimes the experience of the void is around a relatively limited aspect of the psyche but at other times the void seems much more global and threatens to engulf the entire personality; the whole individual psyche then seems threatened by the possibility of dissolution into nothingness.

The void experience may result from the early failure of external objects to meet the needs of the developing ego, which leads to the sorts of primitive terrors that Winnicott described, or it may result when the Self itself seems threatened with annihilation, which may be more to do with a rupturing of the ego–Self axis. In the first case the fear is of disintegration, whereas in the second the experience is one of the living dead, as though the individual is cut off from her life source. But more than that, the intrusion of the void into the conscious experience of so many of us implies that its occurrence is not only the result of severe trauma but also a necessary aspect of the individuation process.

Drawing on the writings of Jung and post-Jungians, and psycho-analytic thinkers such as Bion, Winnicott, and Bick, as well as on poetry, mythology, and art, and illustrating these ideas with dreams and other material drawn from my practice, I hereby attempt to illuminate some of the compartments of this immense space. As Estragon comments, in Beckett's *Waiting for Godot*, "there is no lack of void", and this book looks at the genesis of this state in the individual in both its pathological and life-enhancing aspects.

In certain of the void states, particularly those arising from severe trauma, memories of past events have disappeared as though sucked into a black hole. In others it is the emergence of the psyche into the white light of a higher consciousness that may be experienced in a threatening way. To feel the presence of the void is to reach the edge of the known world, inner or outer. It is a liminal state that extends backwards from the far side of memory yet continually emerges from the forward edges of our experience. It is by nature frightening and, usually, well defended against.

I will describe some of the defences employed against experiencing the void and suggest ways of helping ourselves decrease the rigidity of those defences so that we can encounter the void and in that process engage with it progressively. My thesis is that the void, frightening as it is, is not something that can or should be obliterated, as that would lead to stagnation. Rather, that hidden behind the "clouds of unknowing" (Bion, 1967) that shroud the void, lie endless possibilities for growth and transformation and an increasingly strong connection with the objective other.

It has seemed to me that the void experience in childhood and early adulthood is mostly associated with fear and can be deemed pathological. In order for the ego to learn to stand alone it appears that it has to deny, or live as though unaware of, the existence of the void. When the void is constellated in these individuals it is often defended against rigidly and what seems to be necessary is to help them find structure and meaning in their lives, i.e. non-void attributes.

Within an older age group, especially with those in post-middle age, the experience of the void is so common that it can be thought of as normal or healthy even. With these individuals what seems to be valuable is the exploration and acceptance of the void. This allows them the space in which they can expand and fulfil as much of their individual potential as is possible in their so-short lives. The fullest experience of oneself implies the loss of certainty and of the known.

The book is constructed in five parts, with the last section mostly composed of clinical material divided into two sections by gender. Hopefully that separation will give some clues as to the different experiences of the void in men and women.

The Territory attempts to articulate the nature of the void experience and the ground I will be covering in this exposition. *Origins of the Void Experience* is concerned with the aetiology of void states in individuals and thus is largely from a developmental perspective. The section on *Amplifications* widens the scope of my exploration using material from different sources: literature, mythology, and personal and spiritual experience. *Treatment* brings together different ideas about the prevention and management of void states and *Individual Experiences* discusses the void experiences of individual analysands.

One of my difficulties, which will be passed on to the reader, is in the language used to describe this immense space. It is often contradictory and confusing; as one looks at the concept of the void, more and more seems to fall within it. For example, at different times the void has been equated with God, the Great Mother, the Archetypal or Collective Unconscious, and the Self.

I have tried to keep to the use of the word Self to describe the God image within, a numinous sense of the ultimately unknowable reality of the totality of the psyche as well as the organizing principle of that psyche. And when I use the word God it means something similar, which is an inner numinous experience. I am not entering the debate about the reality or not of an external-to-the-psyche God.

The word self, with a small s, I use more loosely to describe the sense of self or sense of identity as felt by the conscious ego. This is a much more time- and place-bound concept whereas the Self embraces both the timeless and the time-bound realms in its meaning. For those who are naïve to Jungian vocabulary there are explanatory notes at the end of the book.

Where possible I have tried to use gender-free language or alternated the genders when I describe patients or analysts. To avoid confusion, if I describe the analyst as male I will describe the patient he is dealing with as female and vice versa. To impart the sense of the ineffable when writing about God I have also tried to use gender-free language and rather than use "He", "She" or "It", I just repeat the word "God". I was tempted to write it as "God?" but felt that it became even more confusing, perhaps I should have allowed that piece of confusion to reign.

None of the patients I describe will be identifiable to anyone but themselves and this only because I have used their own words wherever possible. The whole concept of "informed consent" is fraught with difficulties but I have attempted to obtain this in as meaningful and thoughtful a way as I could. I am extremely grateful to the individual patients who have taught me so much over the years and have given me their permission to publish their material for what they, and I, consider to be the greater good. Some of my colleagues too have obtained permission to pass on material that they thought was relevant and I am grateful to both them and their clients.

I think that the void is one of the most under-explored and certainly under-referenced aspects of psychotherapy, which, given its importance in depth psychology, is surprising. I will count this book as having been successful if, hereafter, book indexes contain references to "void" somewhere between "vision" and "von Franz". At present Jung's entire *Collected Works* has only three of those references!

THE TERRITORY

Being an exploration of the general void landscape.

It is nothing but a breath, the void.
And that green fulfillment
of blossoming trees: a breath.

(Rilke, 1987, p. 273)

CHAPTER ONE

On the territory of the void

There is no lack of void.

(Samuel Beckett in *Waiting for Godot*, 1956)

In exploring what is meant by the word "void" and from what it can be differentiated, I will mention and define some of the wide range of terms that have similar connotations. These words include abyss, gorge, maw, emptiness, chaos, darkness, and blackness. And what individual people may experience subjectively would be loneliness, emptiness, hollowness, disconnectedness, loss of or lack of meaning, an unknowing, and, as a more active event, a feeling of falling, into something or out of somewhere. Archaic yet evocative words such as maw and gorge are not much used in modern man's descriptions but do occur in poetry and myth.

The word void, as a noun, means a space that is unoccupied, empty, or lacking in. As a verb, void means to make empty, to evacuate, to go away from or get rid of, to render ineffective or to nullify. Being nullified suggests a state of having been made into nothing. So the void is a state of nothingness, a place where no thing is. Although not explicit in the dictionary definition of the word, it often has a connotation of falling; the long drop from out of the arms of the mother, out of safety, out of the known. One dictionary gives the origin of the word as being from an Old French word *voide*. This means bereft, suggesting the state of desolation following the loss of someone dear. (Macdonald, 1967)

Other words used in this context are hollow, empty, vacant, vacuous, insubstantial, immaterial, flimsy, worthless, ineffectual, and, to describe the process, annihilated, rubbed out, eradicated or ended. Words that suggest the sound of emptiness or hollowness, such as reverberate or echo, or the absence of sound, e.g. silence or stillness, are also part of the void vocabulary.

The pleroma, on the other hand, is about fullness or abundance, the opposite of the void, it first seems. In its fullest form it refers to "the Divine Being filling the universe and including all the aeons emanating from it." (Collins) It is that which has existed since before time and space, i.e. any-thing, began. For Jung the pleroma contains all the opposites but in such perfect harmony that they cancel each other out and thus cease to exist as separate entities.

The first split of the pleroma would result in "effective fullness", which is perhaps energy, and its opposite, "effective emptiness" which suggests negative energy. (Jung & Basilides, 1916) This effective emptiness is the void. Because the pleroma itself contains no identifiable manifestation it is also a state of no-thingness and yet it is a state out of which everything may come. The pleroma contains everything *in potentia,* including nothing.

The things that crystallize out of the pleroma, taking on their discrete identities, are called creatura, literally the created. The word God is sometimes used as more or less equivalent to the pleroma but Jung equates God with "effective fullness" and thus as of *creatura.* What lies behind God would be Godhead, universal ground, ultimate unknowable reality, etc., ideas that are all closer to the pleroma.

When dealing with a void experience one may not be sure whether one is dealing with an experience of the pleroma or whether one is dealing with a differentiation of the pleroma, i.e. the void as effective emptiness. The pleroma can be thought of as the void in its own right (because it contains no-thing) or as containing the void, and one always needs to ask oneself whether this particular experience of nothing contains nothing at all, or is "the All".

The universe consists of all existing matter and space considered as a whole, whereas the cosmos is the universe regarded as an ordered system. Cosmos suggests order as opposed to chaos. It implies a created universe and we can usefully ask whether it was created, i.e. ordered or arranged by God, or whether it is the human propensity to categorize things that has resulted in our conscious experience of cosmos; i.e. has it been defined by human consciousness? Or is order an *a priori* state that "just is"? In mythic times man had a clear sense of the cosmos as having been created by the gods or God but with the rise of science and the "death of God", the idea of man's scientific ordering is what often rules. Cosmos may be thought of as a product of what Freud called secondary process thinking, whereas chaos is an experience of primary process or dream thinking.

Chaos is about confusion, muddle, undifferentiatedness, and yet one of its meanings too is the void. In some ways it represents a too-muchness, and in another an absence or emptiness. This is really the first unformed state of the universe before it was reduced to order by the Creator. Jung sometimes calls chaos the *massa confusa*, which describes it well. Chaos is the name of the first of the Greek gods from whom all else originated. Chaos has its origin in darkness or blackness and it has the sense of a space into which things might vanish or out of which they may appear. In Greek *chaos* means "yawning" (Graves, 1955, volume 2, p. 385) which suggests a gaping or open space into which things might fall.

Neumann in the *Great Mother* writes of the volvas or sorceresses. (Neumann, 1963, p. 173) These wise women yawned while they were spouting an oracle and that is when they were connecting with the depths of the unconscious. (*ibid.*, p. 251) Wisdom surfaces from the yawning depths, out of the chaos that links both the all and the nothing. (I return to this theme on and off throughout the following pages.)

The abyss or abysm suggests a deep hole, something threatening. It has connotations of the underworld, darkness, and bottomlessness. It seems more sinister, less neutral than the void. Whereas the void extends in all directions the abyss' extremity is its depth. Patients often talk of the abyss of despair or the pit of depression. ("In the pits" is a colloquialism for being depressed.)

Gorge implies something deep and narrow-sided but it does have a bottom and thus does not have as frightening connotations as abyss. That is unless it is used as maw. Gorge and maw, usually as "devouring" maw, are the mouth, throat, and/or stomach of an animal. They imply that which can swallow you down into the dark interior of something; Jonah by the whale, Hiawatha by the great salmon, the child by the All-Devourer, the sun in its nightly sinking.

These images of the hero being swallowed by the dragon link with the fear of the masculine being engulfed by the feminine, consciousness by the unconscious. A child in my playroom arranged for a small snake, "a child", to be swallowed by a crocodile. A "python" then crushed the crocodile, and python, crocodile, and child-snake sank into "quicksand".

Hel, an early Norse figure who gave her name to our hell, was described as the gaping abyss that swallows up mortal men. (Neumann, 1963, p. 170) Hel was sister of the Midgard serpent, the uroborus that girds the earth, and of the devouring Feris wolf.

Chasm also suggests a void space but with connotations of a yawning emptiness as well as an opening into something. (Macdonald, 1967) Jung describes the chasm as the entrance to the underworld or into the Mother. (CW 5)

Darkness is that which is without light, is obscure, secret, unenlightened, ignorant; it is "the dark abyss of not knowing". (CW 13, p. 219) In the dark we do not know whether we are dealing with chaos or the void. Darkness may be used to blanket ourselves against seeing what frightens us or it may constellate an emptiness within which our worst phantasms can grow. In complete darkness, within a deep cave for example, we can see nothing at all. Whether our eyes are open or closed makes no difference to what we perceive, and we can easily imagine emptiness receding into infinity, and yet we can also sense the solidity of substance or matter, so that when we light a candle and the rock springs into existence a few feet away we are not too surprised. With some reactions to the void experience, it is as if we are waiting for someone to switch on a light so that a presence rather than an absence will be revealed.

Like most of these images darkness has multiple dimensions, as the darkness of ignorance and unconsciousness, for example, it has the negative connotation of blind brutishness. As the darkness of mystery and secrecy it suggests a special kind of knowledge, something worked for or at, something given but also attained. The Rig-Veda speaks of darkness holding everything *in potentia*. "Darkness there was: at first concealed in darkness this All was undiscriminated chaos. All that existed then was void and formless: by the great power of warmth was born this unit." "This unit" refers to "That One Thing . . . apart from which was nothing whatever." (Ballou et al., 1939, p. 3) Notice, in this quotation, the linking together of so many void words—darkness, undiscriminated, chaos, void, formless, nothing—and they are connected to pleromatic words such as All and One Thing.

Not-knowing is another word that is close to darkness in one of its meanings. On a small boat in the middle of an ocean, assailed by the sense of my own ineffectuality and smallness, I could take refuge in my sextant and sight reduction tables. They enabled me to gain a sense, in spite of my inability to affect the universe, of at least knowing where I was on the earth and where the sun was in the heavens and what the relationship between us was. Knowing those details meant that I could turn my back on the enormity of what I did not know. Like the famous picture by Blake, *The Ancient of Days*, in which we see God reaching out from his circle of redness with a pair of compasses in his left hand. He is starting to measure off the darkness outside, turning chaos into cosmos. As we look at this picture we imagine God inhabiting a minute corner of this space-unlimited. He has walled himself off from the black void of the unknown in his tiny circle of red light.

In reference to this work, Sister Wendy Beckett suggests that the darkness is a space that could be filled with the imagination— had God, or man, the courage to let himself fall into un-knowing. (Beckett, 1999, p. 40) Darkness may be a place of fullness waiting to be revealed to you, just as the void may be a place of emptiness where you can be revealed to yourself.

On a more mundane level under cover of darkness is an excellent way to experiment with oneself. Getting to know one's shadow side, particularly if one is heir to paralysing shame or a punitive super-ego, by asking oneself: "If no-one could witness me now, what would my impulse be? Is that what I want, who I am?" Darkness keeps us hidden and yet may allow us to see.

Blackness too is associated with emptiness, a loss of vitality and meaning, and also evil. It is strongly linked with death; "dead black" we say. The more distant we become from a religious understanding of life after death and the less we are held by those structures that give meaning to the mysteries of life, the closer death comes to the black void. Absolute darkness and blackness are unusual in nature and evoke God's face being turned from one, or the feeling of being inside of something that shields us from any light, buried in the mother perhaps. My first experience of total darkness was being lightless inside a deep cave. Night is only truly dark when there is deep cloud cover, otherwise there is always enough ancient light for us to make our way, especially if we don't try too hard to focus.

Neumann refers to both darkness and blackness as being symbols of the unconscious and, of course, of the Great Mother. (Neumann, 1963) One of my clients speaks of blackness as being closed and dead whereas darkness teems with life. Kandinsky writes: "Black is something burnt out, like the ashes of a funeral pyre, something motionless like a corpse. The silence of black is the silence of death." He refers to it further as "complete non-resistance, devoid of potentiality." (Kandinsky, 1955, p. 61) We can fall into or be swallowed by black. In the astronomical concept of the black hole not even light can escape its gravitational pull.

Meaninglessness is another state that can be experienced as void; a space that is not bounded by meaning or that is empty of meaning. Whenever we come up against something that we do not understand, we are touching the void. One of the most efficient defences against that void is to attribute significance or meaning where none obtains, but that defence itself constellates a state of closure that is empty of deep meaning.

I once spent a few days in the bush in the presence of another psychotherapist. He had the gift, or the curse, of being able to "understand" and give a formulation about everything. There was no room left for awe or uncertainty or unknowing, for the experience of emptiness or nothingness that can presage newness, and I began to realize the critical importance of letting go of the claustrophobic clutter of facts and theories in order to embrace the void. As we grow, our understanding of the world shifts and falters. Our new understandings do not fit into our previously firm framework and this requires re-visioning and letting go of previous assumptions. They may go up in smoke, as in the alchemical process of *calcinatio*, or dissolve, as in *solutio*.

Whenever there is dissolution this implies the liquefaction or loss of shape or discreteness of something and a return to the swirling waters of the amniotic sac or the dark waters out of which the creation occurred. The ego no longer has solid ground on which to stand.

Whiteness can evoke a sense of the void and yet it can also symbolize the pleroma. Death without God is imagined as entering darkness or blackness, and death when with God, as entering the light or perfect whiteness. According to Kandinsky, and this thought has also been expressed by one of my clients, white is "like a cold, indestructible wall going on into the infinite." (Kandinsky, 1955, p. 60) I imagine that the wall extends laterally and prevents one seeing into the depths. In that sense it obliterates emptiness, but it also gives rise to an intuition that on the far side of the wall is nothing, i.e. it evokes the void.

Outer space we think of as black and empty except for the pin-pricks of starlight, but in fact it is filled with light that only becomes "visible" when it illuminates an object. Paradoxically, in space, darkness is filled with light, emptiness with energy.

There are also paradoxes in what the void stands for. Apart from emptiness and fullness it is also equivalent to the Great Mother, the Archetypal Psyche, God, the Self, and the Collective Unconscious. It particularly refers to the ego's relationship to those concepts, the ego is as nothing compared to them and when it engages with them it is in perpetual fear of dissolution or death. If the ego can relate to them, this brings a sense of connection and meaning to it. What happens when that relationship is lost is imaginable if we think of what happens when our mother dies, or when God is dead, or when no Archetypal or imaginal images can come to one.

In practice

In writing this material I have noticed the following process that links with the creation myths. (see below) It starts with nothing, the emptiness or darkness, and then in the "wide wandering" (see Eurynome in Graves, 1955 volume 2, p. 391) exploration of that comes a mass or mess of material. Some of this seems to link together and some does not, this is the phase of chaos. As I work with it, trying to make a structured "cosmos" out of it, I am drawn to make links, put things together, and, more than that, I am attracted to those things that do link and repelled by those that do not.

To help me tolerate what seem to be unlinked bits, I keep reassuring myself that the ideas or bits have come together around this particular theme and that even if I, as ego, can not see why yet, there is another centre that has arranged this. It seems that I need to wait, in a state of reverie perhaps, and some realization will come. Knowledge should be a process not an achievement and it may cease as a process once "I know".

The void state as described or experienced in the psycho-therapeutic setting is a subjective state that recurs time and again in both analyst and analysand. When they use the word "void", different individuals are describing a very similar feeling state, but it is a state that may have very different origins and destinations. The differentiation of the type of void experience that this particular person is having at this particular time is thus of major importance.

The void state is not always experienced with terror or despair. Sometimes the emptiness is actually sought for as with drugs or alcohol, or individuals may flirt with the void, as in bungee jumping, or leaping off high buildings with a parachute; any of the extreme sports challenge the limits imposed by nature. "I can float down the abyss in my parachute or hang-glider, it is not so bad." The *puer* response to limitation is to try to deny it.

In the clinical setting I would say that the most commonly expressed void feeling is one of emptiness or a fear of falling into something vast or bottomless. The main differentiation is into emptiness within and emptiness without, or outside of oneself. As an internal state it may feel like a lack of something definite, a vague incapacity, or the loss of something once had. As an external state it is more related to a feeling of disconnection and lack of protection or containedness or holding. Actually most of these features obtain to both conditions.

Void language

To alert the reader to the feel of the void, especially its pervasive ordinariness, and expand on what I use the term to encompass, I have included a short description of a film and underlined words or phrases in it that describe aspects of the void experience. It will be noted that some of the words portray dead emptiness of one sort or another, and others the feeling of being cut off from possibility, and others the often frightening potentiality that may be contained in the unknown.

The movie is *Good Girl*, and in it a young, <u>childless</u> woman is <u>locked</u> into an unrewarding job and married to a man who "<u>speaks but never thinks before he speaks</u>". She suddenly has the realization that none of her dreams have panned out. Completely <u>disillusioned</u> and only thirty she feels <u>alienated</u> from others who are actually <u>in the same box</u> with her. The arrival of a highly disturbed young man, a <u>would-be</u> writer who calls himself Holden in a <u>puerile identification with</u> the hero of *The Catcher in the Rye* (Salinger), seems to offer the chance of something new.

The viewer can see what a mess Holden is, dependent, narcissistic, manipulative, and <u>living in a fantasy realm</u> to <u>escape the dreadful reality</u> of being forced by his inadequacies to live with his two <u>self-absorbed</u> parents. Our heroine, attracted by the fact that he, unlike her husband, actually talks to her, comes to an emotional <u>crossroads</u> where she must choose either to <u>stay with her known life</u> or reopen the <u>doors of possibility</u> into a <u>space</u> that she describes as an <u>alluring emptiness</u>. In the film, that option would be concretized by her <u>eloping</u> with Holden, but to go down that road would be to <u>tumble</u> with "eyes wide shut" into a <u>new prison</u>. This would be a journey into <u>nowhere</u>, made possible only by <u>closing her imaginal eyes</u> to the truth, the truth that has been so obvious to the viewer.

Painfully, she comes to feel the <u>emptiness</u> and glimpse that it could be properly filled only with <u>something novel</u>, a new attitude. Armed with her recent <u>acceptance of what is</u> and with a <u>baby growing inside her</u>, Holden's baby, she returns to her far-from-adequate husband in what we hope will be a fresh relationship. Certainly she enters a <u>new relationship to herself</u>. The <u>empty space</u> has become a <u>creative possibility</u>, a <u>fresh canvas</u>, a <u>darkness</u> to be filled with the <u>light of the imagination</u>, and the weight of feeling. <u>Cosmic order</u>, broken down briefly into <u>chaos</u>, has been reinstated, but in a new way.

Some of these underlinings may at first seem not to fit one's view of the void but they do need to be considered from the view of "for whom is this a void experience?" Is it void for the conscious self, or for that which seeks to express its wholeness? It may be for one or the other or both. For example, embracing a new attitude will at first seem like a loss for the ego (a void) but is a growth for the whole personality. Closing the "imaginal eyes" may keep the sense of identity secure but limits the expression of the individuating self.

Reactions to the void

The affective reaction to any of the void experiences ranges from chronic boredom through dissatisfaction, to a state of despair or horror. There seem to be stages where the experience of the void is normal and healthy, a necessary stage to be embraced and worked through. These would, in particular, be stages of transition, such as adolescence, midlife, and approaching death, and, in more gentle increments, the whole individuation process, in fact being alive. Fordham writes of a process of deintegration being necessary for growth to take place, deintegration being followed by reintegration of the deintegrates. (Notes) Piaget, so many years ago, coined the terms assimilation and accommodation. We take in new ideas and knowledge about the world by assimilating them but when those ideas don't fit in with our schemata we have to change those schemata to accommodate the new. We have to destroy our old ways of seeing to build new frameworks.

There are phases in life when the encroachment of the void is cata strophic. Experiencing the implacability of the universe as a mature adult with a well-developed ego may be unsettling, but having that same experience as an infant or a person with a fragile personality structure will require the mobilization of massive defences. The lack of defences may permit the leaking away of identity, or the impingement of another's reality, either of which may make the person "empty of herself". (see chapter *Empty of Oneself*)

But the experience of emptiness may also be brought about by the defences themselves. Especially those defences that are too extreme or too inflexible, such as the autistic defences defined by Tustin (1988) in her work on psychogenic autism, or the defences of the self, the self-care system, elucidated by Donald Kalsched (1996), or the schizoid defences. (see below) In these conditions the individual is sequestered from a full experience of himself and others in the outside world.

Whole societies may be subject to the void as in the anomie suffered by the socialist Mother-Nations such as Sweden, Denmark, and Great Britain. Anomie refers to that sense of meaninglessness that arises when you are too well-taken care of and not allowed to define your own limits by, for example, falling out of a tree, or off a jungle gym or out of a paying job.

Repressive regimes, and of course repressive parenting, may inhibit, through fear, the full growth of a personality. In these situations an individual may be too frightened to explore her own individuality, resulting in a feeling of emptiness. It is as though one's individuality has been squeezed out of one and there may be no room even for one's own thoughts.

I wonder whether pop culture is part of the void or a defence against the void or even both. It seems to be like a self-care system that protects one from emptiness while making sure one is also protected from the experience of fullness, the meaningful. In pop music, the lyrics may be meaningless but the mechanical beat holds things together, rap gives words and thus a semblance of meaning to the drabness of everyday experience, and raves are highly efficient boosters of serotonin on a communal level. It is not surprising that in the music shops the so-called "alternative" music is kept well separated from the pop nor that it includes subversive anti-establishment singers such as Marilyn Manson who sing or rant about obscene, violent or abusive themes, hate rather than love. This is the shadow aspect of pop, but an aspect that is needed to complement the often too-sweet one-sidedness of that culture. Each extreme, on one side or the other is a void experience.

Modern astronomy's view is that complete nothingness, absolute emptiness or void was a pre-Big Bang phenomenon. Before the Big Bang there was no time, space, energy nor mass, there was nothing. And yet, in that nothingness was, *in potentia*, everything that we know today. We grope for some sense of meaning but perhaps we should accept that meaninglessness, itself part of the void, is an essential aspect of life's structure. In our incessant asking of questions we are hoping for definition that will obliterate the void or at least place it under our control. A borderline child in my playroom spent his first three months asking "what?", "where?", "why?" He was trying to blot out the emptiness that he felt and define the space that we shared.

And experiences of it

For most people then the void is to do with emptiness, aloneness, and a sense of falling, and their experience of it is distressing. The most extreme examples are where the child, or adult, feels completely abandoned, as if he were alone in outer space. He feels as though he has nothing inside himself and that there is nothing and nobody outside of him. He is "nothing assailed by nothingness". Something similar would be the child who feels so cut off from her world, perhaps through her autistic defences, that she assumes that only she exists. This is an extreme form of the omnipotent position but, like most attempts at omnipotence, is extremely brittle and any impingement by the world is experienced as catastrophic. Such a child is able to nullify her parents and will attempt to nullify her therapist too to stop that impingement; "if you don't exist you can't hurt me" she seems to say.

More common than these extremes are the experiences of empti-ness or pain that form part rather than the whole of our existence. It is often because of psychic pain that we form a no-go area around ourselves that will become an area of emptiness, a place that we will attempt to avoid so as not to plunge unexpectedly into it.

Balint describes a case (in *Empty of Oneself*) in which the void was experienced in the presence of the mother. Although her case is extreme, the sort of formulation she suggests is applicable to a wide range of cases. It shades into what we could call normal misattunement, where the parent does not, for one or another reason, validate the whole child, and instead denies the existence of some aspects of her. Those aspects are made to seem so awful that they must be repressed. What is tolerated forms the "false self" (Winnicott) or an amalgam of ego and a persona (Jung) that creates a sense of identity. What is not tolerated is extruded into what will become a personal shadow, or else denied so radically that it is split off or dissociated from and projected elsewhere. Both these routes result in a lack of fullness in the personality, an in-authenticity, a depletion or emptiness. (Hester Solomon, 2004, describes something similar in a recent article. She names it the "as-if" personality.)

It is only when the therapy gets close to, or stumbles by chance onto, one of these areas of emptiness, that the vertiginous feeling of tumbling, into or out of something, occurs. As that feeling of falling can be increasingly and consciously tolerated, something like an expansion of the personality and a shrinking of the void is achieved.

As touched on above, an important question to ask about the void experience, as one would ask in relation to a dream, is, "For whom is this a void experience, for the ego or for the Self?" Where there has been a loss of "the prevailing spirit", Desteian's (1989) term for the parental and societal values that have been lived by, or of "the ruling ideas and dominants", to coin Jung's phrase, the ego, in its process of coming down to size in relation to the greater personality, will initially experience these lost "instructions" as a loss of meaning or an emptiness. It has been said that every developmental step has a loss attached. With time, however, and if an adequate inner connection exists, an expansion of the personality takes place through the incorporation of previously unconscious material, and a sense of fullness will replace the felt loss.

Some examples

I see a young woman whose life is a constant struggle against one or another aspect of the void. As a child she had learnt to suppress all desire and much emotion, i.e. separate herself from her Self, in the hope of procuring some nurturance from her mother, and she became a compulsive caregiver, looking after her mother and anyone else who needed her, to her own detriment.

Her connection to her inner world or structure remained undeveloped and as a result of that lack came a deep and pervasive sense of emptiness and a feeling of aloneness. To gain respite from the loneliness she makes contact with her mother, but that interaction serves to increase the distancing from the Self and deepen her experience of emptiness. The Self needs her, one could say, but her ego-persona complex needs her mother; whichever way she turns, an aspect feels the pull of the void.

My father, an efficient thinker and benevolent patriarch, had, as a young man, a dream of playing golf. He slightly mistimed his drive and struck up a divot of grass and was then amazed to see blue sky where the clod had been. He quickly replaced the grass and continued his game. This dream stayed with him unshared for the next 50 years. It did not fit in with his worldview and he was ashamed of it in some way. Was it the thinness of the ground on which he stood so firmly that unsettled him, or the idea of heaven being so close by but covered over? We do not know; but to have embraced the *numinosum* that the dream offered, required more courage than he, at that time, possessed.

Alienation, fragmentation, and defence against dependence

Pathological narcissism, perhaps the disease of our time, is one of the commonest causes of the void experience or is at least often associated with it. In a severe narcissistic disorder the individual frequently experiences a profound sense of alienation. This can be an alienation either from the Self, or from others, or both. The way I think of it is that the narcissist fluctuates between the following positions. "I, including the Self with which I am identified, am all there is, there is nothing else besides me." And: "The other, the world or the objective psyche, is all there is, there is nothing else besides that. I am nothing." In its most extreme form this is similar to a Bipolar disorder, a manic defence on the one side and annihilatory anxiety on the other.

In Borderline states, the situation seems to be more of an ego feeling adrift in space, which attaches itself to whatever complex has the most gravitational pull at a given moment. There is little sense of coherence or history, or knowledge of the Self or one's self. (see notes) The shards of the splintered psyche are so scattered that they can give no sense over time of "this then is me".

One of my analysands, early on in her therapy with me, drew a picture of a childhood scene. It had the appearance of having been drawn on a sheet of glass that had then been dropped, leaving shards and splinters almost in the right places but not quite. Paradoxically, when there is a beginning of coherence in these patients there arises too a rejecting sense of "but this is not me". This is because there are so many bits that do not fit in with the tenuously cohering core. Whatever is identified with at a particular time feels the lack of the other parts (that are not being identified with) so that the sense of alienation and emptiness is unrelenting.

Norman Doidge (2001) wrote a prize-winning critique of the novel and film of *The English Patient* in which he explores the literature about the Schizoid patient. He refers to Guntrip's key schizoid characteristics that include self-sufficiency, loss of affect, loneliness, depersonalization, and regression. Although the schizoid's affect is constricted he may have an explosive reaction to felt emotion so that "the smallest surge of emotion is like a bomb going off". (*ibid.*, p. 285) Schizoid individuals seek treatment because of a chronic sense of futility, meaninglessness, and deadness. At core is an intense but usually hidden dependence. Without meaningful relationships they feel enervated, futile, and lifeless, but they protect themselves from relationships because of a fear of losing themselves within the other so sustaining a loss of identity.

The schizoid individual uses the fantasy of self-sufficiency to cover up the feelings of ineptness, loneliness, and emptiness. Feeling effective in their world is the *sine qua non* of a person's (particularly a man's) existence. Feeling inept or incapable renders him or her into nothing. It is to protect against that that the fantasy of self-sufficiency is constructed.

In a relationship, "the pent up wish to merge and cling that . . . was never satisfied in childhood . . . gives rise to a fear of losing the external boundary between oneself and the exciting love object." The schizoid may feel possessed by the love object as by a spirit. (*ibid.*, p. 287)

Doidge makes another point that the schizoid withdrawal is not only from external objects but may also be an intrapsychic withdrawal, which results in fantasies of being buried within oneself. He refers to Hopper's 1991 article on "Encapsulation as a defence against the fear of annihilation" and suggests that there is related imagery that, *inter alia*, includes tortoises, crustaceans, insects, armour, and animals in holes. These are all defences against the void that aggravate the feeling of the void. Becoming alerted to the defence helps the analyst intuit the emptiness behind it.

Both Doidge and Emanuel (2001) refer to J. Steiner's concept of "psychic retreats" as described in his 1993 book: *Psychic Retreats: Pathological Organisations in Psychotic, Neurotic and Borderline Patients*. These retreats may take the imaginal form of buildings that offer safety, or they may appear in a "semi-personified way, as an organized gang, a totalitarian regime, or the Mafia, all of whom provide 'protection', but at a cost." (Doidge, p. 288, note 4) They offer defensive containment that is pathological, resulting in isolation and stagnation. Remaining at all costs in stable employment may also be a retreat.

One version of these retreats places them conceptually close to the claustrum as described by Meltzer (1965); in this version the retreat can be into a space inside the object or inside a part-object like the breast, womb or rectum, even the head. (see notes) Another retreat that Emanuel focuses on is the world of grievance and resentment. He describes a patient who would visit ancient grievances in her sessions with him, and their linking of that retreat to states of feeling "nothing" or "a nothing".

Some clinical material

One of my patients, Alan, was twelve years old when he entered therapy for the second time. He had had a traumatic early childhood at the hands of an abusive father. Brought up by an over-concerned mother and a caring but passive stepfather, he was thrown into disarray when his biological father reappeared in his life when he was aged eight. Unable to tolerate his feelings of love for his mother, which now appeared to be a "betrayal" of his father, he repressed them and felt nothing but a sense of emptiness and despair. His retreat from that emptiness and feeling of being a nothing was into an extreme rage against his mother, whom he accused of all manner of neglect and abuse. In the playroom he used up balls of string in his attempts to construct a secure web, replete with booby traps, that would warn of threatening invaders.

Another patient, an adult, who had little sense of self-worth or even of self, described the rage that she had started to feel against the husband who had abandoned her. "It is like a thorn-kraal (see notes) inside of which is a still calm centre." When threatened by feelings of intense vulnerability she could retreat to this protective kraal and experience some relief.

In her case, the feelings into which she retreated seemed to me to be necessary and unlikely to lead to a "fixed" retreat. They were appropriate, should have been felt before, and were protective of her growing self-awareness and individuality. In spite of her having to "rediscover" herself in this new way as someone capable of intense rage, she felt that within the affect lay something of her own essence. With Alan on the other hand, his rage seemed to be a cover-up. It was something that hid his emptiness and vulnerability and stopped him falling into an abyss of despair, and yet it distanced him from the mother who loved him and the internal object as well, leaving him bereft and alone. There seemed to be scant possibility of his resolving the despair because it was sequestered within his brittle rage.

On having a skin

Many of the void dwellers have boundary difficulties that may be thought about in relation to a skin, which can be too thick or too thin. In his introduction to Rilke's *Letters to a Young Poet*, Mitchell discusses Rilke's need for solitude. He states: "whereas we find a thick, if translucent, barrier between self and other, he was often without even the thinnest differentiating membrane." (Rilke, 1986, p. xii)

A hypersensitivity to stimuli may occur in a variety of conditions such as autism, the schizoid states, and children with ADHD or bipolar disorder. (Doidge, 2001, p. 291) The stimuli to which the individual is sensitive may be in a variety of modalities, such as sound, touch, taste, sight, and/or smell. The distress experienced can be of two sorts. Firstly a feeling of being impinged on; the "skin" cannot keep out unwanted stimuli which are thus experienced as intrusive, and, secondly, that the "skin" can not hold the individual together, that they may fall apart or leak away.

A proper functioning "skin" should be able to contain but also breathe and allow for flexibility of movement and also growth. The castle-wall type of "skin" leads to a claustrophobic encapsulation that generates its own aloneness by separating from others, whereas the diaphanous membrane type of "skin" may not be able to stop one spilling away into outer space, or dissolving into another.

Bick first wrote about the Second Skin defences in her groundbreaking paper of 1968, and she has been widely quoted and her ideas expanded on since then.

> The thesis is that in its most primitive form the parts of the personality are felt to have no binding force amongst themselves and must therefore be held together in a way that is experienced by them passively, by the skin functioning as a boundary . . . The optimally containing object is the nipple in the mouth, together with the holding and talking and familiar smelling mother.
>
> (Bick, 1968, p. 484)

If she had added the visual component to her description, she would have covered all the senses, which suggests to me that the "containing object" is formed mainly from sensory experience. Bick goes on to assert that "this containing object is experienced concretely as a skin", and that if the "development of this primal skin function" is disturbed, the "development of a 'second skin' formation" may take place as a substitute for it. "Dependence on the object is replaced by a pseudo-independence, by the inappropriate use of certain mental functions, or perhaps innate talents." (*ibid.*)

An example

A young woman presented in a state of collapse some months after the birth of her second child. When she was a child both her parents had been alcoholics. She had managed to ward off her anxieties at that time by achieving spectacularly on the sports-field, "proving" in this way that she had no need of them. Later, work in a welfare department had the same function for her; caring for others reinforced the feeling that she had no need of care herself. Both her sporting prowess and her social work acted as second skins. It was only when she was attempting to care for her small child, and feeling unsupported by her husband in that attempt, that she experienced the fragility of her primal skin function and felt that she was falling into a void and was in danger of dropping her child too. She had been forced out of her defensive second skins.

Defences such as these are used to ward off primitive anxieties and may also take the form of hyperactivity, or muscularity, which may be verbal as well as physical, or of an adhesive identification, where the patient seems to stick to the analyst like Velcro, or may, in an intrusive way, even get right "under" her analyst's skin. In other words, patients can ward off their anxiety about the absence or thinness of their own skin by intruding into or sticking onto another or by creating a skin of their own through action, doing rather than being.

Another example is of a seven-year-old child whose mother was dying of cancer and whose father was preoccupied with his work. In the playroom he constructed an impenetrable barrier around himself by bouncing a ball vigorously about the room. The sound, and the constant movement, made him seem present and yet unreachable and I could only hope that he was weaving a temporary cocoon rather than a permanent shell. In the countertransference, my feeling was that I had to keep close to him but could not make contact with him.

Over-investment in work or sport, obsessive running or exercising, and most addictive behaviour, may be examples of that protective skin, and Emanuel even suggests that being attached to strong feeling states may also function in this way. (Emanuel, 2001) Whenever that skin is damaged or penetrated the individual feels vulnerable to annihilation or to simply leaking away.

Much of the rigidity of a personality is a result of this second skin function. By means of it we are enabled to keep the void at a safe distance or ourselves at a safe distance from the void. With a properly functioning primary skin, or containing object, we can allow ourselves to let go enough to experience the multitudinous and often contradictory aspects of our natures without losing a sense of our own coherence. Through the experience of the vastness of the unknown and of ourselves in it we somehow come to experience the fullness of a self that has not been denied. Fullness and emptiness are no longer worlds apart.

Summary

I hoped in this chapter to give a sense of the multifaceted nature of the void of which there is no lack in human experience. The differentiation of the void is of great importance in learning to live alongside it. The remaining chapters in this section continue with that differentiation.

CHAPTER TWO

A walk on the wild side: connecting "the void" with people

There is a void outside of existence, which if entered into englobes itself and becomes a womb.

(William Blake)

There is a paucity of literature, especially Jungian literature, on the subject of the void and yet the experience of emptiness is endemic to the human condition. It has even be posited as being "at the root of the human psyche". (Charles, 2000a, p. 5) Milner is quoted as writing of a "pregnant emptiness", suggesting that the absence of something is what contains the potential for development. (*ibid.*) We need emptiness in order to take in something new. The emptiness of the pre-gravid womb is a potential space within matter.

Void, being a condition of nothingness or a lack, implies the state before or the state after, a not having had or a loss of what has been had. It suggests too the act of getting rid of something, either emptying oneself in the Buddhist sense or getting rid of excrement. When we void shadow aspects from our consciousness only a persistent sense of inner emptiness remains. The feeling may be that if you are shit you will, like shit, be expelled; goodness though is kept inside and thus being good may keep you safe. Projection empties us of parts of our selves and repression and dissociation do something similar. We are emptied of the unacceptable. Emptiness may be a defence against the experience of our own hostile projections and a way of avoiding identifying with what has been projected onto or into us. When we do not feel like a "container-contained" but like a "receptacle" with a "foreign-body" in it, as Gianna Williams calls this experience, we will attempt to rid ourselves of that foreign body leaving emptiness in its place. (Williams et al., 2003, p. xiv)

The emptiness may be experienced as outside oneself, as in "I am completely alone", or within oneself, "I am nothing, I do not exist", or both, as in "I am nothing in nowhere". Less extremely it is a feeling or condition of loneliness or deprivation. "Being in a void" may be seen as a continuum, leading from being as if "nothing in nowhere", through a state of feeling that nothingness within or that there is nothing outside of one, to the experience of islands of emptiness within or without. In the most frightening of the void states there is a complete immersion in nothingness, and in the less severe states there is a feeling of distance from that. Patients may then say, "I feel lonely," as opposed to, "I am completely alone in the universe," or, "it feels like I am in a void," rather than, "I am in a void."

Emptiness may also be something we unconsciously seek for, following a compulsion to repeat our childhood experience.

What was yearned for and not found in infancy becomes the void. It is both familiar and ineffable and often has the feel . . . of "home". It therefore becomes difficult to move beyond the safety of (this) encompassing womb—no matter how toxic or empty it might be.

(Charles, 2000b, p. 133)

This is such an important point. We need to differentiate this sort of void, that we reconstitute around ourselves in order to feel its familiarity, from the void that arises when we try and match up our idea of how the world should be with our realization of what it actually is, and also from the void that is the openness of a world untrammelled by our expectations.

From a subjective view, being voided implies being got rid of, dropped like a baby from the arms of its mother. Suddenly there is no containment, no container to contain and keep separate, no container to be contained. All can run together or drift apart. The arms of the mother, of the human mother or the Great Mother or the various societal mother substitutes, have not enclosed you, or have let you go, and the terror is of falling forever or of expanding into nothingness; like the elements of the universe speeding away from each other at an alarming rate ever since the BIG BANG. In developmental terms, the child, witnessing the primal scene and seeing his parents locked up in their own universe with him on the outside at the "lonely end of the triangle", is thrust towards aloneness. *The Loneliness of the Long-Distance Runner* was what one movie was called; the loneliness of she who walks by herself, the individual.

The word "vacant" is another void synonym. It conjures the stare of the depressed mother or the blank gaze of the therapist who has lost empathic connection with his patient. Imagine peering eagerly into a mirror to examine yourself only to discover that you are not reflected. That mirror may be like a hole in space opening into a world of ever-receding objects, or else it may reflect back everything except the observer, like a family portrait where one of the members, the black sheep usually, has been carefully expunged.

In *The Book of Laughter and Forgetting*, Milan Kundera (1980) describes the erasure of a man, Comrade Clementis, from an official photograph. He describes this as a metaphor for the power of the state, or the mind, to effect the "truth" of remembered events, our continuity in the world, in other words. And our continuity in a particular way often requires something about ourselves being blotted out, made to disappear.

During a balcony appearance in freezing weather the solicitous Clementis had taken off his own fur cap and set it on the Communist leader Gottwald's bare head. This event became the subject of a propaganda photograph.

> Four years later Clementis was charged with treason and hanged. The propaganda section immediately airbrushed him out of history and, obviously, out of all photographs as well. Ever since, Gottwald has stood on that balcony alone. Where Clementis once stood, there is only bare palace wall. All that remains of Clementis is the cap on Gottwald's head.
>
> (Kundera, 1980, p. 3)

In *The Family Orchard* by Nomi Eve (2001) is another story, this time of a family's attempt to forget their child. The severely afflicted five-year-old son is sent away, "for the good of the other boys".

They tried to forget him. They pretended that he did not exist. In time, he became buried. Buried like the roots of a tree, for, like roots, he pressed up into their lives unprovoked. And with their roots all tangled up, and under bent boughs, they sank into a theology of namelessness. They called the child nothing. They never again called on God. And they knew not what to call themselves anymore.

(Eve, 2001, p. 176)

Nomi Eve poetically describes how the two brothers of that child learned to

fill up the space where the other one once had been. They would stand up extra straight or puff out their chests to take up more room when they heard the emptiness in the house begin to roar. They became the best joke-tellers in the village, the best song-singers, storytellers, they were constantly trying to be amusing, to attract all attention so that attention would fall on nothing else.

(*ibid.*, p. 177–8)

These extroverted defences are defences against the emptiness that also prevent the emptiness being filled. The void is almost palpable beneath them, and its potential for being deforming, through entanglement with the very roots of being, apparent.

The loss of the child, the emptiness where the child had been, became filled with a silence that crept into the house where the remaining family lived. "The silence came blowing, airless and thick, blowing from out of their own lives . . . blowing not to destroy but to protect." (*ibid.*, p. 208) And the effect of that silence was to create a "grave" in which the possibility of them being the sort of parents who had not sent their child away, lay buried.

By not facing aloud the absence of their child and their responsibility with regard to that absence, they created an emptiness surrounding who they were. So there developed a void in both their being and in the possibility of their own becoming. They became walled off from a full experience of themselves.

An experienced loss will, in time, be filled with grief, but this abandoned loss opens up an emptiness that can never be filled because it cannot be grieved. This loss or emptiness may be felt to be on the outside of the individual, or in her interior as part of her subjective experience of herself, or both.

A friend, with whom I had been discussing the writing of this paper, felt that the whole idea was nonsensical, as the void could not be thought about. How can one think about nothing? It will make you crazy! The sermon-giver in *Seven Sermons to the Dead* says something similar. "In the pleroma there is nothing and everything. It is quite fruitless to think about the pleroma, for this would mean self-dissolution." (Jung & Basilides, 1916, p. 7)

My friend's thesis, too, was that as you are the centre of your own experience of the universe, everything you experience is self-referenced. Thus your being in a void obliterates the void because if you are there than there is no longer *nothing* there. Perhaps he was defensively attempting to deny the existence of the void or perhaps he intuited that thinking about the void creates a sense of boundedness that contains it, turning it into a lacuna rather than an expanse of nothingness that extends to infinity.

The feeling of emptiness can be consciously held away through logical thought. Thinking both separates us from and connects us to others and from what we know and do not know. Thinking can begin to define, through differentiation or ordering, what is or can become known. It does not deal with that which is unknown and extends to infinity, but it forms a felt boundary around it or around itself. "As far as I know" is how the expression goes, and thereafter is "heaven only knows".

The void has a shore or edge, on the void side of which there is nothing that is known or has been known or, this is the feeling, will be known. This space is outside of our awareness or our experience or our memory. It may seem that the world of our conscious perceptions is a kernel within that void, rather than that the void is encapsulated within our consciousness. But actually in this paradoxical place both visions have a truth, the emptiness bounded by thought or feeling is like a lacuna within the kernel of consciousness that itself is surrounded by a great emptiness. The expression "bigger than big and smaller than small" begins to make sense here; infinity, the ultimately unknowable, extends on both sides of our time and content limited consciousness.

At the recent IAAP congress in Barcelona, which was titled *Edges of Experience: Memory and Emergence*, the theme of what lay beyond those edges emerged in the morning Dream Matrix. The Matrix, a forum for sharing dreams dreamt at the congress, was set up in the form of a spiral, curling anti-clockwise from outside to inside. One participant sat regularly near the centre, and on the last day it was suggested by one of the facilitators that she sit near the outer edge, to experience what it may feel like to be at the "Edge of Experience". I think that the facilitator missed the point that the spiral has an inner and an outer edge, one can fall deeper in or further out, and both are void.

A person may simply have an experience of something missing, he knows or intuits that there should be something there, something felt, but there is nothing. And that nothingness is like a space opening up which he dare not approach too closely or examine too thoroughly. And this is one of the difficulties in regard to the void space, without the courage or hopefulness to peer into it, it becomes walled off so that it becomes unreachable, or else stood back from so that it seems to extend or expand. In this way the void maintains its position "at the root of the human psyche".

Surrounding skins

A trainee analyst attempted to convey the tension of the void experience in a painting. On the right side he painted a misty figure whose boundaries melted vaguely into space as his or her silent scream echoed out into the empty reaches. On the left was a figure in the deep red of pain, compressed beyond endurance, boxed in, "you will be like this", empty of itself, squashed out of its own authentic existence by an encroaching world. Arising out of the space between these two opposing figures was a mountainous island newly emerged from the surrounding ocean, its verdant slopes and plains comfortable between a setting sun and a rising moon.

The picture as a whole portrayed his intuition that the secure inner world can come into being somewhere between the poles of abandon-ment and intrusion, and perhaps a further one, that it can only come into being through the conscious experience of those poles. That it is out of the experience of the void states, which I think these extremes represent, that a solid sense of identity or belonging in the universe can emerge. It is necessary to have felt and survived the emptiness and experienced and resisted the intrusion and closed-off-ness.

Where there is not enough containment or too much pressure, two possibilities arise. One is that there is no chance for the individual personality to accrete because there is not enough of what Daniel Stern (1985) calls "affective attunement" to give rise to the feeling that one is part of a community with whom one can share or communicate. That is, that can give one the feeling that one is not alone in a universe of which one is the centre. The other is the feeling that one's inner experience or individuality is wrong and that to belong requires a suppression of that. In both cases the "skin" is missing and what is necessary (as discussed in the previous chapter) is a "skin" to protect the individual from intrusion and/or to hold him together; a "skin" that can keep you in shape, your shape.

An image that arose in the therapy of a man with severe Obsessive Compulsive Disorder was that his symptoms represented a sort of shell that he developed to protect himself against the demands of an annihilating mother. She was a mother of the "compressive" sort but one who was also unable to contain because of her emotional absence at other times. For him, as for another analysand who regularly dreamed of crayfish, the shell was a necessary expedient. It protected him from violation and at the same time imparted a feeling of shape, of identity.

But to grow or change or develop was a major threat to this feeling of integrity, as it required dispensing with the carapace, leaving him vulnerable to penetration from the outside, or to spilling away into space. The carapace acts as an exoskeleton and, as he had not yet developed an endoskeleton, without it he feared becoming a shapeless, identity-less mess. In this context the crayfish shell represents a rigid mask with which the individual has identified and behind which he can hide.

This scenario is beautifully amplified in the Danish fairy story *Prince Lindworm*, discussed by Donald Kalsched (1996). In this story the princess might well follow the fate of the previous brides of the "worm" and be devoured on her wedding night. But she has armed herself with sage advice from the wise-woman, and presents herself arrayed in nine petticoats and considerable courage. To see her naked, the worm must first slough his skins, his "shell", one for each of the petticoats that she will remove. The removal of her skirts will leave the bride naked and exposed but not deeply threatened, she will have shed some of the external or public aspects of her identity, but the worm's "disrobing" is much more than that.

The story details his suffering, a suffering that increases with each skin shed until he becomes just a shapeless mass. He must still endure being whipped and washed in lye by his young bride. Sloughing his multiple external skins the lindworm loses his individual shape and becomes formless.

In the story both princess and worm now fall asleep, the dream sleep of the unconscious where time stands still, yet hastens onward. When they awaken, minutes or years later, the worm has been changed into a handsome prince and the marriage can be consummated. What is so important here is that the girl actively addresses her situation and the worm submits to the process. Instead of simply having his will of the girl, he elects to suffer the loss of his known identity, his shape, and thus open himself to the powers of transformation.

This submission to fate is a critical aspect of each person's journey but it is made more difficult when there is a felt emptiness in the centre of an individual's being. Perhaps the Borderline person's horror of approaching the centre is that he has an acute awareness of the emptiness that is there. The intrinsically difficult access that most of us have to the centre is because we have built walls that prevent us from knowing about that emptiness. When the walls collapse chaos ensues, but within that chaos is both the nothing and the all.

On metamorphoses

In nature when the skin needs to be shed the animal uses the protection afforded by the environment to enclose it during its most vulnerable time, it will crawl into a hole, or under a rock, and the earth, the Great Mother, will succour it. Perhaps one of the evolutionary aspects of depression is that the depression creates a hole into which we can crawl, be still, and endure the shedding of our old skin and the growing on of the new. According to Julian David, a Jungian analyst and writer, depression forces us to be still, rooted to the spot while the metamorphosis takes place; the mythological examples are legion. Nature points to the idea that we need a protective environment, in human terms a good relationship, if we are to endure the loss of ourselves.

Ovid, in *The Metamorphoses*, relates many examples of trans-formation, and also some of its dangers, of which the most obvious is that the changed person can become fixed in her new form, for eternity. He also communicates the sense of impending doom that precedes the event, its irrevocable nature and the unpredictability of the results. It is one thing becoming a bigger and bigger crayfish, briefly losing one's shell to accomplish that periodic growth spurt, but a much more severe trauma is to lose one's exoskeleton and change into a human being when it goes against one's whole life experience and self knowledge. For this involves entering the void of unknowing.

In the film *Monster's Ball* (2001, director Marc Forster, USA) the protagonist, played by Billy Bob Thornton, is drawn between the embittered racism of his father and the open-minded humanity of his son. He avoids making his own moral choices and maintains a sterile disconnected life. This is imaged in one cold scene as having an unfeeling union with a prostitute from the rear; face-to-face would have been too intimate.

He meets and befriends a young black woman, Leticia, played by Halle Berry, and the shell of his life falls away from him as he falls in love with her. His son is dead, the first crack in his shell, and he perforce separates from his intolerant and intolerable father. Under the influence of Leticia as a transformative object he starts life anew. But that new life implies the fragmentation of his old one and the loss of the way he used to think, feel, and interact with himself and his friends.

In Euripides' *The Bacchae*, it is not the old men Cadmus and Tiresias who resist the new god Dionysus. Rather it is King Pentheus, Cadmus' grandson, who cannot bear the loss of the established order. He must wrap around himself the cloak of certainty and attempt to banish by force the upstart god. In contrast, his grandfather and the blind seer, wise through their years, dress themselves up in fawn skins, grip their *thrysi*, and set off with a modicum of cynicism to pay their respects and see what is up. They are mature enough to allow for difference, and can accommodate change without the loss of their identities. Tiresias has, by this stage in his life, undergone many metamorphoses himself.

So, the two old men do not attempt to disguise themselves but simply dress appropriately for the occasion. Pentheus, on the other hand, pretends to be something he is not. He dresses up in women's clothing and attempts to spy on the Maenads. When they notice him, exposed by the god on a tree, they dismember him. Without his kingly appurtenances he becomes nothing, there is an emptiness behind his public mask which is easily exposed by those who refuse to follow the established order, and he ends up in bits.

What happens to those bits? If the myth were to be "dreamed onwards" I imagine that they would be buried and that out of the grave would come a tree. This is what happens in many different examples from the symbolic realm, e.g. Munch's *Metabolism* paintings of 1899 and 1916 (see below in *The King's Scarifice*), various alchemical drawings, and also various fairy story images. These latter include the tree that develops out of her mother's grave, watered by Cinderella's tears, or that which grows from the buried bones of the dismembered son in Grimm's *The Juniper Tree*.

In both the Dionysian and the Christian myths the tree of death, i.e. the Cross, leads to resurrection and eternal life. The tree is symbolic of the state of wholeness within the individual, the Self in Jungian thought, and this state can only be aspired to once the external or mask aspect is no longer identified with. The death of the old order is necessary for something new to sprout. New life arises within the void created by death.

It is excruciating that Agave, Pentheus' mother, should be punished by the fates in such a dreadful way, that as a member of the Maenads she should dismember her own son. Perhaps she represents unconsciousness here, her following of the Maenads was done in a blind way, she became immersed in their orgies, lost herself entirely, and thus stands as an opposite pole of the same complex that Pentheus represents. He cannot give up his conscious viewpoint and be informed by the "other" world and she loses all consciousness and cannot see what she is doing at all.

So both Pentheus and his mother are engulfed by the void. He, terrified of the change that Dionysus represents, tries to ward it off, but ends up dismembered and his remains burned; he ends up as nothing. She, too blindly accepting the Dionysian way, experiences the worst loss that a mother can, that of her own child by her own hand; this is an emptiness that can only be filled through a lifetime of grieving.

The combination of the old warrior king and the blind seer affirm the more helpful attitude of a healthy respect for unknowable chaotic forces but without letting go of consciousness. Tiresias may be blind in the "real" world but he can "see" in the inner world. Together they have the wisdom of age without the one-sided rigidity that sometimes comes with age.

An experienced analyst in the Kleinian tradition, secure in her knowledge of the importance of the frame and the necessity of powerful interpretations, realized one day that this form of psycho-therapy does not work with badly traumatized patients. She felt the loss of certainty as if the ground had opened up underneath her feet but was able to draw on her own wisdom and let go of her "knowledge" and through that find a new way to be with these very damaged patients. (Valerie Sinason in a seminar in Cape Town, 2003)

The covering

In one of the Greek creation myths a union took place between darkness and chaos and out of this union sprang Night, Day, the Air, and Erebus. Graves translates Erebus as "the covered (pit)". (Graves, 1955, p. 33) I suggest that the covering of the pit is the way in which we attempt to make sense of our world, either through our own efforts or through following the "prevailing spirit", the parental and societal voices of our childhood. (Desteian, 1989) These ways of knowing give us a sense of solid ground under our feet and in this way defend us against the experience of the great emptiness beneath. Conversely, when the covering is rent it is as though we are poised to tumble into the deep unknown, "down the godless plunge of the abyss" as D.H. Lawrence describes it. (Lawrence, 1950, p. 124)

A man described his experience on medication as a feeling of being suspended in a hammock of webbed filaments just strong enough to bear his weight. There was always a fear that something could give and he would plummet. Just turning around could be catastrophic. What holds us above the pit can be medication, as in this case, or "knowledge", which may be factual or wishful, or faith perhaps, or hope, or paralysis, or even "functional" blindness, the refusal to see.

In his book, *The Mystical Way*, Johnston tells us optimistically that: "The void is no mere negation but a state of consciousness full of spiritual wealth." (Johnston, 1993, p. 289) I would stress that it is not usually felt to be full of spiritual wealth. The void, because it is so empty of known things, either by design or "fate", is a place of darkness or lostness. It may be filled with "spiritual wealth" at some time or another as part of a mystical experience, but even if it is, one of the essentials of a mystical experience is its evanescence. (James, 1960) For the most part the void is experienced as a spiritual wilderness and even though we may find God in it, try as we might, we will lose God again.

As suggested above, when meaning is lost it is as though I fall out of some container and nothing holds me. That nothing may be experienced as the absence of God or, in Eckhart's sense, as the presence of God (see below in *The Dark Night of the Soul*). A fullness within me and without me that flows into a oneness, a unity with "The One"; or an absence that pervades and surrounds me, embracing "The None".

And even if that nothing is experienced as "the ultimate reality"— called "nothing" because of its unknowable nature—the separation of the seeking soul from that reality may be experienced as utter desolation. The denial of the Nothing or the attempts to defend against it or ward it off leads to the negative experience. If we can accept the nothingness and its position as the interior of a womb, we can feel held by it and watch in awe as something forms itself out of silence, expands, and evolves in that womb, before it metamorphoses, through a new nothing, into something else. Where will we be when the process ends, what will we be when it begins again? We cannot consciously approach the void sanguinely but we can approach it with "faith on tiptoe" (John Freeth) with a tentative trust in the long-term view.

CHAPTER THREE

Primary or secondary?

All the lonely people
Where do they all come from?
All the lonely people
Where do they all belong?

(The Beatles)

This chapter took shape through my trying to articulate an answer to the question of whether the void is a primary or secondary experience. As I explored the issue I realized that the question is about as meaningful as asking, "Where is the beginning of a circle?" The thoughts that follow are fated not to come to a conclusion.

The capacity to experience the void is dependent on having a certain degree of consciousness, an awareness of self and other. In those cases of structural deficit that result in an inability to process information in a core way there may not be much consciousness of either presence or absence, in other words of the void or its opposite.

If a foetus has survived to birth, a large amount of its original environment must have been adequate. In this environment the foetus experiences, at the least, shifting pressure, smell, sound, and sight, and presumably also taste and touch in its different modalities, and even a sense of itself as a body in space with an upside and a downside.

The foetus is bathed in a fluid of changing consistency (or consistent change), yet one that is maintained within certain limits. She receives information from the maternal circulation too so that she will experience inner sensations such as those brought about through the effects of adrenaline, the fight or flight hormone. To be born alive implies having experienced containment, being with, and being within. So if a small infant shows an awareness of the terror of the void, this will be connected to a sense of the loss of something once had.

Pulling the plug

Piontelli (1992), in her fascinating study of the foetus *in utero,* has shown that the developing foetus has an awareness of its muscularity and ability to manipulate its environment. She cites the example of a foetus of mid-term gestation who had been active and exploratory of its space and who seemed to enjoy tugging at the umbilical cord. It looked like someone trying to get the bath plug out and it did indeed nearly "pull the plug" on itself because the pregnancy was threatened by bleeding from behind the placenta.

According to Piontelli's account the foetus became subdued from then on, looking withdrawn and too scared to act, a behavioural trait that stayed with her for some years after birth. It seemed as though she "knew" that something had gone seriously amiss and that it had something to do with her. However, this was mediated, presumably biochemically, she had become "aware" of the possibility of oblivion and shrunk behaviourally to preserve herself from that awareness, that threat. In other words, she defended herself against the void, and locked herself into another compartment of it.

A friend of mine likens the experience of an anaesthetic to "being lost down the plug hole". It is a gentle way of experiencing the pull of the Black Hole, the inexorability of one's expulsion from whatever is into nothingness, from a state of awareness into the dark. It is the transitional state that holds the terror, the state where one is still aware of both the structure and its dissolution. This has been described as "the penumbra". (Ladson Hinton, IAAP congress, 2004) For my friend this was a frightening experience, but William James describes a sort of mystical experience that was entered under anaesthesia and seemed to be associated with a loss of ego-consciousness but with the experience of another centre of awareness. This loss of the known opened the individuals who experienced it to a new universe of understanding and, for some, it became something to be sought after.

So the void here is not a primary experience but implies the loss of something had, it is entering the unknown from the solid ground of the known, it involves the experience of something being wrested from one, or of one being wrested from something. And it involves some grades of defence that further cut one off from experience, from the experience of being held, either physically or emotionally or by a sense of meaning.

Won from the dark and formless infinite

And yet, seen in another way the experience of the void is a primary experience and it represents what Lacan would have called an experience of the "real".

Bion states that the idea of infinitude is prior to the idea of the finite, that the finite is "won from the dark and formless infinite". (Bion, 1967, p. 165) The sense of finitude only develops out of an engagement with oneself and one's limitations and it is through this developed sense of finitude that one can intuit the nothingness that came before and will come again.

John Dourley writes of the "Mystical Anamnesis of the nothing" and develops the idea that we are drawn to re-experience that "Nothing out of which All may grow". (Dourley, 2004, quoting CW 10, p. 75) Perhaps this seeming paradox is resolvable if we think of the need to develop some sort of consciousness in order to experience a sense of the void. We come from the nothing but our awareness of it is dependent on being a something.

In a review of Rose-Emily Rothenberg's book in 2002 I wrote the following paragraph:

> A major question raised in me through reading *The Jewel in the Wound* was about meaning. In becoming conscious are we beaming a light into the darkness and finding illuminated there rare texts and exquisite jewels, a fullness of things that was always there, awaiting only our torch to make it manifest? Or are we painstakingly, from the edge of a void, constructing an edifice, stone upon careful stone and thought by precious thought until the emptiness is obliterated? Is truth discovered or constructed? I would like it to be the first but fear that, in this story at least, it is the second . . . probably it is both.
>
> (Ashton, 2002, p. 54)

Yes, probably it is both in the sense that in our seeing we also shape, we give form to our experiences, we construct our reality out of a reality that is already there. And the sharedness of our realities arises out of our shared relationship with those around us, particularly our early caregivers.

As mentioned above, Piaget wrote of the linked processes of accommodation and assimilation, suggesting that we acquire new knowledge through assimilating it into our schemata but that we repeatedly reach points where those schemata are no longer large enough to hold the often conflicting data and a new schema must be found to accommodate those.

Daniel Stern (1985) argues for a more linear model of changing or developing ways of experiencing the world and has coined the word RIGs for internal Representations of Interactions that have become Generalized. It is a very useful descriptive model for systems that change by slow accretion but does not address those systems where change is by a quantum leap into something different.

Michael Fordham's idea of "deintegrates" captures the more experientially true idea that knowledge acquisition proceeds through loss or collapse or breakdown of the known in order for a reformulation, the new, to take place. As a friend once said, "it's as though just as you are beginning to understand God (or the universe, or the psyche, he might have added), God changes the rules." (This is a bit like the series of DSM manuals, just as you have mastered one of them it undergoes a transformation that needs to be accommodated within a new framework.) The importance of this idea is that it captures the loss, the sense of floundering, that must occur as we push into the emptiness of the unknown. Each accretion to our knowledge is like a small addition to an existing scaffold that inches its way into the unknown; but any leap into this darkness is like dropping into the void. It is uncertain whether this will become a generative space, generative of something new, or whether one will simply fall down into it, dwindling eternally.

The problem with new knowledge is that, to be acceptable, it must be seen to connect back with what is known, otherwise it is felt to be meaningless, at best inapplicable, and at worst crazy. Each new discovery exposes vistas of unsolved problems. (Bion, 1967, p. 166) When you are mapping an area as vast as the psyche there may not be readily accessible connections between experiences or concepts, which may, nevertheless, be true.

An image I have had, particularly when working with dreams, is that of pebbles dropping into different areas of a large pool. Each pebble makes its own expanding set of rings that move over the surface. The sets may be far apart initially but ultimately a web of interconnecting ripples will cover the surface. One can extend the metaphor downwards and imagine the rings at different levels forming a three-dimensional matrix; eventually they will interweave through outer or inner space.

So, a dream image resonates with another, perhaps very different, image from the same or a different dream, and then with the diverse things talked about during a session, which, while seemingly disconnected as they first appear (daily events, fight with the boss, walk with the dog, the impending war, etc.), suddenly seem to join hands, or rings, near the end of the session, and what had seemed like wisps of mist take on solid substance, a chunk of a new reality. But this can only come out of permitting the fall into not-knowing. Admitting to one's self that "I have no idea what is going on here!" often opens the door to a new understanding.

The expansion of knowledge through holding on to what is known is a slow, yet safe, linear process, but that which obtains when we allow ourselves to freely embrace all possibilities is exponential. Looking with the yet unknowing eye is like peering into the void; it is trusting that something will appear if you wait long enough and look in all directions but you don't know yet what that is.

"Three Colours Blue"

I would like to digress into some thoughts about the French film *Three Colours Blue*. In this film, Julie, a young mother played by Juliette Binoche, loses both her only child and her husband in a motor accident. Devastated, but unable to express much emotion, she withdraws from the world, leaving her home after jettisoning its contents, and abandoning her close male friend, Patrice. She rents a flat in a seedy part of town and when asked what she does, she aptly says, "I have one thing left to do—nothing"; the sub-text is, "for I am now nothing". She has entered a void within the world, withdrawn connections from outside of her and, one feels, is filled with emptiness. But by entering and engaging with the void she permits something new to happen

Early on in the film is a hint that she was in fact the covert composer of her husband's famous music. She now turns her back on that by refusing to continue with "his" current big work, and by destroying, so she thought, the musical scores for it. This work was to have been a Chorale to be performed at the upcoming ceremonies celebrating the unification of Europe.

Julie's fall into the void is vividly imaged in the film when she goes to visit her mother in a frail-care home in the hope of being seen and contained by her. But her mother is demented and fails to recognize Julie, and her slipping out of the "arms of the mother" accelerates. In the background we see an image on a television screen. An octogenarian plummets in free fall from a small aeroplane, bungee-jumping! From the viewer's perspective it is the fall into space that registers not the fact that the cord will hold him . . . hopefully.

Ensconced in her safe emptiness Julie resists attempts by various people to connect with her. She is protected by what could be thought of as a "hard autistic object" (Tustin, 1988), a mini-chandelier in blue glass that she has taken with her from her daughter's room, and she regresses to a diet of coffee and ice-cream. What finally breaks through her autistic shell is music and feeling, and her capacity for connection, for love, and for charity.

At moments of extreme stress, when she closes her eyes, thus opening her inner ear, she hears the grand opening chords of the *Chorale for the Unification of Europe*, and at another stage she hears a mysterious street-musician playing one of its melodies on his flute. These impingements, acting on her inner and outer ears, reconnect her both to her responsibility to the outside world and to her creativity within.

She is lured out of her flat to befriend a stripper and through that act comes across photographs, taken before his death, of her husband in the arms of another woman. Julie follows that up and discovers that the young woman is pregnant by her deceased husband. It is as though her suffering caused by her husband's betrayal, and the conflict that she feels in realizing the girlfriend's distress, and her feeling for her and her husband's as yet unborn son, all conspire to break through her defences and both her feeling and her creativity are restored.

She returns to Patrice, who, as her husband's erstwhile partner is still busy working on the score of the Chorale. She is fired up to produce with him what we know will be a great work. Instead of accepting her creativity as a gift that inflates him, as her husband had done, he gives her the choice to either own her own work or accept his inferior attempt. As he puts it, his object too has been "to make you feel. Say 'I want', or, 'I don't want'."

The film ends with a *coniunctio* image "seen through a glass, darkly". The viewer is outside and Julie, seen through a window, is being made love to by Patrice. This scene resonates with what Dimitri describes (see below) in his vision of a man trapped in a glass box, and yet it is a very different image. In Dimitri's story the man is "boxed in" by the glass, here Julie is contained by it but symbolically connected with the world through its transparency. Julie's hand explores the glass, her face touches it and her flesh moulds to it; she is contained but she is not separated from herself or others.

As they make love we hear the great chords of the Unification Chorale. The massed choirs are singing Paul's deep affirmation of love as expressed in his letter to the Corinthians 13, and the camera briefly highlights images of the people whom Julie has affected or who have affected her over the previous months. A boy fingers a crucifix she gave to him, the stripper comes into view, her mother slumps in her chair at the old-age home, and her dead husband's girlfriend views the new life within her on an ultrasound. This child will be taken home, to the home that Julie has given her, for "love is patient, love is kind, Love beareth all things".

"Though I have the gift of prophecy, and understand all mysteries, and all knowledge; and though I have enough faith to move mountains, if I have not love, I am nothing," sings the choir. And we sense that it is by means of love that Julie has been rescued from the void. Not only the love that radiates from her to others, but also the love that she has learned to have for herself, and that was sparked by Patrice's faithful attempts to reach her during her despair. And also the love expressed in the reaching out that came from the others in her story, the boy, the stripper, the girlfriend even; all of whom connected with her in some way.

Yet it is not solely love, but pain too that has reached through her encapsulation, as when she witnessed a man being assaulted and her friend's grief, experienced the posthumous betrayal by her husband, and arranged the destruction of some rat babies in her flat. Psyche was also at work in the synchronistic way that the flautist's playing of the theme music and the inner surges of sound penetrated her defences, forging new links across her formed barriers. She had allowed herself to love and to feel loved, to feel the pain of disillusion-ment, betrayal, and loss, and to be open to psyche, and in this way the void around her has filled.

Boxed in by vision

As mentioned elsewhere in this book, the idea of closed eyes is an important one; when one's mind is full of ten thousand things it is impossible to hear through the static. About seventy-five per cent of sensory input, and the arousal that it causes, is visual, so with eyes wide open the inner world of the imagination, the unconscious, becomes much less accessible. Having one's eyes open shuts one off from inner experience, intuition does not work well when one is immersed in sensory stimuli. A child was once asked which he preferred, television or radio. His prompt response was, "Radio, because the pictures are prettier." William Blake would have agreed, for him the world of the imagination was more real than the "real" world. This "real" world is usually thought of as the visual world or the world of the senses.

> How do you know but every Bird that cuts the airy way
> Is an immense world of delight, clos'd by your senses five?
> (*A Memorable Fancy, The Marriage of
> Heaven and Hell*, Plate 7)

Blake felt that only the imagination could lift the "veil of illusion" that masks reality and could put us in touch with our true energies.

A friend believes that to fully enjoy a film one must arrive after the beginning and leave before the end. In that way one can avoid being boxed in by someone else's meaning or vision and experience as many different outcomes as your imagination is capable of. As in the classic *The Thousand Nights and One Night* where one story is embedded within another and has another embedded within it in an extravagant display of interconnectedness, or the looser postmodern novel by Italo Calvino (1981), *If on a Winter's Night a Traveller*, where no chapter is definitely concluded but leads rather into another domain, a new vision or parallel reality.

The sorts of vision that restrict are both the undiscriminating vision of the generalization-based world of the media, as well as the discerning or over-discriminating vision of the philosopher or scientist, which may whittle away substance until there is nothing left. The first creates a sort of white noise or haze that may look alluring, but which, like the blue sky, prevents us from accessing a view of the myriad individual scintillae embedded in the vastness. The second may lead to a "brilliantly lit cul-de-sac" (Ian McCallum, personal communication), a pin-point of light in the darkness, a spark of knowledge that may nevertheless be devoid of meaning. These sorts of "creation", being lacking in substance, fall into the category of "void".

On the other hand there are visual images, paintings or sculptures that stimulate the inner eye, setting the imagination vibrating, and rending the "veil of illusion". Poetry and literature can do this too, where words mean more than they say and meaning expands to embrace ever more truth in its womb.

The use of pictures as tools to develop the imagination or to reach into the world of psyche is a widely used technique. It shortcuts the process of symbolization in that the subject does not have to construct her own symbols but uses a variety of supplied images in her own symbolic way. In this technique clients are shown an array of images from different sources, paintings, sculpture, or photographs from newspaper articles, as an art form, or simply as snapshots. Out of this array they are asked to choose one or more that seem to resonate or call to them. These are then circumambulated, i.e. discussed from different aspects such as what it pictures, how it could ideally be, what changes would be necessary to get it from what it is to how it would be preferred, etc. This is a powerful way of undercutting the critical voice of reason without foreclosing the creative process with the analyst's well-meaning knowledge.

An analysand had a dream in which he was stumbling through the darkness looking for a place to obtain food for himself and his young child. He peered with increasing desperation into the darkness to no avail. He re-entered the darkness in an active imagination and as he closed his eyes he was transported back into a hotel room where he felt safe and hopeful. In his life at that time he was trying to make up his mind whether or not to leave the secure but unfulfilling job that he had held for fourteen years and start a venture in an area where he had no expertise but had been offered the supportive guidance of a mentor.

My initial interpretation of the dream was that it was perhaps to do with his overzealous looking for the right way, and that letting go by shutting his eyes and trusting in his own interior or third eye brought him back to safety. I came to understand later that the looking represented a stalwart attempt by the ego to confront the real difficulties looming as the result of his choice to take the hero's path and that closing his eyes brought about a collapse of that heroism and a regression to the hotel as symbol of womb and paradise.

Sometimes, peering into the void, attempting to see into the darkness or through the "Clouds of Unknowing", must be done from the ego position, holding on with one hand while you part the mists in front with the other, and sometimes it must be done by letting go of that position, closing the eyes and awaiting an image to bubble up from the deep recesses. The first is the active way of the hero and the second the contemplative path of the mystic and both have their time and place.

Many artists paint to music or with music in the background, and novelists too may use music as a "portal to the source". Music seems to aid contemplation. Words, inner chatter, even following a musical score may all inhibit the creative function, the listening to what arises from within, the expression of the imagination. That inhibition is a secondary void experience.

"Love is all you need"

What Paul is on about in his wonderful letter to the Corinthians used in the Chorale in *Three Colours Blue* is the unifying nature of love. Prophecies, knowledge, understanding, even language, are all incomplete; they are all "in part". "But when that which is perfect is come, then that which is in part shall be done away." As children, he suggests, we knew things wholly, naturally. "But when I became a man I put away childish things. For now we see through a glass, darkly; but then face to face: now I know in part; but then shall I know even as I am known." (1 Corinthians 13)

I love that linking of the past tense with the future tense, suggesting that it is only the present that is different, that it is consciousness that divides and separates, that when we re-experience the world as a unity, as perfection, as wholeness, past and future collapse into one. Love is the connector, the mediator. Love embraces all things. And knowing discriminates.

"Intimations of immortality"

Wordsworth's theme of lost unity with God, in his well-known *Ode on Intimations of Immortality from Recollections of Early Childhood* (Smith, 1921, p. 111) is similar to the theme in Paul's epistle, but in this poem he does not yet see the possibility of being recognized in that "even as I am known" way.

> There was a time when meadow grove and stream,
> The earth, and every common sight,
> To me did seem
> Apparelled in celestial light,
> The glory and the freshness of a dream.
> It is not now as it hath been of yore;—
> Turn whereso'er I may,
> By night or day,
> The things which I have seen I now can see no more. (Lines 1–9)

In the next stanzas he extends the images of earthly beauties that excite him but returns to the idea that something has been lost.

> —But there's a Tree, of many, one,
> A single Field which I have looked upon,
> Both of them speak of something that has gone;
> The pansy at my feet
> Doth the same tale repeat:
> Whither is fled the visionary gleam?
> Where is it now, the glory and the dream? (Lines 51–57)

And then the great fifth stanza:

> Our birth is but a sleep and a forgetting
> The soul that rises with us, our life's Star,

> Hath had elsewhere its setting,
> And cometh from afar: (Lines 58–61)

He describes the gradual loss of the paradise that surrounds us in our infancy, is still accessible through the joys of childhood and, as the vision of possibility, attends the youth on his way. However,

> At length the Man perceives it die away,
> And fade into the light of common day. (Lines 75–76)

What Wordsworth is saying is that we are born with a remembered connection to the divine (or the pleroma, or the Self), and that connection is primary. As we grow up we separate from that and experience a loss, a loss that reaches its nadir in adulthood. We can suppose that it is pre-midlife adulthood that he is referring to. For this is the period of the ascendancy of the ego, the time of the greatest distancing from the divine as the Self. It is only in the latter half of life that a reconnection is offered to or thrust upon one.

In fact a poem written sixteen years later, when Wordsworth was 48, explores again the connection between the worlds of mortals and of the divine. Called *Composed upon an Evening of Extraordinary Splendour and Beauty* (*ibid.*, p. 130), it describes just that, and Wordsworth's musings on the theme of both transcendent and human reality. He feels the vision of this evening has been sent,

> That frail Mortality may see—
> What is?—ah no, but what can be! (Lines 7–8)

He harks back to a time before adulthood and the images of the Ode as discussed above but indicates that the lost knowledge of the divine radiance has been rekindled by this new experience.

> Oh, let Thy grace remind me of the light
> Full early lost, and fruitlessly deplored;
> Which, at this moment, on my waking sight
> Appears to shine, by miracle restored;
> My soul, though yet confined to earth,
> Rejoices in a second birth! (Lines 73–78)

What is powerful now is not angelic, celestial choirs appearing on earth, but the way that the earth is illuminated by a divine radiance so that what is visible is more than earthly and more than divine, the new sum is greater than its parts. There is even a hint that some of the beauty is from the infernal regions:

> —From worlds not quickened by the sun
> A portion of the gift is won;
> An intermingling of Heaven's pomp is spread
> On ground which British shepherds tread! (Lines 37–40)

And what this beauty does for Wordsworth is open a spiritual stair,

> . . . steps that heavenward raise
> Their practicable way. (Lines 51–52)

> And tempting Fancy to ascend,
> And with immortal Spirits blend. (Lines 47–48)

On offer is a return to "Immortality", not as some remote place that is unattainable from the depths of humanness, but glimpsed from that humanness, and appearing accessible, even if distant. He is describing a numinous experience, the recognition of spiritual heights that is felt in the body through the emotion of awe.

It is man's loss of the memory of the experience of God, the felt loss of God's love, which Wordsworth mourns in the first poem. In the second poem there is a sense that the reconnection is coming from God's side, although man must be receptive to the call.

Wordsworth had been plagued by a sense of immateriality in his early life, as though he merged into the universe or into the void. "There was a time in my life when I had to push against something that resisted, to be sure there was something outside of me. I was sure of my own mind: everything else fell away, and vanished into thought." (Smith, 1921, p. 204) And again: "I communed with all that I saw as something not apart from, but inherent in, my own immaterial nature. Many times while going to school have I grasped at a wall or tree to recall myself from this abyss of idealism to the reality." (ibid., p. 203)

What Wordsworth felt initially was a sense of oneness with the All, or with infinitude; what some may think of as a void experience. He then felt a separation from that oneness, a disconnection from it that he experienced as a deep loss. Finally he learnt to be with both "the abyss of idealism" and "reality"; to feel connected to both.

In *The Varieties of Religious Experience*, William James quotes the experience of a man who felt that he had always known God in God's grandeur until one day he stood below and looked up at the Niagara Falls. He felt the waterfall's enormity, and those thundering waters, only a tiny activity in the scale of our small earth, changed his scale forever. God must be so much bigger than what was so huge, and the man was filled with awe. (James, 1960)

True awe takes us to the brink of the void, in the vastness of that experience we can no longer think of ourselves as being in God's eye. We have fallen from the cosiness of paradise and now experience God's absence more than God's presence. The immediate space where God had been present is no longer filled; outside of me may be nothing.

Conclusion

To return to the beginning of this chapter, the capacity to experience the void is dependent on having had a certain degree of consciousness, or awareness, of self and other so that one can experience their loss. And similarly the capacity to obliterate the void or to lose one's fear of it, is also dependent on being conscious of both oneself and the other. Embraced by that consciousness and the feeling that the other has us in mind too, we may be able to willingly let go enough to glimpse, from our contained finitude, some of the infinite space and possibilities for being that make up the void. Or we may simply be thrust into the void through the vagaries of fate or the intervention of God "that force which goes against my will". Which came first, the void or its absence, remains uncertain.

CHAPTER FOUR

Psychotherapy and spirituality

The Buddhist creed of emptiness ends "Gone, gone, totally gone, totally and completely gone, enlightened, so be it."

(Moore, 2003)

In my attempt at bringing the ideas of the mystics into some sort of relation to the ideas of analytical psychology, I am leaning heavily on an accessible and coherent chapter in which Ken Wilber articulated his early ideas. This is Chapter 11 of his book *Grace and Grit*. (Wilber, 1991) Originally espousing many of Jung's ideas, Wilber later came to feel that Jung did not go far enough in his thinking and had got some things wrong. I doubt whether Jung would have disagreed with him had he been alive today.

Early on Wilber quotes Gary Trudeau: "Trying to cultivate a lifestyle that does not require my presence." I first understood this on the level of the avoidant individual who attempts to live his life without ruffling the surface or engendering others' notice or envy, or the life so well-organized that it requires no further input. But by the end of the chapter I felt it referred to that advanced psycho-spiritual state where the ego has been brought down to size in a new relation to the Self and is no longer the centre of attention or the organ of action. That "relativization" of the ego may be felt as an annihilation of the "I", it becomes as nothing.

Exoteric or esoteric

Seeing exoteric and esoteric religions as different, yet lying on the same developmental continuum, Wilber attempts to define them.

Exoteric religions are "outer" religions, based on belief rather than evidence and supported but also constrained by dogma. They are mythic religions but the myths are taken concretely and must be accepted simply on faith. Wilber takes issue with Joseph Campbell, who, he feels, interprets the myths as being allegories or metaphors for transcendental truths. His issue is that the original believers did not take their beliefs as myths but as truths and he feels that Campbell is, in a way, mixing metaphors by interpreting them. I don't think that is Campbell's aim. What he does is indicate the psychological value or meaning within the myths, their internal rather than external truths, and he is demonstrating their value for a consciousness that has moved beyond the mythic. The fact that they were originally developed out of a mythic perspective does not prohibit them from being understood in this more rational way.

Esoteric religions are inner and hidden, revealing their mystical meanings only to those with spiritually enlightened minds. They are the result of direct experience and personal awareness and thus are akin to science, in that both mysticism and science depend on direct consensual evidence and experimentation. In the esoteric religions the experiment is a personal one and consists of meditation or contemplation. The results of the experiment are hidden from those who will not perform it and yet are shared with others who do. The esoteric religions, the world over, are in many ways identical, what Wilber calls "the transcendental unity of the world's religions". (*ibid.*, p. 177) (See also James, 1960, in his chapter on mystical experience.)

Form versus formless

Jung and the mystics, such as St Augustine and Meister Eckhart, meant something different from each other in their use of the word archetype, says Wilber. For Jung, archetypes "are basic mythic *forms* devoid of content (and) mysticism is *formless* awareness". (*ibid.*, p. 180) For the mystics, on the other hand, the archetypes are the first subtle forms that appear as the world manifests out of formless and unmanifest spirit. They are "nothing but radiant patterns or points of light, audible illuminations, rainbows of light and sound vibrations—out of which, in manifestation, the material world condenses." (*ibid.*) In this sense the archetypes would also correspond to that which is left when the world dematerializes, under the mystic's gaze, from the condensations of matter, to vibrations of light and sound (the archetypal resonances), and thence to "formless and unmanifest spirit", the void.

Wilber goes further than Jung with archetypal theory and he proposes, for example, that collective elements should be further differentiated into collective prepersonal, collective personal and collective transpersonal elements. We dwell in the personal, although we have arisen out of the prepersonal and some of us at least attain the transpersonal. For Wilber, the only Jungian archetype that is truly transpersonal is the Self as it has an ultimately nondual character. In one of its aspects the Self seems to coincide with "the ultimate oneness".

He asserts that real mysticism is first finding the light beyond form, then finding the formless beyond the light. In the language of the mystics from many different origins, there is much repetition about achieving an awareness of "no-thingness" or "nothingness", "emptying", "formlessness", the "clouds of unknowing", etc. Beyond these may be glimpsed the "ultimately unknowable reality", "light", or the presence of that which fills but has no form and is indivisible, "the ultimate oneness" or "the universal ground".

It seems to me that the individuation journey, the journey towards wholeness, is akin to the mystic experience in that it too ultimately involves the disappearance of egohood. But, as Jung states in his forward to Suzuki's *Introduction to Buddhism*, ". . . it frequently happens with us also that a conscious ego and a cultivated under-standing must first be produced through analysis before one can even think about abolishing egohood or rationalism." (Jung, 1969, p. 554) This implies that ego-consciousness must be differentiated out of the darkness or formlessness, the prepersonal, before the state of transcendence, the transpersonal, can be sought. This coincides with the experience of many analysts that the initial stages of psycho-therapy focus on the strengthening of the ego. It is also akin to the idea that as developing persons we must obliterate the void, become separate from the darkness of the maternal interior, as an initial step that allows the later phase-related return to the void in the second half of life.

In an attempt to clarify this process of the development of consciousness, Wilber has contrived a scheme of stages that extends Jung's ideas of the development of consciousness and of the psychoid barriers; those barriers that separate psyche from the matter of the body on the one side and from spirit on the other.

Wilber places his stages in a hierarchy of ten steps that begin in matter and end in "absolute spirit". They embrace, in the successive in-between levels, mind, body, and soul. His idea is that we must, in our development, "differentiate from each lower stage, identify with the next higher stage and then integrate the higher with the lower." (Wilber, 1991, p. 183) So there is an implication that even in the later stages of high spiritual development there is a connection with the preceding, more mind-body levels. It is not a case of pure mind floating away into the ether but of spirit connected through soul to mind, to body, and, at the furthest end of the spectrum, to matter. The ox-herder of the ancient Chinese pictures does not remain dematerialized but he returns to the market place a lot heavier than when he set out. (Ref: The Zen Ox-herder pictures from twelfth-century China. Internet site http://www.4peaks.com/ppox.htm.)

As Jung says, "consciousness is always only a part of the psyche and therefore never capable of psychic wholeness: for that the indefinite extension of the unconscious is needed." (Jung, 1969, p. 556, my underlining) And the unconscious extends into matter on the one hand and spirit on the other. The ground of our being surrounds both the beginning and the end.

Wilber is at pains to differentiate the prepersonal experience of "adualism" or "oceanic or protoplasmic awareness" of the lowest stages from the transpersonal experience where "awareness transcends the subject/object duality". (Wilber, 1991, p. 189) He feels that both Jung and Freud misapprehended the two states as being quite similar. (ibid.) Jung errs by elevating the prepersonal in the kind of way that Wordsworth does when referring to "trailing clouds of glory do we come from God who is our home." (Ode on Intimations of Immortality from Recollections of Early Childhood) Freud errs by negating the transpersonal as being simply a regression. In fact Neumann and other Jungians such as Edinger also warn about the danger of the spiritual or mystic experience being a return to the mother, an example of "uroboric incest". (Edinger, 1985, p. 49) In other words, they too seem to see it as a regression.

In The Seven Sermons to the Dead there is a collapsing of the two states, the prepersonal and the transpersonal, into the all-encompassing concept of the pleroma that is ultimately unchanged by the activities of the *creatura*. As with infinity, the pleroma can be added to or subtracted from without changing it. Also, in *Aion* (Jung, 1959), Jung describes a cyclical process where energy and matter meld into each other.

Wilber's levels

In Wilber's level one, which he terms the Physiological self and which seems similar to the "emergent self" of Daniel Stern, the self is undifferentiated from the "mothering one" and the material world. It arises out of matter, long before consciousness occurs and is a state of protoplasmic awareness or adualism rather than individual awareness. He stresses that this is not a state of union but an indissociation, a global undifferentiation. What union there is, is only a fusion of a sensori-motor subject with a sensori-motor world. It is really the opposite of a mystical state and in fact represents the greatest point of alienation or separation from all of the higher levels or higher worlds whose total integration or union constitutes mysticism. Thence comes the Christian mystics' idea that we are born in sin or separation or alienation, which can only be overcome through evolution out of matter and towards mind and into spirit. (Wilber, 1991, p. 188) This first primitive level is characterized by *participation mystique*.

Development is then into the second or Magical level in which there is a sense that the world can be influenced by thinking or wishing. Levels three and four are concerned with a more differentiated sense of self and other, including world. The initial passive feeling that God will influence the world if I please him, a Mythic belief, gives over into an attempt at pleasing the Gods through manipulation of the environment, e.g. through sacrifice. This is a Mythic-rational way of thinking. In level five, the stage of Rational Scientific Materialism, we can think about thinking and start to deconstruct our world-view so that our myths lose their sense of meaning. Level six is the last of the personal levels of consciousness, it is Humanistic and Existential and tends towards integration rather than the splitting that obtains in stage five.

Once the transpersonal levels of consciousness are reached, awareness develops of "the multidimensional, divine universe, that is theocentric". (*ibid.*, p. 195) There begins a realization that one's awareness is not confined to the individual body–mind, it goes beyond or survives the individual organism. Wilber brings in the idea of the "Witness" or transcendental soul, a different sort of consciousness, one not sited in the ego complex. (*ibid.*) In another context Jung suggests this is like being viewed from another planet.

This stage can lead to a direct identity with spirit. Attention becomes freed, both from the outer world of the external environment and the inner world of the body–mind, and awareness transcends the subject/object duality. There is a growing realization of the illusory nature of the world of duality, a realization that duality is a product of mind rather than "real" in and of itself. (*ibid.*, p. 195) This new realization is a manifestation of spirit, and precedes, firstly, mind's communion with that spirit or divinity and then, at an even higher level, mind's union with spirit, in the *unio mystica*. (*ibid.*, p. 196) This is a state beyond individuality. This state of non-duality is akin to the obliteration of the opposites through the coming together that, in the *Mysterium Coniunctionis*, is referred to as the third stage of the *coniunctio*. (Jung, 1963)

The "Witness" then is beyond ego and as the name implies it is not a do-er or agent of action but a be-er and observer. Yet a part of the ego too functions as a witness. Jung quotes from the Apocryphae (presumably this is God talking): "What you are, I have shown you. But what I am, I alone know and no man else. Behold me truly not as I have said I am, but as you, being akin to me, know me." (Jung, 1969, p. 282) This suggests the idea that the knowledge of God, God's identity, is given truth or substance by an observing consciousness, and that both God and the individual are indispensable in the joint process of witnessing each other, of identifying each other. God and man, Self and ego, are needful of each other in this mutual process of becoming known.

What is implicit in this quote is the concept that the maturation of a stable ego is a prerequisite for the further development of a higher consciousness and ultimate union with the divinity. This is not a process that can be side-stepped by suppression which would lead to a depletion of consciousness, but involves the fullest experience of ourselves, leading thus to self knowledge and an increase in consciousness. This is the individuation process which can only be experienced over time and not without the suffering of feeling.

The puer's *relation to the Self*

In an article entitled *The Puer Aeturnus: The Narcissistic Relation to the Self,* Satinover (1980) makes the points that the inflation–deflation cycles of narcissism are states, respectively, of identification with or alienation from the Self. Identification with the god-image or Self is an inflation that leads to a sense of grandiosity and God-likeness whereas dis-identification from it leads to a felt alienation from our deepest selves. In its most extreme forms these are the equivalents first of an early at-one-ness with "the mothering one", a state of non-duality, where the "I" and the "not-I" differentiation has not occurred, an early god-like state, versus, second, the very human condition of feeling abandoned by God, not only separate from God but distanced too ("dissed" as the modern teenager might say), i.e. the primal void experience of being nothing in relation to no-one. Satinover contrasts these opposing positions with that of the ego being in relation to the Self, where the ego–Self axis is intact and functioning as discussed particularly by Edinger and Neumann. This state of inner connectedness or relationship is the antithesis of the void.

Although mystical experience may be achieved by means other than meditation or contemplation, e.g. through drugs, deprivation or near death experiences, unless that experience is allied to a broader consciousness it may not be deeply transformative. A mystical experience of these sorts may lead to a search for a higher meaning, through a realization of something different being possible, but if it simply leads to more drugs or ego-driven activity aimed at achieving paradisal oneness, the experience is unlikely to result in what the mystics seek through meditation or contemplation. Rather than discovering the formless beyond the light, they may find the formless before the light, chaos rather than "generative uncertainty", God without the consciousness necessary to apprehend God.

One of the important points that Wilber makes is that science is a critically necessary stage in the growth towards spiritual maturity. This is because science strips us of our infantile and adolescent views of spirit, i.e. the pre-rational views. Under the influence of science the world may start to look like a meaningless collection of material bits and pieces of no value, and we may look with a yearning nostalgia back to the days of mythology, or magic even, when the world was imbued with meaning. (Wilber, 1991, p. 201) But if we are forced forward rather, into the "clouds of unknowing", a transrational way of understanding eventuates that may give access to a new experience which is of the single divinity that lies below the surface of manifestation. This may only be reliably accessible through meditation.

This unmanifest or formless Godhead is the ultimate source of all lower levels of awareness, of what Jung, in his *Seven Sermons to the Dead*, called *creatura*, and the mystic, Meister Eckhart, termed "the created". (Fox, 1991) Moving towards the source we move out of our defined world of *creatura* into an experience of the world that is beyond "thingness", the world as no-thingness, the world empty of any-thing and yet full, complete. The paradoxes become almost unbearable for the rational intellect, cannot be understood by logic and can only be expressed in symbols or grasped intuitively.

Jung attempts to articulate this understanding in *Aion* (Jung, 1959), one of the few places where he uses diagrams to help express his ideas, and Murray Stein translates this elegantly in *Jung's Map of the Soul*. (Stein, 1998, chapter 7) What he describes is the paradoxical idea that as we descend from the highest level of psychic development, imaged as "the Anthropos quaternity, an expression of ideal wholeness at the spiritual level" (*ibid.*, p. 164), down to the lowest level, we extend deep into matter and thence into energy. This pure energy takes us "back into the realm of ideas, which is the world of *nous*, of mind, of spirit". (*ibid.*, p. 167) So sinking down into the darkness of matter we come out in the light.

But what about the other way? If we rise up into the realm of the Anthropos are we then close to the darkness too? Jung's drawing (Jung, 1959, p. 248) of this dynamic circulation shows it as uni-directional as though he did not want to believe that the hard-won light could be extinguished.

Christ, as "the Word" or Logos or consciousness, suggests he who constructs knowledge, takes us out of the darkness through new-built realms of the spirit into one-sided union with the "good" God. Verbal consciousness both connects and separates. Through the shared meanings of language we connect with others, and yet language is also a mechanism that we can use to lie or distance ourselves from others and our own feelings.

The act of differentiation made possible by verbal language extracts us from the one-ness of the no-thing. Enduring the opposites so created may lead to a higher order of being, a transcendent position that obliterates emptiness. But the rejection of one of a pair of opposites creates a lack or void. Repression of the bad, a particularly Christian habit blamed on St Paul, forms the shadow, that "abyss of darkness in human nature" (Samuels et al., 1986, p. 138), whose unconsciousness leaves us empty of that which is ours, separated from ourselves.

Lucifer, the "light-bearer", is more linked with the revelation of what is; he shines a light into the darkness. This seems to be related to the idea of the integration of shadow. By shining that light into our own souls, the boundaries of the known are extended. Lucifer is also the name given to Venus, the morning star, who heralds the dawn. And Venus is likewise the evening star who ushers in night. There being thus an equivalence between Venus and Lucifer, perhaps one can say that it is through connection and acceptance, attributes of the goddess of love, that the growth of a revealed consciousness is enabled.

Satan comes from a word meaning "adverse", and this suggests another way of filling one's own space and that is by opposition to "the prevailing spirit". This implies leaving the known and accepted road and discovering one's own path. A movement away from what seems the fullness of the illuminated and into the void, but with the possibility of occupying that emptiness with one's own found reality.

Rational consciousness skirts rather than fills the void, and this is especially true of collective consciousness. By demonstrating commonly accepted truths it establishes islands of "light" within the sea of darkness and ignores the dark spaces between, but, as in Astronomical reality, there may be more matter in the "emptiness" between the stars than in the stars themselves.

In Wilber's thought, from the Godhead as the source or ground emanates the All, including God and Satan. Jung would say that out of the Pleroma arise effective fullness and effective emptiness. God is effective fullness and the devil effective void. God relates to life and light and the devil to death and darkness. The Pleroma is known by itself and the Void is unknowable. The ego can only know about itself and the world, about *creatura*. It is the organ of differentiation and neither the Pleroma, which transcends differentiation, nor the

Void, which is undifferentiated, can be known by it. The Void as the great unknown embraces both ideas, i.e. both pleroma and void. The Self as the totality is both the organizing principle and that which it attempts to order, i.e. chaos.

The void in this process

There are many ways that the void is constellated in this process and it can refer to most of the changing states of consciousness articulated here. Both the end and the beginning (the Godhead, the universal ground, the archetypal psyche, and the Great Mother, which are all synonyms) are void states in that they are conditions of no-thingness, states of non-differentiation. In Wilber's first two levels, consciousness has not definitively precipitated out. The "mystical participation" is not conscious so that there is no clear sense of self and other. Thus, it would only be in looking back from a more developed consciousness that the sense of being lost in the immensity would be manifest.

In Wilber's third and fourth stages, man loses that sense of participation or oneness with and instead becomes aware of his smallness in relation to the enormity of the Other. What in later times we would think of as mythical preoccupations do contain us by generating the feeling of being embedded in meaning. With the rise of rationality though, we enter another void state, that of cosmic meaninglessness side-by-side with "known-ness". It is only with the advent of vision combined with logic that we enter another phase of mind–body and inter-individual integration where meaning and value arise through interrelationships.

Following this stage of felt connection, we may enter a phase of forward-looking to the Other whom we are not. The sense of emptiness arising from this drives the desire for communion with that other but the bliss felt when communion happens is short-lived because of the very painful realization that "I am not that". (Or not yet anyway.) The final stages of uniting with God and then being one with God involve the loss of the ego entirely and thus the void experience of the "loss of myself".

As discussed elsewhere, I think it is important to be aware that this is not a linear journey, the immersion in the nothing (or all) will be followed by a return to the separated state; the separated state can be followed by a return to the immersion in the nothing. The movement in either direction is one that is painful because it conjures the void either in the sense of absence of the "I", or in the feeling of the absence of the Other.

And the analyst in it

The analyst's role is to be a courageous witness to her analysand's progress and this is aided by her awareness that the stages of psychological growth are both cyclical and impermanent. The analyst can not know where it will all end but she does know that whatever is happening now is not the final point in the journey. Each dream listened to, each Active Imagination performed, each encounter with the archetypal psyche in whatever form, involves an immersion and return, and the analyst can be of use, both by not preventing that immersion and by recalling the patient to the time-bound present.

The difficulty with this as a psychoanalytic process is in maintaining an analytic attitude that is neither consciousness driven nor completely without the differentiating function of consciousness. Ideally the analyst should accompany her analysand during his immersion in the nothing and yet "live to tell the tale", that is act as a reminder to him about what he experienced. Dourley (2004) has articulated that the mystic's return from his or her immersion in the nothing is as important as his or her descent into it. The analyst can aid that return but also help keep alive the insights gained during the descent.

ORIGINS of the VOID EXPERIENCE

Where does the river come from?
From the bottom of the nothing pool
Sargasso of God
Out of the empty spiral of stars
A glimmering person.

(Ted Hughes)

Introduction to ORIGINS of the VOID EXPERIENCE

All the lonely people
Where do they all come from?
All the lonely people
Where do they all belong?

(The Beatles)

Most of the material in this section is about the pathological aspect of void experiences and reflects my own position as a Psychiatrist and Analyst, as well as the focus of the psychoanalytic writers from whom my material has been gleaned. However, I would like to stress again that the experience of void states can also be non-pathological, in fact an indicator of psychological health, in that sometimes these states are a necessary part of the individuation process, and, indeed, of any meaningful psychological growth.

In health, emptiness is a prerequisite for any "taking in". Underlying all capacity for learning as well as eating is a tolerance of emptiness. A readiness to receive is implied and this suggests the state that is present before starting to fill up. It may be contrasted with the state of being too full to take in, as well as the failure that can be expressed as "nothing happening when it might have", e.g. the emptiness which results when the longed for and then "hallucinated" mother is not followed by the appearance of the "real" mother. Via failure, the state of emptiness then becomes a condition to be feared. (Winnicott)

To permit oneself the experience of the void once one has overcome the deep emptiness and sense of nothingness that accompanies the conditions discussed below, requires both courage and determination as well as an openness to the enormity of psyche itself. Tolerance of discovered aspects of oneself and submission to the sovereignty of the unconscious are likewise important psychological achievements that can be developed over time, with or without the benefit of a good-enough psychotherapeutic process.

Although the following chapters deal with rather extreme examples they do have significance on a less global scale for many different individuals. They are principally about the origins of some of the void states but also touch on aspects of both the delineation and the treatment of those states. What follows in this introduction is a brief synopsis of other conditions that may present as being connected with the void as well as some further remarks on the "healthy" experience of the void.

A mother (or parent) has certain conscious and unconscious expectations of, and desires for, how her child should be. The child has certain requirements to be fulfilled. When all goes well, there is a "goodness of fit", the child can be close to whom he is destined to be, and have that identity affirmed while having his needs met. The "gleam in the mother's eye" lets him know that all is well. (Kohut)

When those needs are denied or are not met for some other reason, or if there has been severe-enough deprivation or erratic mothering, the underlying structure of the personality is disturbed. There is a lack of connection between different parts of the personality, and complexes and archetypal constellations are most in evidence. Because the archetypes have not been humanized they remain one-dimensional and undifferentiated and they give a lopsided shape to the personality. The ego may identify with one or another of these fragments of the whole and because they remain unattenuated, each fragment is larger than life and when identified with seems to close down other possibilities of being. Somehow these archetypal fragments need to be incarnated, made more human. As one man articulated about his therapy: "I used to feel enormous (but undefined). Now I have come down to size but feel more substantial." Integration of different aspects of oneself is an achievement.

If her basic needs are only met conditionally, the infant learns to repress those aspects of herself that meet with disapproval. With a sure-enough sense of herself, a solidly cohered ego, what is repressed becomes what Jungians refer to as the shadow or the personal unconscious. Being outside of consciousness the shadow is removed from one's awareness of oneself, it is usually projected onto others. Because it is projected out of oneself it is not experienced as part of the personality and what is experienced in its stead is an absence or emptiness. On the other hand when the ego is weak or not sufficiently differentiated from the Self it becomes "over-shadowed". (Kathrin Asper lecture, 2002) Because it has to not know about or not respond to its instinctual desires or feelings, it learns to separate itself from them more forcibly. This results in a splitting-off from the core of the personality, a dissociation, resulting in an experience of loss or a feeling of something missing.

There is another level of void for this sort of child. The conditional mother, who is often abandoning, still represents the only possibility of obtaining what the child needs: food, warmth, being clean and dry, and above all, being loved. He becomes reliant on the tidbits he receives but is never fully satisfied. Because of the lack of connection to an interior sense of being "OK" he remains dependent, for that sense, on someone or something outside of himself. Paradoxically, he must often also supply the mothering that he needs himself to the actual mother, to keep her alive and responsive. Because her presence cannot be internalized, when his mother is not available he experiences her absence as a void.

One 25-year-old client of mine was unable to close the door of her room because that would separate her from her mother elsewhere in the house. This "elsewhere" mother veered between being over-intrusive and abandoning. My client became a compulsive caregiver but when people did not accept her care she experienced a terror of the void which resulted from a fantasy that without her care her mother would die, leaving her bereft.

As she tentatively began to form a relationship with her own interior (equivalent to a strengthening of the ego–Self axis) being in the presence of her mother undid that connection and led to a different kind of void experience. The new connection to herself was incompatible with her bond to her mother.

When the self-reliant defence of the schizoid patient cracks, through the admission of need, the individual may be flooded with intolerable affect. Feeling his desires and that he may be forced to act them out may bring on a fear of dissolution as the image of "who I am" starts to crumble. But, once he can tolerate them, fully experiencing his desires starts to delineate more certainly "who I am", and thus obliterates the void. "Hollow" is the word a man of the cloth used to describe the emptiness he felt when he no longer cared for his parishioners and wanted to follow a calling of his own.

Emptiness may also result from the parts that have been denied. They are denied for many different reasons. For example, in a girl or woman they may be denied because they are like her mother, or because they are not like her and would displease her, or because they are like negative aspects of the Great Mother and she wants to be a "good girl", or because they are like positive aspects of the Great Mother but too powerful to be seemly. (See *Individual Experiences*)

Too much of an identification with the mother is another way that personal identity is lost. This is more likely to occur in a female than a male and result in a sort of equivalence "I and my mother are one" with consequent loss of the sense of self or ego-identity. Thus, a void state may eventuate where a woman identifies too closely with her mother, or where a disidentification from her has taken place, and it may also arise from a denial of her need for a mother.

Torture puts the victim in the position of dependent child to a witch mother. The sense of a caring mother is lost and an indifferent, or frankly abusing, mother is constellated. Also there is the loss of the "container contained", a loss of meaning, and an experience of the "dark side of God". Trauma of any kind may precipitate the feeling that God or the universe is either malign or indifferent, and even indifference can be frightening. For some, the intuition of the presence of a watchful other is alarming; for others his or her absence is the ultimate emptiness.

Story telling may be a healthy form of individualistic self-expression by the teller, leading to self enhancement in the listener, but it can also be a process that is driven by collective values and that serves to boost a one-sided image of ourselves, or how we "ought" to be, and denies our deeper wholeness. Much of what is portrayed on television and other mass media is an example of this latter sort of story, and it is devoid of substance. The sort of art that carries a particular political or social message which subsumes the real purpose of art, which is to expand the boundaries of our awareness not constrict them, can also be mind deadening. These too are apprehensions of the void.

Absence of "proof" is another void experience that connects with loss of memory. It is a horror for many individuals not to be able to clearly recall what has been done to them and to mistrust the memories that they do have. This is particularly so with child sexual abuse where the adult survivor is unable to be intellectually certain if, what, and by whom things were done to her and yet she knows throughout her body that they were done. There is then a longing for a shred of evidence from outside her that would fill that emptiness. As one client put it, "If I could grasp one speck of dust of memory it could make the ground more solid." This person also named her "fear of the empty echo" a phrase which seemed to refer both to her lack of clear memory of past traumatic events and to the lack of responsive mirroring by her caretakers.

Another abused woman was deeply moved by the Grimm's (1975) fairy tale of *The Robber Bridegroom* in which the heroine tracks her future husband to his home in the forest and witnesses him and his band of robbers dismember a corpse. A finger becomes dislodged and flies into her lap where she lies hidden. Having made her escape she is able to show the finger as evidence that leads to the undoing of the bridegroom-to-be. For my patient, the finger represented a piece of tangible "flesh and blood" evidence, the sort of evidence that she lacked and the absence of which kept her from coming to some sort of terms with what she "knew" had happened and thus with whom she was.

The absence of memory links with the loss of time intervals and of the sense of continuous identity that occurs with dissociation and its extreme variant the Multiple Personality Disorder. Here there are lacunae in the fabric of a person's experience of himself that can be extremely distressing.

One female client who had the experience of being brought up by a "dead" mother, one who was probably severely depressed, once dreamed in terror that her mother was standing over a drain grating and leaking away into it. Her response to her chronic feeling of emptiness was to take a course in public speaking thus creating an external structure with which she could engage the world.

In an article, *The Therapist with her Back against the Wall*, Margaret Rustin (2001) describes a fourteen-year-old boy who had been left by his mother at the Social Services offices when he was eight. He believed that she had left him there temporarily and then been unable to find her way back to him. It was preferable to feel that he had been lost rather than that he had been abandoned. He hardly demonstrated any feelings about anything, as though waiting in a state of "lifeless inertia—sitting as if in a timeless world without movement or sound for extended periods." (Rustin, 2001, p. 280) It was as though if he moved, his mother would never find him again.

This "boy without a mind", as Rustin called him, showed no capacity for thinking or feeling and was experienced as being empty. It was as though the boy felt he would lose his thoughts as his mother had lost him, and his state of meaninglessness was being communicated to the analyst who then felt that she had nothing meaningful to say. Rustin described her countertransference feelings as fluctuating between a "drift into mindlessness" and a desire to "probe and prod and demand a response" from the child.

What helped in the psychotherapy, apart from having patience and the courage to face her own despair and not-knowing, was the therapist's sense of connection with an external support network and an internal working self. The therapist was not in a void, she was connected to both the external world and her own interior.

Stern has a lot to say about the alienating effects of language as a means of self-expression. He suggests that non-verbal experience may be a "conglomerate of feeling, sensation, perception and cognition". (Stern, 1985, p. 175) Verbal language on the other hand excludes whatever is not directly addressed. He gives the example of the experience of a patch of sunlight on the wall, which will have intensity, colour, warmth, shape, and the pleasure it evokes, as part of its experience. "Look at the yellow sunlight" immediately makes it into a visual experience only.

Language such as poetry can evoke an experience that transcends words, but usually words fracture a modal global experience or send it underground. "In learning a new word, a baby isolates an experience for clear identification and at the same time becomes accountable to mother for that word." (*ibid.*, p. 180) Accountability for the meaning of a word can lead to a denial of the non-verbal conglomerate, which then becomes unconscious. In this way the self is unavoidably divided by language. Verbal language is obviously a powerful tool and one by means of which we can learn to share our personal experience of the world with others but it is also a mechanism that separates us from the fullness of our own experiences, alienates us from ourselves. Both art and music will bridge that division.

The sort of void experience that is part of our healthy repertoire of experiences is more associated with mid-life and thereafter. It involves the process whereby the ego, gradually and incrementally, or sometimes abruptly, experiences a fall from the grace of certainty and enters the dark wood that Dante finds himself in at the start of *The Divine Comedy*, or the *Clouds of Unknowing* that the English Mystic describes. In order to endure this unknowing, either willingly sought or painfully submitted to, implies a strong sense of who one is. It goes with that toughness of spirit that has developed over a long period of continuing with life in spite of its felt meaninglessness or emptiness.

That "strong sense of who one is" is usually shattered or dissolved in this post-midlife process resulting in a feeling of becoming nothing, and yet this loss of ego-identity may also lead to a sense of burgeoning, and "that green fulfilment of blossoming trees". (Rilke, 1987, p. 273) The coming to know one's true self implies both a death and a rebirth.

CHAPTER FIVE

Empty of oneself

But listen to the voice of the wind and the ceaseless message
that forms itself out of silence.

(Rilke)

In Enid Balint's book, *Before I was I*, is a chapter entitled *On Being
Empty of Oneself*. (Balint, 1993) In this chapter Balint discusses
patients who demonstrate an important differentiation of the
Void experience. In the formulation that she offers, the patient feels
something opposite to a sense of being full of oneself or identified
with who one is; instead he may feel "empty of himself". Balint does
not use "self" in the Jungian sense of an archetypal organizing
principle around which the developing individual coheres but more
in the sense of the conscious feeling of "this is who I am". The person
who is "empty of himself" may have an inchoate feeling of "this is
not who I am", and is likely to dread human contact and resent
receiving help from others which exacerbate that feeling.

Such people, feeling inadequate, empty, and awkward, may lead
an outwardly normal social life although they are likely to feel
dissatisfied with their involvement. At the extreme end of the
spectrum they may withdraw completely from everyday life and this
is liable to aggravate their state of mind and lead to a sort of
confusion. They seem to feel safest when not alone nor <u>actively</u> with
anyone. Balint notes that this disturbance is more common in women
than men, and is often linked to a feeling of being full of lifeless
rubbish.

Balint developed her ideas through her work with a patient she calls Sarah. According to her mother's view, Sarah was problem-free until she left her home on the continent and arrived in London at the age of twenty-four. At this time she disintegrated psychologically, becoming confused and highly anxious. She then entered what turned out to be a difficult but productive therapy with Enid Balint.

For a long time Sarah experienced her relationship with her therapist and any interpretations made by her as meaningless, and she felt as though she was not seen or recognized. She became more withdrawn and suicidal yet seemed eager to find out if the therapist could perceive her distress. More terrifying than her nightmare world was the fear that the therapist would be like her mother and subjugate Sarah to her own world, by, for example, making her go back to work. Her mother's world she experienced as a complete void and that void she dreaded more than anything else. To be as her mother wished her to be, was to identify with what Winnicott called the "false self".

Over the years Balint pieced together a formulation that went something like this. From an early age and throughout her life, Sarah's mother had been unable to give Sarah adequate feedback about herself or supply the needed "echo" or mirroring. Because of the lack of feedback, Sarah felt that her true or core self went unrecognized and thus that she was "empty of herself" and had, perforce, to live in a void. She felt alone, but, being ignored, relatively safe. To have something, Sarah created a nightmare world, which she located in her head. This chaotic world was presumably preferable to the void experience. Sarah's attempted adjustment, in order to satisfy her parents, finally led to unbearable feelings of unreality and the breakdown when far from home.

In the early part of the therapy Sarah had regularly used to dissociate. Over time Balint became aware that the void from which Sarah was retreating was constellated by her lack of understanding of Sarah, "because that meant that I saw only the external shape of her body . . . but not what really mattered—herself." Thus, Sarah's felt sense of an intolerable internal emptiness (or absence of herself) was confirmed.

During the therapy, which lasted about six years in all, Sarah went through the following phases. She started off with a feeling of being empty of herself and of living in a void or emptiness, with a constant fear of impending catastrophe. After about eighteen months she started making drawings, first dots and dashes and later of increasingly developed part objects and body symbols. After about three years it was as though she started to fill up, actually experiencing feelings in her body. As she filled up, the world filled up. In spite of her persecutory anxieties she made some adjustment to reality.

What makes the article particularly striking, is its modernity with regard to ideas of mirroring by the mother, which Balint calls "echoing", and also the concept of feedback, that implies a response by the mother to an action of the child's, a response that is then fed back to the child. She does not quote Bion and this is long before Kohut was writing. In describing her impressions of Sarah's mother she states: "for her, mothering was an enveloping manipulating activity, where the infant herself had no potential, but was a kind of empty object into which she could or even must put her own self, so as to gain satisfaction and reassurance; she could not see her child as an independent person in her own right." (*ibid.*, p. 51)

Balint also makes the point that "this feeling of being empty or of 'being empty of herself' is more frequently found in women than in men." (*ibid.*, p. 40) It seems to me that this may be because there may not be a clear-enough differentiation between mother and daughter, as there necessarily is between a mother and her son, and that this easy over-identification with the mother leads to a lack of connection with oneself. The child's essence as an individual being is not validated and this may be not only because the child for some reason identifies with somebody outside of herself, but also because the projections she has to carry are so strong.

Amity

A few cases with very similar dynamics have been brought to my attention. The first also involved a young woman in her early twenties. She had been a model daughter and student, and she left home for another city to experience something different in her world. Within a very few weeks, Amity had become virtually catatonic, hardly able to communicate and seemingly dissociated. She was brought back to town and absorbed once more into the family home. The decision to let her continue there, as it was felt that her breakdown had been precipitated by being away from the family, nearly proved fatal, due to a sudden and serious suicide attempt. This necessitated her hospitalization.

Both her psychiatrist and psychoanalyst felt that separation from the parents was an urgent necessity, so that Amity could, in a secure but non-demanding environment, start to find herself rather than the self that she felt her parents wanted. Her parents, on the other hand, seemed bent on formulating her problem in a way that was counter to the opinions of most of the psychological staff involved in her clinic stay and regularly broke down the separation plans, so that they could "mother" her, even inside the clinic.

Having read Balint's paper and thought further about the case, I feel that something like the following is what obtained. It had been vital in the family system for Amity to be a certain way, to be happy, healthy, successful, and well liked. She initially appeared to be all those things and caused no ripples to appear on the smooth surface of the family pool. What happens in this sort of constellation is that the person does experience a sort of mirroring, but not of her Self, rather it is of her false self or persona. But it is the mirroring of something, so that while she is in the presence of the mirroring object/s she has some kind of identity. She must make do with having fragments of herself seen, a selective mirroring, or "echoing", for that is better than nothing; she may even start to know herself as she feels her parents want her to be.

When Amity was separated from her family that tenuous link to "who I am" broke down and, in its stead, all sorts of previously not-experienced, threatening, and shameful feelings welled up. These were not assimilable, yet they were her very own. This experience of chaos rapidly became too much for her resulting in her retreat into a dissociated state. Her doctor's initial experience of her was of a young girl who was trying to be sweetly compliant competing with a self-state that was disorganized, confused, and full of shame.

When first assessed, Amity had denied suicidal impulses, but moving back into the "caring" home environment precipitated a void experience that was unendurable. She became aware of being empty of herself and yet could no longer feel recognizable to her mother. She was cut off from any form of being known by an outside other, while at the same time being unknown to herself; she was nothing in a state of nothingness. Much later, when she was well again, she was able to describe how, when she had been away, she had had the "knowledge" that people were trying to steal bits of her soul or innermost being. Yes, she had been stolen from herself.

A striking aspect of the case was the way the parents sought hard to find a "medical" cause for her symptoms. An organic cause for her illness might have been less difficult to accept than this intangible sickness which demanded from them a new way of being with their daughter. Balint puts the requirement clearly, "What was needed was a human being who realised that she (the patient) was in another world and did not force her back into his world." (*ibid.*, p. 52) Balint meant the therapist but could equally have been referring to the child's parents.

It sometimes had seemed that there was a war on with Amity's treatment, with the psychological staff on one side and the family on the other, each vying to have their view of Amity accepted and worked with. This resulted in an escalation of tension within the system. As one senior member of the team found herself saying in reference to the parents, "Do I have to kill myself to get them to listen?" (This is a perfect countertransference encapsulation of Amity's problem.)

Some difficulties

One of the problems with dealing with a patient who is so "empty of themselves" and one that must obviously be made conscious in the therapist, is that the emptiness generates a desire in the therapist to obliterate it. This may be in the way suggested above where the therapist "knows" what is right for the patient and finds him or herself filling the patient with well-meaning interpretations or explanations, instead of allowing the slow accretion of self-knowledge to occur. Or it may be experienced in a concrete sexual way with the therapist, usually male, feeling a desire to "fill the hole" inside his patient in a literal way.

Whether in a literal or figurative way, that desire to fill the emptiness must be stood against. Neither the capacity nor the right to do that belongs to the therapist but rather to the patient. She is empty of herself because what she is has not been recognized or not been accepted. Instead someone else's imaginings have been forced upon her or into her, so what she most needs now is an alert receptivity from, rather than an intrusion by, her analyst.

I remember in my early dealings with such a patient suddenly realizing the "phallic" nature of the way that I was interacting with her. As she had been sexually abused by father figures, this mode was particularly inappropriate, although understandable. I resolved to try and be the opposite and in order to achieve this put myself in what I imagined was a receptive posture, relaxing deeper into my chair, letting my legs spread and my hands cup each other in my lap while I took some deep slow breaths and made myself available to listen. It needed this rather concrete enactment for me to achieve the sort of felt attitude that was necessary to just "be there" for her.

Another danger is that of shutting out the patient and her distress, not allowing them to touch you. By distancing ourselves from our patients we can pretend that their emptiness does not exist, but by doing that we exacerbate the void that they feel.

And solutions?

What is required of the therapist is witnessing, mirroring or echoing, and the supply of a space or container where the seemingly unendurable can be endured. The void inside has been formed, *inter alia*, through the denial of negative experiences, through defending against them. Those negative experiences are thus often the first experiences to be laid down within the previously empty space. The patient cannot and should not be protected from that, but she can be accompanied through the experience.

This process requires from the analyst, as from the analysand, qualities that the alchemists of old defined as patience, courage, honesty, and staying awake on the job. (Jung, 1966; Stevens Sullivan, 1989) Those aspects are what are needed as you witness the changes rather than ring them. It is difficult to peer impotently into the darkness or emptiness, glimpsing only the fragments shown to you and not what you wish or hope you could see, and to stay awake while you "do" nothing. But, for these patients particularly, this is the most critical attitude and aspect of treatment, the gradual, witnessed, filling of the void in the presence of the (mother)/ therapist, with that which belongs to the child and not with that which belongs to the mother/(therapist). For this to happen requires the receptive presence of an analyst at the right distance.

Whose cocoon?

A child of three was brought into play therapy with a colleague, by her parents, because of severe tantrums. Robyn, as I will call her, had been the second child in a family where the first-born son was adored and where the mother had been expecting and hoping for another boy. Her mother was depressed and preoccupied during her infancy and, as Robyn grew up, she used to follow her brother about and play with his toys and friends. Unlike most children she did not like to hear stories about herself but preferred those that focused on other family members, her brother particularly. She seemed to see herself as him.

When she used the word "hollow", in relation to some experience, her therapist felt that she was describing her own inner emptiness. In identifying so thoroughly with her brother, she too had become "empty of herself". After some years of a difficult therapy she asked her therapist to draw a caterpillar, cocoon, and butterfly, all on one page. This gave her much satisfaction. In a succeeding session she fantasized that the cocoon was already full and that the caterpillar would have to find its own cocoon. At one time, perhaps, she may have thought that both caterpillars could have fitted into the one cocoon but she was becoming painfully aware that each needed their own enclosed space in order to become themselves, to develop their own individualities. Like a hermit crab without its shell, the solitary caterpillar left out of a cocoon is alone and vulnerable.

I think it is significant that the already occupied cocoon was one drawn by her therapist. Perhaps it represents both the allure of the "space" in her mother's mind, in which she could become as her mother wished (and what she fantasized that her therapist wished), as well as the danger of losing her true identity, becoming what she was not. The big question will be, "Will what emerges from the therapeutic gestation be acceptable to my parents?" Meaning both the external parents, and the internal ones, who may be even more difficult to satisfy.

We could say that this child was empty of herself because, not being what her mother desired, she was forced to identify with what she was not, i.e. with an elder sibling. Another child may become empty of herself because of an identification with her mother. Another possibility, particularly in boys whose father is absent, is that not having a father to identify with, the child may identify with the absence itself. Being inadequately mirrored, by someone who is blind to the identity of the child, may also lead to this impasse.

The replacement child

The "replacement" child may also be a child "empty of itself". A good example is the poet Rilke, whose sister died in babyhood before he was born. His mother called him René Maria and dressed him in girl's clothes and it was only as an adult that he formally changed his name to Rainer, an unambiguously masculine name. Throughout his life he was deeply aware of being impinged on by people, prompting his advice to form a "vast solitude" around oneself. This solitude would protect an individual from the impingement of the other's need or opinion of him.

In his prose writing, *The Notebooks of Malte Laurids Brigge*, Rilke suggests that the story of the Prodigal Son is "the legend of a man who didn't want to be loved". In the eyes of his family, and his dogs, "he could see observation and sympathy, expectation, concern; . . . he couldn't do anything without giving pleasure or pain." (Rilke, 1987, p. 107) In order to be himself he must, of necessity, leave home; leaving the felt pressure to be what they wished him to be and what they loved him for. Rilke senses that we love in our own images, love our projections and not the individual; and we are loved, not because of who we are, but because of what others project onto us. Thus, to find ourselves we must leave those who love us.

When the Prodigal Son returns and is warmly greeted he is at first terrified that he will be ensnared by the family's love. But he has a sudden realization that enables him to stay; he is not understood, not encompassed by their "knowing" him. "(T)heir love . . . had nothing to do with him," he realizes. The passage ends: "How could they know who he was? He was now terribly difficult to love, and he felt that only One would be capable of it. But He was not yet willing." (Rilke, 1987, p. 115)

Rilke did long to be loved. As Mitchell states in his introduction to *The Letters to a Young Poet*: "You can see it in his eyes: the powerful intuition of the state of being that is called God, the huge oppressive longing for it, and the desolation." (Rilke, 1986, p. xii) What he longed for was to be embraced by a knowledge that was not limiting; a knowledge into which he could grow. The sort of knowledge that only the Self can have of one. His desolation arose from his awareness of his separation from that state of being, from God, from the Self. He was like the mystics whose awareness of God is tainted by their knowledge of not being God and being separate from Him. His intense yearning was what many feel for a deeper connection with the Self, the yearning that fuels the individuation journey. It also has the flavour of man's exquisite intolerance for imperfection and for intuitions of limitation that make the individuation process so difficult.

> "Who, if I cried out, would hear me among the angels' hierarchies?" he wrote. "And even if one of them pressed me suddenly against his heart: I would be consumed in that overwhelming existence."
> (Rilke, 1987, p. 151, from *The Duino Elegies* no. 1)

Who can hear me? This is one expression of being in a void. Feeling consumed by another's existence, is another.

Summary

Being empty of oneself is one of the void states and it may come about via a number of mechanisms. First is that state where the individual identity, the true self, has been ignored by one's parents, and the image of what they assume one to be has been inserted instead. Second is a condition where another identity seems more alluring, perhaps it is felt to be more attractive to the individual's caregivers or perhaps it seems safer or to carry more prospect of reward. Third, and there are many varieties of this, the individual identifies with only an aspect of themselves or another, and this may even be of someone absent such as a dead sibling.

   In the first case the feeling of emptiness will be exacerbated by being close to one's parents, especially after a break from them. (This has some resonance with the Winnicottian idea of early "impingement" by the primary object that leads to a retreat to what he called "secondary isolation".) In other cases, being with parents or with others who reinforce a one-sided view of you will feel temporarily satisfying and it is leaving them that may precipitate a void experience. It may only be after considerable work, and suffering, that one can attain the position of feeling connected with oneself both when alone and when in the presence of another.

CHAPTER SIX

The void in psychogenic autism

... if one of them pressed me
suddenly against his heart: I would be consumed
in that overwhelming existence.

(Rilke)

In a 1988 article, *Psychotherapy with Children Who Cannot Play*, Frances Tustin summarizes her theories about "psychogenic" autism. She suggests that this variant of autism arises from the combination of an extremely sensitive infant with a mother who is unresponsive, usually because of depression. This early lack of responsiveness is so traumatic that the child becomes cut off and encapsulated by autistic practices that block the capacity for play and for relationships. (This chapter is not about autism per se but about Tustin's model for a variant of it which I think is highly applicable to those suffering from one of the Void states.)

Autistic objects

Tustin coined the name "autistic object" for the hard objects that autistic children carry round with them, and she suggests that each of these hard objects is experienced by the child as a part of his own body, a part that keeps him safe. The stability of structure and the resistance of these objects to change are what allow them to function as protectors; and their real or shared functions, as keys or toys for example, and also their symbolic meaning, are irrelevant. As being "'me' objects (they) help the child to feel that he exists and that his 'going on being' is ensured." They also shut out distressing flashes of awareness of what is felt to be "not me", an awareness that seems to threaten both the existence and the safety of these children. (Tustin, 1988, p. 94)

Experience of another person is felt to be catastrophic and thus guarded against as effectively as possible. This is a very different situation from that of most children whose knowledge that they exist is tied up intimately with their experience of the "other", with "the gleam in the Mother's eye" to use Kohut's phrase. Here an infant looking into the mirror of the maternal gaze sees himself reflected and comes to know both himself and his mother. Even if the mirror distorts, as it so often does, and the image reflected is not a true one, the effect is not as catastrophic as that caused by the mirror that does not reflect at all. For many, indifference on the part of the other is the worst experience of all as it implies "you do not exist for me".

In some autistic children, the terror that "I do not exist" arises simply from being in the presence of another. Any intrusion of the "not-me", as the other may be experienced, accentuates that fear of non-being. The autistic objects are barriers to the "not-me" experience. Tustin contrasts them with Winnicott's "transitional objects" which are a combination of "me" and "not-me" and help to link the two together, i.e. the transitional objects form a bridge connecting the "me" to the "not-me", whereas the function of the autistic objects is to maintain a distance between them.

Autistic shapes

Another defence used by autistic children is the production of what Tustin calls "autistic shapes". She feels that the stereotypical movements that many of these children make have their origin in soft bodily sensations arising from the flow of fluids, such as urine or spit or even diarrhoea or vomit, around the body. One can imagine how comforting the spreading warmth of urine released into the nappy might be, for example. These comforting sensations can later be engendered by holding an object loosely, or pressing against it, or by rocking, spinning, or making stereotypical movements of the hand or body. Unlike the hard autistic objects, the autistic shapes are soft, fluid, and evanescent. They function as a bodily generated form of tranquillizer, soothing and calming the child and preventing impingement from the outside world. (*ibid.*, p. 94)

Like chemical tranquillizers, such as alcohol or the benzodiazepines, autistic shapes prevent emotional and cognitive development by attenuating interaction with the outside world. My understanding is that the autistic objects are like a hard shell or armour whereas the autistic shapes are more like deep layers of cotton-wool or downy duvets, but that both function by keeping otherness at bay. The hard shell protects from intrusion while the duvets soothe and comfort, allaying anxiety. These result in the void experience of being distant from others, as in "you/they do not exist", while protecting the child from the void experience of "I do not exist".

Origins of the black hole

One of Tustin's ideas is that when the infant feels the withdrawal of the mother, he feels not only that she is going away, but that part of him is being removed too. Because he experiences that she and he are one, if she has gone it is as though part of himself has also gone. Tustin describes her understanding of a four-year-old's revelation to her that as an infant he had experienced the nipple, or "button" as he called it, as an extension of his tongue, i.e. as part of himself. When the nipple was withdrawn this was experienced as the loss of the nipple-tongue, causing the shocking realization that it was not always present, and that its presence was not under his control. His description of this loss, and the burning rage that it aroused, was that his mouth had become "a black hole with a nasty prick".

Tustin quotes Winnicott as saying that in a more organized state "the same loss of the mother would be a loss of object without the added element of loss of part of the subject", i.e. in this case the child would experience the loss of the nipple of the mother but not of his own tongue. (ibid., p. 95) The nipple-tongue as the source of warm nourishment is felt as a vital part of the infant's body, and his experience of it guarantees both his safety and his going on being. The loss of it and the consequent "shell-like vacuum of nothingness" cancel out all hope, so that these patients are in a state of helpless despair, assailed by nothingness and yet protected by nothingness. (ibid., p. 98–9)

Another way of saying this, is that there is a lack of separation or differentiation between the infant and external objects. When the object withdraws, because of depression or even as part of "good-enough" rather than "perfect" mothering, not only does the infant lose the object but she also loses part of herself. This loss gives rise to a "black hole" or void within the child, and at the same time to a loss of omnipotence, even of agency; she has become powerless to prevent this happening. The response to this trauma is the walling-off described above so that the autistic child becomes the omnipotent ruler of her "castle of nothingness".

One of the patterns of anxious attachment that Bowlby described is that of compulsive self-reliance where the infant and later the child or even adult takes over the care of itself and also, often, of its primary objects. The autistic child cannot fall back on the illusion that he does not need anyone or that he could look after everyone necessary, because that very solution implies the sustained recognition, and the threatened loss, of something that is other and thus outside his control.

Because the loss of the other is intolerable, it is walled off from conscious awareness and never mourned, which Tustin feels is one of the autist's main problems. (ibid., p. 95) In fact, the autistic object or shape "is" the lost object, has become identical with it, so loss of the object is never experienced and thus cannot be mourned. It is only after the child has learned to mourn (mourning implying the conscious experience of loss) that the capacity for symbolization, and thence thinking and speech, can develop. Thinking is a symbolic function that is only made possible through separation, separation between subject and object, and without thought we live in a void. (There is a story that one day Descartes was sitting on an aeroplane on the way to a congress on the Philosophy of Mindfulness, when the stewardess approached him. "Would you like a drink?" she asked. "I think not," replied Descartes, and disappeared.)

The obliteration of the presence of the other results also in the lack of empathy that is so characteristic of these children. There is no feeling connection with another because the other cannot be allowed to exist.

The nothing barrier

Stern (1985), in his book *The Interpersonal World of the Infant*, discusses infant development from the experience of what he calls the

Emergent Self through the Core Self, the Subjective Self, and thence to the Verbal Self. Mario Jacobi (Seminar) has linked these concepts to the Jungian ideas of Typology, suggesting that these "selves" give rise, respectively, to the functions of intuition, sensation, feeling, and thinking. The impossible areas for the autist are feeling and thinking. Their walling off of the core self, hiding the emptiness from themselves under a shell of sensations, separates them from others, prevents empathic connections with those others, impairs the acquisition of language, and thus the development of thinking. To think is to have a relationship with oneself and that suggests a sort of duality that would be threatening to the world of "perilous-sameness" that the autistic child inhabits.

The autistic child's immersion in an ever-present sensory world protects them from experiencing loss so that they are never stimulated to call to mind absent people or objects by means of pictures, images or memories. (Tustin, 1988, p. 97) What the autistic child does is live in a world of ever-present physical contact of the hard or soft varieties. Only what is tangible and physically present is felt to exist, and, as memories, images, fantasies, and thoughts are intangible, these constituents of mental life cannot develop and without them imagination is blocked.

Being unable to tolerate the experience of being separate from the outside world, the autistic child lives in a state of non-differentiation from the world around him. He cannot clearly differentiate what is me from what is not-me, inside from outside, real from imaginary. Whereas, in more normal infants the missed or longed-for breast is temporarily substituted by means of sucking digits, the fist, or a comforter, and later by the image or memory of the parent, in the autistic child the breast is replaced and the nurturant mother blocked out of awareness by the hard autistic objects. These effectively render the mother and her caring ministrations null and void, so that both mother and child are surrounded by nothingness. (ibid., p. 99) In fact he feels a nothing, embedded in nothingness, and nothing but nothing.

The autistic child surrounds herself with nothingness or void and the experience of that too is painful. She is in a no-win situation. If the awareness of the lost nipple-tongue is allowed into consciousness that is a reminder of having things stolen from her, being diminished, or not being in control. The defences against that give rise to the feeling of nothingness but it is a nothingness that, like the pleroma, contains all there is. If there is no difference between myself and another, then neither of us exist as separate beings. As in the primordial oneness of the biblical beginnings when everything was "without form and void", yet somewhere in the background, or foreground, or filling everything, was God. Massive anxieties arise when the intuited presence of another fractures the pleroma and being "all" reduces itself to being "nothing". Not surprisingly, when patients can be rescued from this autistic state and begin to speak, they may refer to themselves as being "God" or the "king", but being a nothing is not far away.

Treatment

Treatment of these patients focuses on the idea of gently but firmly creating a frame in which the child can be helped out of his idiosyncratic universe of self-imposed darkness and into a world of shared meaning. Tustin uses the word "common-sense" a good deal; this word suggests both the low-key nature of the work and the idea of the commonality of experience between individuals. The frame, when it can be endured, results in a decrease in the sense of autonomy and control, and an awareness of an alive other with whom one can be in relationship.

By refusing to be blotted out, made null and void, the therapist makes her presence as a separate object felt by her patient. This fosters the dissolution of the sense of oneness and the growth of the feeling within the child that he exists as a separate being. Coincident with this, dawns the realization that the therapist's absence, and, via the transference, the absence of the nurturant mother, cannot be avoided by the use of autistic objects or shapes. Tustin quotes Bion as saying "the wanted breast begins to be felt as an idea of a 'breast missing', and not as a 'bad breast present'" (*ibid.*, p. 102), i.e. it is experienced not simply as a "black hole" or an "emptiness" *but where something has been and should be*. It is an emptiness that contains the shape of what is missing rather than a void without end. Both the child and her objects begin to be sensed as being within their own protective skins. This definition of her own boundedness and her separateness from others, leads to a space beginning to open up between herself and others, and within her own mind. It is within this space, that fantasy and symbolic thought begin to emerge. With this new capacity comes the potential for play and, finally, language.

Autistic objects and shapes vs. skin

Autistic objects obliterate the surrounding world, fostering a sense of going-on-being through their hardness and immutability, and autistic shapes obliterate boundaries and edges, where things start or finish, through their soothing softness. But a skin contains and separates in the presence and in the absence of another. A skin allows some interaction across its boundedness. The castle wall type of barrier that exists around some very violent children, because of its inflexibility and impermeability, may prevent a child from learning what is happening on its other side. So he lacks affective attunement to the other, lacks empathy, and obtains no practice in the modulation of his own affect. This leads to abrupt expressions of aggression when his defences have been breached.

Hopefully, the therapeutic container will be able to adequately hold the analysand so that the castle walls can be breached without undue harm, and thus he may learn more about those on the outside of his world and about his own reactions to them. He can learn, through commonality of experience, to connect inside with outside and himself with another, and visit, as Winnicott articulated in another context, "the seashore of endless worlds (where) children play."

CHAPTER SEVEN

Another "black hole"

The emptiness is endless
Cold as the grave.

(Bob Dylan)

The "black hole" is an idea borrowed from astronomy and refers to the intense gravitational force that occurs when a star or even a galaxy collapses in on itself. This causes such a powerful pull that even light waves become sucked in *once they get too close*. There is no escape once a particular threshold is reached and as far as any distant observer is concerned, what enters a black hole simply disappears. Pecotic (2002), in an article entitled *The "black hole" in the inner universe*, describes how an experience of a "black hole" may express itself as autism. In this article, she describes how the "black hole" may be constituted inside the object as opposed to within the subject as Tustin described. She suggests that the child's autistic withdrawal occurs when the child turns away from the object that contains a "black hole" to avoid being sucked in.

Pecotic noted that when the young child that she describes started coming out of his autistic withdrawal there would be moments of closeness between the two of them but that these were followed by an abrupt change where the child would seem terrified of her. She realized that that terror was precipitated by the child looking into her eyes, an act which would be a normal way of confirming a shared experience, looking for the gleam as it were. But he seemed to see there something completely annihilating and would scream in terror. He pushed her away with one hand yet held on in desperation with the other.

Various drawings of his helped her piece together what was happening. The first two of these were drawn on both surfaces of one page, which seemed to indicate that he wanted her to see them in conjunction, as two sides of himself. On the one side were two animals, a zebra and a giraffe, seemingly in communication with each other. Apart from the zebra (on the left of the picture) leaning a bit away from the connection while the giraffe leant towards him, the figures seemed quite happy.

On the reverse side the feeling was very different, this time the figure on the left was a small circus elephant (remember they never forget). It was facing right but leaning backwards as though skidded to a sudden halt. In front of him was an irregular oval structure, like an egg standing on its end, with a darker oval inside it and within that, an area of deep blackness. This right-side figure looked amorphous and vaguely threatening and was somehow associated with eyes. It was as though this "eye" with its "black hole" distorted the elephant's picture and threatened to suck it in, and the elephant resisted that suction.

The child's mother had suffered from clinical depression and even become psychotic at times. Pecotic understood that this mother was present enough for her child to relate to, but that suddenly and unpredictably she would collapse, lose all hope, and threaten to suck her son into the emptiness of her cosmic despair. He would have needed a strong sense of individual being to withstand her collapse; while enmeshed with her he was unable to withstand the pull into nothingness. So to protect himself from the terror of that pull he turned away and took refuge behind autistic defences. As Pecotic notes: "If you go dead, you cannot disappear; if you kill not only the attachment to the object, but even the awareness of it you cannot be pulled in and annihilated: there is nothing out there to do it to you." (Pecotic, 2002, p. 52) But this does mean that you begin to dwell in the void.

Eye/Witness

The boy began to draw eyes during his therapy and the initial ones were drawn completely blacked out. Gradually, more and more white appeared in them, until only a small area of blackness remained, like an offset pupil retained within the white iris. One of these later eyes he labelled "eyewintiess" (sic); it carried the idea of being witnessed by an outside object, presumably his therapist.

Pecotic felt that a shift took place during the therapy, from the extremity of a "black hole" swallowing the good object (mother or therapist) and threatening to suck the child in too, to one in which the "black hole" was contained within the good object who also bore witness to the child's existence and growth. The good-enough therapist was mostly able to be an adequate witness of the child's identity, but that capacity could be lost, and the child could not fully rely on it. This represents a move from the "unformulated fear of annihilation (being sucked into a 'black hole') to fear of loss of identity in a world full of chaos." (*ibid.*, p. 46)

There is a difference between the sort of void space that Tustin described and this one. In Tustin's cases the original trauma, the "black hole", is experienced as the loss of part of oneself, the soothing nurturant part, the nipple-tongue, giving rise to the terror of leaking away or losing more of oneself. This fear is re-awakened whenever someone is experienced who is not part of the self. Anything that constellates the feeling of another's presence in the universe is intolerable and the universe is maintained as a safe but insular place through the defensive exploitation of hard autistic objects and as a tenuously comfortable one through the use of autistic shapes.

The great wall and closed gates of his defences seal off an empty paradise so that there is nothing inside and nothing outside that could suggest, first, the presence of another, and, second, dependence on that other. One of my adult patients, sitting stiffly in the soft rocker in my rooms, could describe how the activity of rocking needed, for her, to be carried out in a hard chair, something *she* could thrust against, creating in that repetitive movement generated by herself a combination of hard and soft autistic defences.

For her to be rocked <u>by</u> the chair was to lose her autonomy and constellate the presence, and threatened absence, of another. This was linked in her psyche to the omnipotent mother who could hold her in her arms, dash her to the ground, let her drift off into space, or simply walk away. It was better to be in control than suffer dependence on such an object!

It is the *aliveness* of the other that is threatening in Tustin's cases, whereas what the infant recoils from, in what Pecotic describes, is the *deadness* of the other. It is not intrusion that is feared nor an active withdrawal, but the feeling that the mother's life has been sucked into a "black hole". The "black hole" then threatens to drown or suck in the infant himself and his only recourse is to turn away.

Too light or too heavy

If there is no such thing as a baby without a mother, as Winnicott has offered, then in the absence of the mother, or in the presence of a "dead mother", as the depressed mother has been called, the child's very existence is under threat. The individual response to different degrees of this deadness may be on a spectrum from acting-out behaviour, a struggling against or definition of identity through opposition, through to the sort of turning away and walling off that Pecotic describes. In between these two extremes and driven by differences such as the age of the infant or child, the severity of the maternal depression, the presence or absence of redeeming or protective others, and the character of the child, would be attempts made by the child to keep her mother alive or to deny the importance of her mother through "compulsively self-reliant" behaviour. This sort of behaviour may extend as a lifetime pattern or come crashing down in a flurry of hopelessness during some episode in life such as a lost-love or a midlife crisis.

One of the symbols of the *puer aeternus*, that state of skirting or flirting with the void, is Peter Pan. The creator of Peter Pan, J.M. Barrie, was a young boy when his elder brother was sent away to a larger centre to further his education. He was not long there when he became ill and abruptly died. His mother, paralysed by grief, took to her bed and spent the next long years in the gloom of her shuttered bedroom. The young Barrie made it his task to enliven her by telling her stories in an attempt to bring a smile to that dead face. Reading the story of *Peter Pan*, one is moved by the almost palpable sense of lostness that pervades the book. Peter Pan has never had anyone to teach him or show him how to play, so that he is never sure whether he is doing it right or not, nor can he adequately differentiate play from the serious business of living. The Lost Boys, who are also the "motherless ones", capture that sense too.

Many of those in the healing profession are products of homes in which depression in one of the parents has been a feature. One can imagine the strong impulse to bring light into the dead eyes of a mother, the *Mater Dolorosa*, so that those eyes may reflect you and thus affirm your own going-on-being. Making reparative gestures is a way of fixing the hole in the maternal container so that she will not leak away, and will thus remain to contain you. The "black hole" compresses voluminous matter into virtually nothing but mass, even light gets sucked into it when it gets too close. Infants of depressed mothers and carers of depressed people are threatened by the fear that their own "light" may be extinguished.

One of my clients, who had a depressed mother and is now in one of the caring professions, fixes me with a gaze that is both quizzical and demanding. It seems to say "if you do not keep contact with me I may die". A demonstration of her aliveness, through her evincing some affect, brings a profound relief into the room. In order to feel that relief, I may attempt to enliven her, perhaps by teasing her or reminding her of some positive or negative events in her life. To feel distress even, is to be alive, and if she is alive then heavy responsibility lifts from my shoulders and I no longer feel the pull of the black-hole. The black-hole seems to exist in the room and its potent pull shifts from one to the other of us.

Some thoughts about mirroring

The eye may be a container or it may be an intruder, it may shut you out from its promise of vitality or suck the "light of your life" into itself. One of its most important functions is as a mirror. When mirrored one can see oneself in the eye of the other but one can also see the other, i.e. one can get to know oneself and the other. If the view of oneself as seen in the mirror of the other is distorted, then, to feel some connection with that other, one may endure that, but "if I look down to see myself," as one woman described it, "there is no one there . . . my shoes are empty." To return to the mirror that distorts you or denies your presence implies that you are distorting the mirroring object or needing some distortion yourself, as in "this is the object the reflection in which matches this view of myself". By maintaining an idealized view of whom one could or should be, one can maintain an idealized view of the mother too, "If I was as I should be, she would be as I wish she was."

If the reflection is defended against, then there is no way of getting to know the mirror either, by shutting out the reflection you shut out the mirror too. It is as though the other has no subjectivity of his own, he is simply an object whose behaviour, or view of the subject, can be manipulated by that subject. The object's behaviour is made explicable only in terms of the subject's behaviour and not out of his own nature; "If I am better behaved, more loveable, slimmer, etc., then he (the object) will meet me on time (or at all)."

These ways of thinking come from the same place that results in the abused child's sense of being to blame and being responsible; "I cannot allow myself to know that my carers are mad or bad, it must be my fault and thus in my power to make it better."

The mirror can give a distorted view because of a distortion in the mirror, some flaw that prevents a true reflection. The mother may simply be blind to certain parts of the child or to some of his experiences. These may be strengths, for example an artistic capacity or a liveliness that the mother is threatened by, or incapacities, such as a physical or intellectual limitation or a personality trait that would sully her idealized view of her child. Due to physical or mental absence, the mirror may give no reflection at all, like a switched-off television the grey screen stares out blankly. Worse is the sort of screen that shows a different movie from that which is played out before it, a movie that the child is forced to watch. Actually, it is difficult to say which is worse. For some the implacable indifference of eyes that will not see is the most terrifying experience of all.

These forms of mirroring can be contrasted with the best mirroring, which is that which is able to demonstrate to the mirrored one a deeper sense of knowing, that can show the person to themselves, not just as they are now but as they could be. It functions in a non-judgmental and yet discriminating way and is a huge help toward individuation. It can arise only in the absence of narcissism and is hopefully a quality of a good therapist. The objective psyche, which shows us to ourselves via the principle of complementarity, may behave in this way and at times seem to be closely involved, while at other times it seems hugely indifferent.

In Balint's case, described above, because of the selective seeing of the mother, which denies most of the reality of the child, the child sees only bits of itself in the mirror. What is reflected is not the Self, not the child's instinctual parts or her potential, but fragments of herself that she can identify with and that serve to give her an initial feeling of being in contact with someone who knows her. In the absence of her mother, she ceases to be mirrored and loses that sense of connection. The imparted sense of identity is not sustainable in the mother's absence because it exists primarily in the mother's imagination. When deprived even of that distorted mirroring the daughter drifts into chaos.

In the psychotherapy Balint felt that she needed to be a presence who could witness and mirror everything shown to her without demonstrating a desire for it to be different or heal quicker. Gradually, the fragments could coalesce and her patient could begin to know herself, the ego–self axis was being restored. Later, in the presence of her mother, that tenuous sense of self deserted her because it could not be seen by her mother, or she did not feel that it could be, hence the "void in the presence of the mother". This fluctuating situation continued until her sense of self had become more firmly established and could survive even when un-mirrored. Then she could exist even in the absence of an external mirroring object. She was now in the stage of object constancy and could evoke the memory of an absent object by whom she could feel seen. She could now mirror herself.

Good mirroring does not cut out the bad either but shows both good and bad aspects to the mirrored one. An autistic child had a phrase that she asked her mother to repeat to her when her world turned topsy-turvy. This was, "The wall collapsed and then there was chaos." She seemed to want her experience of chaos to be witnessed by her mother and held by her without panic in much the same way as a mother might indicate, "That looks sore but it will get better."

Poor mirroring may be a result of parents deliberately not seeing an aspect of their child, a severe birth defect for example, or, conversely, focusing on a particular aspect, that defect or a specific strength, that excludes a whole view of the child. Whatever is not reflected becomes part of the void or the void itself.

Explanatory doodles

My patient Mary made the following doodles:

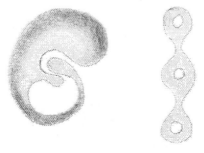

Figure 1

The figure on the left represented Mary herself as a self-comforting, self-nurturing system, and that on the right represented the non-supplying mother. She spoke about her feeling with regard to the uroborus that its eating of itself would be painful and that it may poison itself. Although, at one level the uroborus represents an ever-present source of nourishment under the individual's control, it also implies that to be fed is to be eaten, to be nurtured is to become depleted.

Figure 2

Thus there is a need for an-other to break that cycle. One can imagine how the pseudopodium in the figure's "mouth" becomes unplugged and reaches across to the erect figure, to feed it or be fed by it. (Figure 2) When that other turns away, because of her own needs and emptinesses, a collapse ensues and Mary becomes increasingly "empty of herself".

Figure 3

In response to Mary's doodles, I tried to express the other material written about here in doodle form. Tustin's case would look like

Figure 3. The infant initially feels that he is the originator of all good feelings, he and the breast are one.

Figure 4

When the nipple is removed, he feels that a "black hole" has opened up where "his" tongue-teat had been.

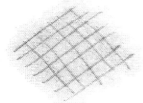

Figure 5

This is catastrophic and results in feelings of annihilation. (Figure 5)

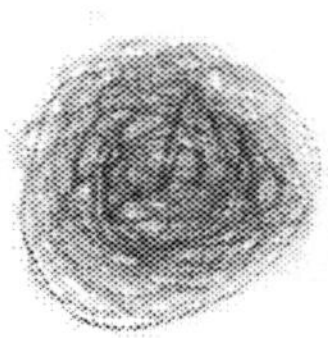

Figure 6

In defending against that he feels (Figure 6) that he is a nothing or (Figure 7) is surrounded by nothing.

Figure 7

This is the all-there-is phenomenon that results in the sense of the individual being the monarch, the lord of all he surveys, or nothing at all.

Pecotic's case I envisage as follows:

Figure 8

Firstly, contented feeding. (Figure 8)

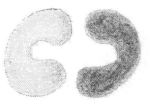 

Figure 9   Figure 10

The mother becomes depressed and withdraws (Figure 9) and the infant feels sucked into the hole that the mother appears to be. (Figure 10)

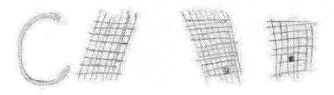

Figure 11   Figure 12

The infant extracts himself on the brink of the void (Figure 11) and builds his own autistic defences to protect himself from the "black hole". (Figure 12)

Figure 13

I feel that something similar happens with the anxious attachment pattern of compulsive self-reliance. (Bowlby) (Figure 13)

Figure 14

Except that the mother's withdrawal (Figure 14) is not experienced as catastrophically as in Pecotic's case. This means that there is not a need to withdraw so radically.

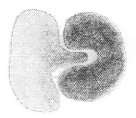

Figure 15

The infant may feel effective in his work of sustaining the mother (Figure 15), and thus begins a lifetime of depletion coupled with a difficulty in separation.

Figure 16   Figure 17

Imaged as fluctuating between the situation in Figures 16 and 17.

Summary

In this chapter I have summarized the views of different writers about the generation of some void states and fleshed their opinions out with material from my own practice. The fundamental attitude of the individuals who are discussed here is one of acute sensitivity to the void and those situations that threaten to precipitate an experience of it. This sensitivity precludes them from having the sort of healthy relationship to the void that allows for a deep experience of psyche and of the generative nothing that constitutes the "positive" void experience.

CHAPTER EIGHT

Memory within the Borderline condition

Well it's flooding down in Texas,
All the telephone lines are down.
I've been trying to call my baby,
Lord! I can't get a single sound.

(Sung by Stevie Ray Vaughan)

Focusing on the Borderline patient, Adler and Buie (1979) describe their ideas of the development of a core state of intensely painful aloneness, emptiness, panic, and despair, and the feeling of hopelessness that things will ever change. These are all elements of the void experience. They assert that these feelings increase with the closeness of the pathology to the psychotic spectrum. (I'm not so sure of that, it sometimes seems to me that the frankly psychotic patient is no longer so alone or is defended from his aloneness by his fragmentation.) For them this condition is a fundamental personality defect as a result of developmental failures. One of the Borderline's core issues is an inability to maintain a state of feeling involved with a sustaining other.

They mention Kernberg's focus on splitting defences, Frasch's ideas of transient reality testing problems, and Chase's stress on feelings of abandonment, and then they give their own definition of the disorder. They describe "borderline patients as people with a relatively stable personality organisation who are particularly vulnerable to feelings of abandonment and aloneness which are precipitated in the context of dyadic relationship." (Adler & Buie, 1979, p. 84)

To alleviate feelings of aloneness, primitive infantile needs on the spectrum of touch through to merger are mobilized. But there is also a fear of merger, or closeness even, with its felt danger of mutual destruction (the collapse of two into one) and this leads to the use of primitive defences such as projection, projective identification, splitting, and a primitive idealization.

That is, vulnerability leads to burgeoning needs that give rise to increasing fears and defences against those fears, and all of these need to be addressed within the psychotherapy.

Aloneness and memory

The feeling of aloneness (the void experience) may arise from one or more of the following routes:

1. An annihilatory (rendering into nothing) rage at the object for being non-sustaining may lead to the felt "death" of the object.
2. Neediness leads to a desire for incorporation, which would result in the loss of self and/or object. The person then tries to distance in a schizoid way thus increasing the sense of aloneness.
3. Intolerable grief at loss, e.g. of the vacationing therapist, leads to denial of the existence of the sustaining other and of the internal object.
4. The absence of the actual sustaining object or <u>an affective memory or 'introject'</u> of it. The sustaining object is not just one that fulfils, for example, oral needs but is felt to be critical for actual survival. That is, it is not just a question of needs not being gratified, and the resultant anger, but a fear of destruction or death that results in panic.

If, during development, there is too much of a feeling of aloneness, the infant will not be able to develop "libidinal object constancy"; i.e. sustaining introjects will be unstable and subject to loss through a process of structural regression. Abler and Buie formulate their understanding in terms of Fraiberg's use of Piaget's six stages of object constancy. Object constancy results in the infant's capacity to <u>evoke</u> the image of an absent object. This <u>evocative</u> memory coincides with the achievement of symbolic thought, increasingly complex speech, deferred imitation of others, and imaginative play. It is usually achieved by about eighteen months of age and is an advance on simple recognition memory, i.e. recognizing what is there, that is achieved anywhere between eight and thirteen months.

Evocative memory may be for persons or things. With good mothering, there is earlier person-permanence and better all-round permanence, whereas with poor mothering, thing-permanence occurs earlier than person-permanence. The achievement of evocative memory is important because it results in a capacity to self-soothe by means of awakened memories and fantasies of real people. Transitional objects are significant in linking recognition memory with evocative memory but the authors stress that the mother must be 'good enough', i.e. available often enough, for the child to use the transitional object effectively. Where she has not been available enough, achieved evocative memory may be vulnerable to rapid regression. Evocative memory is not only in relation to the mother but is concerned with any affective object relationship.

Rage and the loss of memory

Adler and Buie think that the absence of evocative memory is the most important lack in Borderline patients; i.e. Borderline individuals have not achieved solid evocative memory with regard to affective object relationships. Thus, when faced with certain stresses, such as the loss of important people or their support, they are prone to regress to recognition memory or even earlier. Separations, especially if lengthy, and the experience of rage precipitated by the loss of adequate support aggravate the situation. The route may be some-thing like this: separation leads to upset, that expands into rage, that leads to decompensation or regression, and feelings of aloneness and panic develop.

They attempt to differentiate two types of rage. The first, milder form of rage, they call "recognition memory rage". For example, with the loss of his mother, there may be anger and regression to the stage of recognition memory. This leads to the child losing from his mind the comforting image of his mother (in her absence) and subsequent despair. With the reappearance of his mother, recognition of her takes place, and with that a mobilization of the rage which is then attached to her image; he then hates and rejects her.

If there has been a further regression, with annihilatory rage, a loss even of the recognition of the mother takes place. This is associated with the production of diffuse anger that is no longer focused only on the mother or on any specific object, but is wide ranging. Because of its felt destructiveness it gives rise to extreme panic.

Tolerance

According to these authors, there seem to be critical times for the effects of good mothering, not only in the first year, but also during Mahler's rapprochement sub-phase of separation–individuation. The child becomes more tolerant of her awareness of what she is missing and learns to trust that what has been lost can be regained.

Where their formulation becomes particularly helpful is in demonstrating the need to find ways of giving support, e.g. extra time, phone calls, even hospitalization, so that the therapist can be kept alive in the patient's mind between sessions or during crises. Also, in helping the therapist deal with her patient's rage through understanding and interpretation and survival, while demonstrating her care and consistency. When the therapist is to be away, they suggest some sort of transitional object, such as a piece of paper with the therapist's phone number on it, or a small gift or loan, such as a book or a journal in which the patient can write down monitored thoughts; anything that will jog the evocative memory. The covering therapist's job is often to keep the absent therapist alive in the patient's mind by talking about the patient's experience of her. Regression at this time could lead to the complete loss of the affective memory of the therapist, and further regression would result in the loss of any memory of the therapist's existence at all. This is where the void experience occurs.

The full cycle would be something like this: in the presence of a soothing therapist, the patient may be able to risk suffering and thus relinquish some of his defensive distancing from her. His dependency needs would then increase. These needs result in an increased vulnerability to feelings of abandonment, increasing rage, which results in destruction of the internal image, and consequent feelings that something is missing. This is experienced as emptiness and reacted to with further rage. This rage increases the sense of alienation and aloneness, with a resultant increase in the rage and, now, panic; especially when the patient is away from his therapist. He now cannot remember the soothing experience, and then cannot even conjure up a memory of his therapist. He has lost evocative memory capacity in this sector of his life and regressed to the stage of recognition memory or worse. In my terminology, he has entered the void.

The therapist's capacity to survive the patient's rage demonstrates what Winnicott has called her "intrinsic survival value". This aids the task in working through, which is to provide an interpersonal experience over time that will result in increments to the patient's evocative memory of the sustaining therapist. So then the patient can be sustained to some extent by his memories with a consequent reduction in the anger caused by the therapist's absence. This results in less of a regressive pressure on the evocative and recognition memory and the therapist is kept alive in the patient's mind.

The aim, for these patients, is to achieve a solid use of evocative memory that is resistant to regression; this represents a shift from the Borderline to the Narcissistic continuum or a movement towards the Neurotic level. Akin to Winnicott, Adler and Buie suggest that the capacity to be comfortable by oneself implies the capacity to have memories and fantasies of positive feelings or of sustaining others in their present or past lives. It seems to me that, in addition, an individual may form a sustainable connection to a creative part of themselves, perhaps a thinking or an artistic part, that is like having a connection to an external object and may itself act as a soothing mechanism.

Clinical observation

At the beginning of his *Inferno* Dante describes a she-wolf "which seemed in her leanness gorged with all cravings." (Klonsky, 1980, p. 25) This describes an aspect of the borderline experience, yet one that many of us can identify with; we seem to be empty of everything but desire; we are too full and too empty at the same time. A young woman patient with restless fingers was given a piece of modelling clay during one session and her fingers produced, quite outside her conscious participation, a small seated figure holding its head in its hands. The figurine had a gaping circular hole in the middle of its torso—an emptiness. It mirrored a chronic emptiness within my patient, a hole that she attempted to fill with food or pain or contact with her mother.

As a young, spirited child she had grown up with a mother who could not tolerate her to have a mind or body of her own. Any bodily function or instinctual urge was deemed to be dirty or sinful, and sinfulness caused the continual re-crucifixion of Christ. So she was completely unused to being in touch with her feelings, let alone naming whatever it was that she felt, whether it was hunger or loneliness, sadness or love. Because she had no words for her feelings, "alexithymia" as Joyce McDougall (1986) calls it, they have been markedly undifferentiated and it has been extremely difficult for her to process them.

In the early stages of her therapy, she underwent a rapid "malignant regression" (Michael Balint) when an extra session was offered to her, her vulnerability collapsing into feelings of abandonment, rage, annihilatory anxiety, and the "death" of her analyst. It has taken many years of analysis for her to tolerate seeing her analyst three times a week and then losing him during vacations.

Early on, during a break, he would simply cease to exist and even cease to have existed, obliterated from her mind by her defences. Later, her pain increased because he could be kept alive but was absent and thus abandoning. Always the return to sessions after a break would be marked by intense rage that was at first inchoate and far from consciousness and only later became more accessible and differentiated. Keeping her analyst alive and "good" was a product of her gradually evolved capacity for stable evocative memory. She no longer needs the sort of transitional objects that Adler and Buie describe, but they were very helpful at stages in the process where they were used to remind her of the existence of her analyst, or simply the possibility of the presence of an-other. Now she is no longer completely alone, even in the absence of anyone else, but she is still vulnerable to feelings of dependence and the cycle of rage, loss, and emptiness that that engenders.

Summary

In summary, some of the void feelings of emptiness and disconnection from another can be understood in terms of the cycle of anxiety, rage, loss of evocative memory, panic, and loss of recognition memory. This results in the obliteration of sustaining objects from the mind of the subject. The lost objects are not only external objects, but may also be internal objects, part of the individual's psychic structure, so that when they disappear it is as though she has become empty within in addition to being disconnected from those around her. The capacity to "retain" in memory an absent object is hard won and results from many successful losses and returns within the therapeutic encounter. It may be assisted through the use of "transitional" objects and also by the gradual connection of the patient with her own imaginal world through imagery and symbolism, her own creativity in other words.

CHAPTER NINE

Trauma as a void experience

Who, if I cried out, would hear me among the angel's
hierarchies?

(Rilke)

Of course, all void experiences are precipitated by trauma of
some kind or another, but what I want to discuss here is that
sense of emptiness and meaninglessness that arises as a
result of severe external trauma in the present or recent past. Also,
to point out that there is often a singular lack when trauma is being
discussed, this is the emptiness that is full of the presence of the
absent perpetrators; their resonance within the therapist and within
the client is usually not explored.

One cannot adequately deal with trauma survivors, or victims as
they probably are at the start of their therapy, without having dealt
with the perpetrators, in one's own psyche at least. "I am human
and I hold nothing human inalienable to me," says Jung. Violent or
sadistic acts are part of the human repertoire. They are archetypally
based and thus resonate within each of us so that both the abuser
and the abused will be constellated when working with victims,
although not necessarily at the same time. Eros in the space between
therapist and client, the positive transference, is commonly worked
with, but *Thanatos*, death wishes between analyst and analysand,
tends to remain in the underworld. How does one think about these
darker impulses: the sly joy at a patient's mishaps, the negative innu-
endos hinted at to a colleague, the wishing them gone, the not-caring

whether they come or not, "a late cancellation . . . I can charge", "late for your session means extra time for me to read", etc?

These expressions of hate (Winnicott, 1947; Stevens Sullivan, 1989) are reasonably close to the surface and more or less easily known to us. They are understandable in terms of some model, such as the need for separation in a too-close therapy, a desire to peel away the presence of somebody who attaches themselves like Velcro in an adhesive identification onto you, or a distancing from those whose assaults on the therapy, through their attacks on meaning and linking (Bion, 1967) or physical attacks on themselves, render you impotent and enraged. We are moving towards the darker side with these images but there is still some kind of understanding that we can bring to bear to make our hatred seem not so bad.

In Winnicott's groundbreaking article *Hate in the Countertransference* (Winnicott, 1947) he focuses on the idea of there being something in the patient's behaviour that makes one's hatred of him or her not only understandable but also acceptable. He also lists seventeen reasons why a mother may hate her infant and convincingly suggests that hatred is important for love; that we can only truly love whom we have hated. He encourages us as analysts to know about our hate and he makes it easier for us to do that through his frank discussion and disclosure of his own felt hatred at times. He writes: "Above all he (the analyst) must not deny hate that really exists in himself." (*ibid.*, p. 196)

The main weakness in this early paper is the implication that hatred is inspired primarily by some act of the patient or else by something unanalysed in the analyst. He makes a supposition that if she has been adequately analysed, hate should not be emanating from her deep complexes. It is almost as though he is saying that it is either a problem in the analyst or in the patient.

In Barbara Stevens Sullivan's chapter on Hatred in her book *Psychotherapy Grounded in the Feminine Principle* (Stevens Sullivan, 1989) there is much more of an idea of mutuality in the causation of the problem, and that there is something in the analyst as well as in the analysand that gives rise to it. This way of understanding feels more honest and the shared responsibility takes some of the load off the analysand. There has been a shift from a Kleinian attitude towards a more intersubjective view. (Melanie Klein suggested that in the so-called paranoid-schizoid position, intense negative affects such as hatred and rage are split off by the infant and projected into the object who may then receive them, introject them, and even act them out. The intersubjective view suggests that felt affect has its origins in the psyches of both parties interacting with each other.)

The first view suggests the relative passivity of the object (mother or analyst) and the second that each, both subject and object, brings something to bear in the relationship, i.e. both patient and analyst are responsible for the feelings that develop between them. This second idea is deeply Jungian, although it has recently been "owned" by the Self-psychologists and gained wider acceptance through the writings of the infant observers such as Daniel Stern.

But we can look even deeper to where hatred, aggression, and sadism can be seen as part of our "normal" inheritance and yet remain unconscious and not acted out until released by some stimulus such as submissive or weak behaviour. Do abused individuals seek out abusive partners or do they release abusive behaviours? Are these abusive behaviours dark sides of man or dark sides of God, shadow aspects of consciousness or shadow aspects of the self as a whole? We need to ask ourselves these questions.

As Jungian analysts we are supposed to be adequately analysed so that we are aware enough of own complexes for them not to interfere in a negative way with our psychotherapeutic capabilities. Generally this refers to an analysis of the personal unconscious or Shadow, which is difficult enough and often incomplete, but it is the deeper darkness, which, perhaps especially in a Jungian analysis, is most difficult to reach.

For most people, acknowledging their frailty, as in weakness, sadness, woundedness, etc., their victimhood in other words, is easier than acknowledging their viciousness or aggression, their oppressor side. (This is not the case with abused or neglected children where hypo-manic behaviour and manic defences keep the fragility at bay.) However, if we believe in the bipolarity of the archetypes, we must know that on the hidden side of the coin of our victimhood is the perpetrator peering into the darkness.

We can feel our way into our patients' suffering but not so easily into their abusiveness and this is because we don't allow ourselves to explore that in ourselves. What would it feel like to have someone on their knees completely at your mercy, unprotected by any taboos or socialization "don'ts"? What happens when we think about it or fantasize about it? Do we expand or contract? Feel more powerful or less? Freud suggests in *Totem and Taboo* (1960) that it is an impulse perceived as dangerous that gives rise to the taboo, which then protects the individual and the society from the acting out of that impulse. There would be no need for taboos if there were no potentially damaging impulses. As "civilized" individuals we may know about the taboos but not about the impulses.

When a recent murder of an 89-year-old woman reached the attention of a family member in England, he was horrified to be told that there is an increase in this sort of violent crime against the comparatively helpless, aged, infirm, and disabled in South Africa and in the world. The frail make easier victims and, in nature, are the natural prey of scavengers. Presumably, my relative felt that the perpetrators should be governed by a moral code, honour among thieves, rather than by impulse. But that "governing body" is no longer listened to by this sort of criminal. Furthermore, as the statistics of child abuse, aged abuse, women abuse, and the abuse of the defenceless and those without a voice, tell us, the abuser or perpetrator is not a foreign species but one of us.

Acknowledging man's potential for violence, Carole Angier writes: "Over and over people drop the moral structures that contain them like chains, exulting in the unlimited power to hurt those they have envied and feared." (Angier, p. 31) She makes the further point that, in the Nazi-created ghettos, children were the cruellest of all, perhaps because they were maddened by their hunger to a greater extent or "convinced by their captors that only criminals could (and should) be punished so cruelly." (*ibid.*, my brackets) This is a point few have dared to raise, we prefer to think of children as angels rather than devils. (Except for Winnicott who gives an unsentimental account of the infant's capacity for hate and aggression and his capacity for concern and morality that protects what is loved from those negative urges. See Davis & Wallbridge, 1990)

In three different reviews of books about aspects of war or genocide in a recent literary journal, the question is asked about how and why it can happen. Carole Angier suggests it happened in Europe because people could not believe that it could happen, let alone that it was happening. How could laws turn against those who obeyed them? "The Jews of Europe were destroyed by their respect for the law", she states. (*ibid.*, p. 32) With regard to the blind eye turned by many to the abuses of the Soviet regime, J.W.M. Thompson describes the "prevailing fog of wishful thinking". And Adam LeBor asked a young Bosnian Muslim for her understanding of man's evil to man. Her reply: "It's from the dark side of the brain." (LeBor, p. 34) The dark side, the sinister side, the unconscious side, which we can't get to grips with because we prefer to accept the prevailing spirit of collective society.

A child psychotherapist from the UK, one who works with severely abused children, gave a seminar on Trauma to a group of Cape Town therapists. One of her opening comments was how releasing or relaxing it felt to be in South Africa where violence is so endemic that it is conscious and can be talked about without breaking through robust defences. Her experience in England was that people would not easily countenance the idea that destructive violence was so alive in their country. In discussing her work, with victims of parental abuse or ritual abuse, in an open forum, she found it difficult to be heard, to penetrate the defences of her listeners, particularly when it came to the fact of mothers abusing their own children. It is as though the very idea of a mother deliberately harming her own child is too much to bear and must be kept out of consciousness. There is an emptiness where Kali the archetypal terrible mother should be.

The what and the why?

Actually, on the more human level, Medea must be the literary figure who takes the prize as the terrible mother. (Euripides, 1910) She slays her own children, ostensibly to revenge herself on her husband Jason who is about to deny his marriage to her and marry the king's daughter. "Why?" we are forced to ask. We need a reason, and in her case it could be revenge on Jason, pity for her children, or envy of them because, if they stayed with their father, they would have a life of luxury while she, being exiled, would wander the world, "void armed for ever". Perhaps she desires to protect them both from the exile that is looming and from the revenge-seekers who will follow her after her killing of the king and his daughter. Briefer explanations would be that she is mad, crazed by grief and loss, or simply bad.

Renos Papadopoulos, speaking at the Florence IAAP Congress on his work with Bosnian refugees, spoke out strongly against psychiatrists and psychologists using their knowledge to generate theories or explanations about the "why's" behind the actions of the perpetrators of the atrocities. Yet, this is often what is demanded of us by the media and, more primarily, by ourselves. We seem to want to make what happened understandable and, ultimately, meaningful. We see this longing too in the consulting room where particular patients are always asking "why did this happen?" or "why do people do this or that?" and I think that it is a defence, in the metaphor of this paper, a defence against the void. Explaining protects us from the experience of the space that opens up around us as our knowing thrusts the ground of our previous understanding away from us.

Asking "why?" also means that we do not really have to accept "that". In the welter of words we can forget that we are dealing with an atrocity, and that it is part of the human condition and of us. We can hold it at a distance, ignore its immediate reality, and we do this because to embrace that reality would mean changing our whole view of the world, and for that to happen we would have to lose our carefully constructed meaning system, break down our awareness of the world as a benevolent, meaningful place, and enter the unwanted empty space beyond. The clouds of unknowing are frightening to enter, the God we are seeking on the other side of them obscure, and the intuitions that we are beginning to have of God intolerable.

Bion, in using the letter "O" to signify this "ultimate unknowable reality", chose a simple letter as carrying no significant projected meaning. "O" does not suggest a sense of agency or individual purposiveness, benign or malignant. This makes it a concept that is non-traumatizing, but also non-comforting, non-supplying. We do not expect much from "O", and are not so shocked when terrible things happen within "O", but when those things happen under the auspices of a "good" God, our world shudders.

One of the remarkable aspects of the Truth and Reconciliation Commission in South Africa, in the post-apartheid era, was its focus on the perpetrators of violence from across the whole political spectrum, from far left to far right. It attempted to separate the idea of "perpetrator" from its embeddedness within political affiliation. The members tried to judge behaviours according to what was done and for what motive rather than from the standpoint of who did it, "them" or "us". This is a view from a higher position, one that gives a wider and more inclusive perspective. It goes some way to healing the splits, by expanding our conscious realization, it moves toward wholeness.

I think it is Ivan, who, in *The Brothers Karamazov*, says something like, "Even if there were a God and he allowed one child to suffer, I would reject Him!" He cannot even think about the contradictory nature of God. The idealized vision of God that underlies this position does not allow for any negatives to obtrude. It is better to reject God than to know God. With an ego position like this we suffer an alienation from God, a rupturing of the ego/Self axis, a disconnection that is likely to be felt as another emptiness. Paradoxically, that void experience contains the possibility of a new relationship with God or the Self stemming from a new understanding; one that can only develop in the space formed by the loss of the known. One could say that in rejecting and thus losing God, Ivan has a chance to discover himself but I fear that, being one-sided, this would remain a partial discovery.

The more politically or religiously correct our world-views are, the more distant we become from our own natures. Living "correctly" means living according to a mask. Living in identification with a mask means being out of touch with our darkness. There is an importance to our being made aware, by activist groups of all kinds, of the negative aspects of so much of our speech, for example, and how unconsciously we may damage another through it; this should be consciousness raising. But that this should find its way into the law books that tell us how we must behave is likely to result in a depletion of consciousness. By simply doing what we are told we can ignore who we are.

I really enjoy Jung's writing on the trickster and the examples he gives that suggest the need for completely "incorrect" behaviour that serves to clarify the boundaries between what is OK and not-OK, while making sure that Shadow is not too far from consciousness. Racialistic and anti-semitic or anti-anything jokes may have a similar important function, especially in someone who is attempting to become more conscious. They serve to highlight in ourselves our own racism and prejudices in a way that we can handle. Knowing those things about ourselves, we are at liberty to make ethical decisions about how we will try to behave.

Traumatic effects

There are many models delineating how trauma affects the psyche, and not the psyche alone, but across the psychoid barriers into the body or soma on the one hand and into spirit on the other. Also, outside the individual, how it affects the social dimension and the individual's connection with his or her world. In the medical model, trauma may give rise to the so-called Post Traumatic Stress Disorder with its array of symptoms stressing the sufferer's increased arousal and invasion by memories or flashbacks of the stressful event as well as their psychic numbing and deadness with regard to feeling. That psychic numbing is in relation to others and, within the individual concerned, towards him- or herself. Both these states take one away from the known sense of who one is or was and what sort of place the world used to be. So trauma affects meaning, in fact it can shatter our meaning systems.

When severe trauma cannot be integrated it results in an emptiness within the psyche and a loss of self-coherence and sense of life's continuity. Life becomes separated into before the trauma and after the trauma with a cloudiness or emptiness in between. Changes occur in self-perception and in regard to self-worth, resulting in feelings of guilt and worthlessness, and, because severe trauma leads to what Winnicott called "unthinkable anxiety" or "primitive agony" (Davis & Wallbridge, 1990, p. 171), it results in a loss of fantasy and the capacity to symbolize. This loss cuts the individual off from her imagination and thus further impacts on her capacity to make life meaningful.

Basic assumptions about the world are destroyed, particularly with regard to the knowledge of the world as a benevolent place that, if it has you in mind at all has you in mind for your own good. After severe trauma the awareness is more that if it has you in mind at all you had better look out. So, on a social level, the betrayal of trust and the dis-empowerment that ensues after severe trauma leads to isolation and withdrawal from others, social avoidance, and diminished bonding that, while keeping the subject safe, increases his sense of aloneness. On a more spiritual level, the perceived betrayal by God, God's abandonment of us, leads to a state of forsakenness from which emanates Christ's cry into the ether, "My God! My God! Why hast thou forsaken me?" (See chapter *On the dark night of the soul* below)

There is a double terror, to be remembered by God is to invite destruction by God's dark side and to be forgotten or forsaken is to be plunged into a spiritual vacuum or void. Gone is our sense of cosy togetherness and in its place appears the cold awareness of our separateness from God. I do not mean this on the level of the mystics for whom glimpses of God in his ineffable oneness led to an ecstatically painful knowledge of separateness, a desire for, yet a knowledge of the impossibility of, melting into a blissful union with God, but on the more mundane level of the loss of God as benevolent parent.

During the course of a long analysis, a very similar process may happen to that described above. Often an analysand enters therapy because of a vague feeling of disconnection and dis-ease. As she works through her material there is a filling out of her personality and an increasing sense of connection with the objective other, the one who knows, the autonomous psyche. The presence of this other is made manifest particularly through compensatory dreams that seem forever to be demonstrating yet another aspect of her personality, showing her to herself as it were. This leads to a burgeoning sense both of "being" and of "being-with", a filling up of the emptiness within, and of the void around one.

But there comes a time when that guiding, benevolent presence seems to turn its back on one, becomes indifferent at best, and we know the experience that ends with the cry "Why hast thou forsaken me?" The emptiness feels more acute, and we seem more alone than we did originally, bereft in the absence of the God we thought we knew. William James, in a chapter on mysticism, quotes material from Starbuck's collection.

> I never lost the consciousness of the presence of God until I stood at the foot of the Horseshoe Falls, Niagara. Then I lost Him in the immensity of what I saw. I also lost myself, feeling that I was an atom too small for the notice of Almighty God.
>
> (James, 1960, p. 379 n2)

Severe trauma is a numinous experience, the sort of experience that leads to dread, awe, and trembling, as though looking on one of the faces of God, God's dark face. It demonstrates to us the far reaches of humanness; man's capacity to inflict suffering, his vulnerability, and dependence on goodwill, but also his resilience and capacity to heal.

When inflicted by human beings, as in rape or torture or severe abuse of any type, trauma is at one level banal and very human, and at the same time both less than and more than human. Less than: in that the perpetrator stands animal-like below the human structures of taboo and moral codes. As with a cat playing interminably with a wounded mouse, the rightness or wrongness of the act does not come into it for him. More than: in that the abusers position themselves god-like outside of human laws. They may have a rationale but it is a rationale that has no regard for the sanctity of the individual person; they behave like gods, with the arrogance of those who have right on their sides.

And yet both sides pray to the same "big" God. As mentioned above, through the Truth and Reconciliation Commission we in South Africa became hyper-aware of the atrocities perpetrated by both sides of the struggle, the regime and the liberation forces. There were undoubtedly individuals on both sides who were acting out their own perversions, but in general the perpetrators were ordinary human beings acting in what they thought was the best way for the "good" of either the state or "the people". The rights of the individual became subservient to the rights of a group and out of this one-sidedness abusive acts arose.

Conclusion

In this exploration of trauma in the context of the void I have attempted to bring to the reader the idea that it is one-sidedness that is void generating. Whether that one-sidedness is through an identification with the mask we wear or with our darkest parts or with some other complex within, or whether it arises through the denial of aspects, either good or bad, of others, or of God, or of the world without, the result is always an incompleteness. The small percentage of the survivors of severe trauma who achieve enlightenment through their suffering, becoming wiser than they were before, achieve this through their capacity to incorporate the unthinkable into their world views. They have looked on the dark face of God and the twisted face of man and know that it is so.

AMPLIFICATIONS

The analyst must cast a beam of intense darkness into the interior of the patient's associations so that some object that has hitherto been obscured in the light can now glow in that darkness.

(Wilfred Bion)

Warning and encouragement

The chapters that follow do not necessarily follow on from each other as they each expand on some theme related to the general topic but are otherwise disconnected. Some of the ensuing chapters require slow reading as they address issues that are far from easy to articulate and understand. This particularly applies to *The Dark Night of the Soul,* and to the chapter *Dimitri's Void,* which, though not as difficult, also requires close reading, especially at its start. The other chapters are much more accessible.

CHAPTER TEN

Myths and legends of the Creation

Being arches itself over the vast abyss.

(Rainer Maria Rilke)

T he Creation can be defined as the universe being brought into existence out of nothing by God, or as God revealing God's self in nature or as nature, or, simply, as God becoming.

The myths about the beginnings of creation often begin with a state called chaos, which is either a dark void or an endless sea. Out of this, something may coagulate, or a primal creator, or pair of primal beings, may emerge. The coagulation may give shape to the universe, or the creator beings fashion it and then give way to other deities who make plants, animals, and the human race. (Wilkinson, 1998)

A frequent image of the creative source is the Cosmic Egg, which cracks apart. One half forms the heavens and the other half the earth. Creator beings emerge from the shell. This happens, for example, in Chinese, Aztec, and Polynesian mythology. (Wilkinson, 1998)

None-ness or oneness

In the pleroma (see *On the territory of the void*) no-thing exists. When the oneness of the pleroma "is" there is no place for another without shattering that unity. It is both a "none" and a "one". One could also say that there is no place for the "I" that arises as a concomitant to consciousness. Without an "I" it is as if nothing exists, there is no consciousness for anything to impinge on or to become known by, no "I" that is separate-from. When the one is separated out from the all, two exist but in a sort of union, when that union is prised apart there is space for the third, consciousness outside of the unconscious. When consciousness collapses we return to "perilous sameness", the oneness of the two, and thence, to the one which becomes none. The terror that arises in autism is perhaps due to the inklings of non-existence, to an incipient consciousness of the dark waters "lapping at the edges of emptiness and the void beyond". Or else to the sense of "there is nothing that exists apart from me, I am all there is". The pleroma exists without an "I" to know it; or does it? How would it be known without an "I"? Perhaps existence itself is an aspect of *creatura*.

From Egypt

Out of ancient Egypt come, among others, the following stories:

In the world ocean existed the "lord to the uttermost limit", called Neb-er-tcher, who later took on the form of Khephri or Ra. Uttering his own name (forming an "I") he established a place on which to stand. He then had union with his own shadow (the "not-I"?) a form of uroboric incest, and the products of that union led to all the other gods and goddesses. (Robinson & Wilson, 1962)

In Heliopolis, Atum, another name for Ra and "the all", began as the chaos that existed before the Gods. He gathered himself into the shape of a human and sneezed into the void, thus creating Shu and Tefnut, the ancestors of the gods. There is no mention of the emptiness out of which chaos itself arose.

Sometimes Atum took the form of a huge snake that would shed his skin at the end of time and emerge to recreate the world, again and again. This contains the idea of a continual process of transformation extending over aeons. "Eternal mind's eternal recreation" as Goethe puts it in *Faust*.

From Ra/Atum came Shu, god of air, and Tefnut, goddess of moisture; these insubstantial beings were the parents of Geb and Nut. From uroboric incest are born a brother–sister pair who incestuously produce their own offspring. Geb and Nut were born locked together in an incestuous embrace, and had to be separated by their father. Thus separated, Geb became the earth and Nut formed the arch of the sky, her hands and feet resting on the four points of the compass. (Wilkinson, 1998) This disruption of the paradisical union suggests the action of consciousness. Shu's name is also said to mean "to be empty", (Ions, quoted in Edinger, 1985, p. 186) suggesting that, when a separation occurs, emptiness is the result. Emptiness may be thought of as a potential space that can be filled with something new.

Logos refers to the word of God or the second of the Trinity and suggests reason or consciousness. Edinger has raised the ideas of the Logos-cutter and Logos–Eros. (Edinger, 1985, p. 189, 191, 200) Separation and differentiation are the cutting, and naming brings about a linking or joining, a *coniunctio* in fact, and a new order of being. "Division was not only a separation but a reunion, for the Logos was the Glue as well as the Cutter; that is it was the principle of cohesion which makes the universe a unit in spite of its manifold divisions." (Goodenough, quoted in Edinger, 1985, p. 189) Nut's feet and hands connect with the earth.

Differentiation is a result of separation, which is both a cause of, and a product of, consciousness. "The creation of consciousness requires that new contents be carved out of the unconscious." (*ibid.*, p. 191) Britton and the neo-Kleinians propound the opening up of psychic space that occurs when the third is added to a twosome, this space then making possible symbolic thought and language. It is to do with the viewing point. When immersed in the split universe we are not fully aware of the splits, we see the "this's" not the "that's", and thus only one side of a paradox at a time. As we separate and look from afar, we feel the unity that each symbol embraces. Just as with the astronomical view of the universe called the Cosmological Principle that states that "at any given time the universe ought to look the same to observers in all typical galaxies, and in whatever direction they look". (Weinberg, 1983, p. 30) This is only true physically when the universe is viewed from enormous distances and psychologically when we look dispassionately.

Whatever Ra thinks of becomes. He thinks of sunrise, the midday sun, and sunset, and this becomes the first day and the birth of time. (Bailey et al., 1981) Before Ra no time existed, just as neither space nor time existed before the Big Bang. That first great sneeze did not just create matter but also time and space into which matter could expand.

From Greece

There are many Greek myths of the beginning, and versions of those myths. In the Orphic tradition Time existed from the beginning but without a beginning, an interesting paradox. From Time came Chaos, a tremendous space containing Night, Mist, and the upper regions of the air, i.e. Aether. At Time's command Mist spun around this airy space at such high speed that the mass took on the shape of an egg and then broke in two. From the centre came Love and the halves became Heaven and Earth. (Robinson & Wilson, 1962) I think we can translate that Love into the idea of a connecting principle, the ideas of Anima as soul, or of Eros. Heaven and Earth may be thought of psychologically as spirit and matter, the twin poles of archetypal reality.

According to Hesiod, Chaos was first, a vast, vacant, undefined, immeasurable space, a yawning gap, a primal void, before which there was nothing. He equates chaos with the void. Chaos gave rise to Erebus, or darkness, and his sisters Nux, night, and Gaea, the earth. Uranus (heaven) was both the son and the Husband of Gaea. (*ibid.*)

In Graves' version of the Olympian creation myth:

At the beginning of all things, Mother Earth emerged from Chaos and bore her son Uranus as she slept. Gazing down fondly at her from the mountains, he showered fertile rain upon her secret clefts, and she bore grass, flowers, and trees, with the beasts and the birds proper to each. This same rain made the rivers flow and filled the hollow places with water, so that lakes and seas came into being.

(Graves, 1955, Volume 1, p. 31)

In a Pelasgian Creation myth as described by Graves:

Eurynome (meaning wide wanderer), Goddess of All Things, rose naked from Chaos, but found nothing substantial for her feet to rest upon, and therefore divided the sea from the sky, dancing lonely upon its waves. She danced towards the south, and the wind set in motion behind her seemed something new and apart with which to begin a work of creation. Wheeling about she grabbed hold of this North wind and rubbed it between her hands, and behold! the great serpent Ophion. Eurynome danced to warm herself, wildly and yet more wildly, until Ophion, grown lustful, coiled about those divine limbs and was moved to couple with her.

(*ibid.*, p. 27, my brackets)

Eurynome, as a dove, subsequently laid the Universal egg, out of which finally "tumbled all things that exist"; "sun, moon, planets, stars, the earth with its mountains and rivers, its trees, herbs, and living creatures." (*ibid.*)

From the North

In the Norse myths there was a bottomless deep called Ginungagap and a land of mist called Niffelheim. From Niffelheim flowed twelve rivers whose waters froze and filled the deep with ice. In the south was a land of fire, Muspelheim, whose warm winds turned the ice into mist. From this mist arose Ymir, the first giant, Audhumble, the great cow whose milk nourished him, and the frost maidens. (Robinson & Wilson, 1962) Again we have the ideas of endlessness or bottomlessness and a misty non-differentiation out of which everything arises.

From the Kalevala of Finland we hear about Ilmatar the Virgin daughter of the air. She floated alone in space for "too long" then flew down to the bottom of the ocean where she remained for 700 years while she created heaven and earth from the seven eggs of a wild duck. She then gave birth to Vainamonen who created most of the contents of the earth by singing them into existence. (*ibid.*)

This idea of singing or naming things into existence is quite a common one, occurring in eastern mythology too, and suggests that language is a necessity for differentiation. "In the beginning was the Word," says the Gospel according to St. John. And separation, the creation of a symbolic space, is the prerequisite for that "Word", for language and for thinking. Naming separates what is named from everything that is not that named thing but it also links or connects that which is named with all else named. Naming is an ego activity and is a form of "making" and defining, separating out the *creatura* from the *pleroma*.

In the Centre

In a Central American story two life-givers hovered over the waters like humming birds. They said the word "earth" and land rose slowly from out of the water. Winnicott suggests that the infant hallucinates the mother and the "good-enough mother" coincides with that hallucination. Rilke in his poem about the legendary unicorn describes it like this:

> Not there, because they loved it, it behaved
> as though it were. They always left some space.
> And in that clear unpeopled space they saved
> it lightly reared its head, with scarce a trace
> of not being there.
>
> (Rilke, 1967, Sonnets to Orpheus iv)

From the South

In some myths of the Bantu it is Bumba who is responsible for the Creation. When he had completed his work he withdrew to heaven and thereafter communicated with man via dreams and visions. (Robinson & Wilson, 1962) In some stories the sky was originally touching the earth and it acted like a sort of flat cornucopia supplying the wants of all the people on the earth. Because the people abused and wasted the sky, tearing off more than they required and throwing the excess away, Bumba lifted it up out of reach so that thenceforth man had to work to sustain himself. An abrupt if lateral fall from paradise, it is reminiscent of the Geb and Nut story.

Polynesia

From Polynesia come a variety of creation stories. In one, Tiki existed from the beginning. He floated on the waters in his canoe until he discovered the land or he made it by digging it up from the bottom of the ocean. (Interestingly, the Polynesian islands in the Pacific Ocean have arisen from volcanic eruptions and consist of high volcanic peaks or else flat coral atolls built on the tips of submarine volcanoes.) Taaroa, another creator God, lived by himself in the heavens, a place outside the sky. He created a daughter with whom he made the earth, sea, and sky. And Io too created himself, as light in the dark universe, and separated the waters that surrounded the earth thus differentiating land from sea. (Robinson & Wilson, 1962) Again, incest, separation, and differentiation are common themes of these stories.

In another Polynesian myth Narroua the elder exists. Nothing came before him and all around him was darkness and emptiness. He did not sleep or eat but sat alone in the darkness for timeless ages. Slowly, by a sort of mitosis, he divided into two. At this stage the earth, sky, and sea were bound firmly together. Narroua the younger, representing an active principle, tapped on this unit three times and the sky opened allowing him to enter his universe.

It was dark still but, by rubbing his fingertips together, he caused a luminous moth to appear and by its light he began to explore. He found people there but they were not moving for they were asleep because of the darkness. He woke them and lifted the sky a little from the earth and a conger eel appeared that completed the separation of the sky from the land. At this stage the father reappeared and was killed by his son. His right eye became the sun, his left eye the moon, and the fragments of his body the stars. (Bailey et al., 1962) So it is the son, the new active principle, who does the creating. Like Lucifer the light-bearer, that paradoxically dark son of the Judaeo-Christian God, who brings the new light of consciousness into the world, Narroua the younger, brings the world into being by illuminating its contents.

From the East

From the Hymns of the Rig-Veda comes the following creation story. It starts from the very very beginning and is full of paradox.

> Then was not non-existent nor existent: there was no realm of
>   air, no sky beyond it.
> What covered in, and where? And what gave shelter? Was water
>   there, unfathomed depth of water?
> Death was not then, nor was there aught immortal: no sign was
>   there, the day's and the night's divider.
> That one-thing, breathless, breathed by its own nature: apart from
>   it was nothing whatsoever.

Darkness there was: at first concealed in this darkness this All
was undiscriminated chaos.
All that existed then was void and formless: by the great power
of warmth was born that unit.

(Ballou et al., 1939, p. 3)

Bailey, in beautiful language, also describes a Hindu creation story.
According to his description, before the world, before the sky, before
space, there was nothing but ocean; a flat rolling lake that lapped
the edges of emptiness and the void beyond. Floating on the water
was a giant water-snake called Ananta the Serpent-King. In his coils
lay the Lord Vishnu, God, asleep. Then a sound . . . "OMMmmm".

Lord Vishnu opened his eyes, it was time, the world was ready
to be born. As he looked out over the calm waters, a lotus flower
took shape before him. In it lay Brahma the creator, another active
principle. The lotus represents "that wherein existence comes to
be and passes away" and also "the universal ground of existence,
inflorescent in the waters of its indefinite possibilities". (Cooper, 1978,
p. 100) Brahma created heaven, earth, and sky, then plants, with their
sense of touch, and animals, who had all the senses known to man
and the power of movement.

To look after the world he made a new being in the form of God
from his own thoughts. Brahma did not move but stayed with his
eyes closed, unheeding the new world. He only wanted to sit
thinking deeply about God. He realized that he would need to use
his whole self rather than just his mind to make a being who could
open his eyes to the creation as well as the creator and so he divided
his own body in two. One half became Manu the wise or man and
the other became Shatarupa the mysterious, woman. The combination
of the two makes up the whole.

From out of the Void issues emptiness, thence the waters,
Ananta the snake, the passive Lord Vishnu, the Lotus, the active
creator Brahma, heaven, earth and sky, plants and animals, and,
penultimately, a thought God-form. To be open to both the creator
and the created, man and woman are made, wisdom and mystery.
Out of nothing comes everything, through the complementary
attitudes of passivity and activity.

A Babylonian creation myth describes "the primeval condition of
the universe when nothing existed except Apsu, the sweet-water

ocean, and Tiamat, the salt-water ocean". Where they met, i.e. where rivers flowed into the sea and deposited silt, other gods were produced from whom creation proceeded. (Hooke, 1963) Here, the undifferentiated sameness of the salt-water collides with the undifferentiated sameness of the sweet-water and from their difference generation ensues.

In the modern West

Before space and time began there was nothing. Out of that nothing came a vast explosion that rent the fabric of the nothing, so creating space in which everything that is could become. For that, time was necessary too, and it became, and so the universe as we know it was created. Heat there was and absolute cold, clouds of cosmic dust and vast spaces empty of everything except light, energy, and invisible, virtually immaterial, dark matter. Things flying apart from that first great event and matter coalescing under the influence of gravity; the vacuity of outer space and the super-density of black holes, all are present. And out of this cosmic source our own earth was born and found its rightful distance from its lord, the sun, whose blind energy made all life possible. And from that life came consciousness, which could reflect on and begin to know and connect with both itself and the universe.

Together

There are many common threads in these myths. In the beginning was either emptiness or nothingness or chaos. This state is symbolized by the flimsy insubstantiality of air, the aether, mist, or fire, or else by night, darkness or blackness. When the first substance is more substantial as in earth or water, it is unformed and un-formable "a flat rolling lake that lapped the edges of emptiness and the void beyond", there is no container for it. So what is needed is either a filling of the emptiness or an ordering or containing of the chaos.

Within the psyche there are two principal ways of doing this. The "masculine", Manu way is through knowing, turning chaos into cosmos by ordering via logical thought. The "feminine", Shatarupa in Hindu mythology, suggests an acceptance of the mystery, the

unknowable, the ineffable, that which is absent from our understanding, the emptiness; the feminine contains through acceptance,
the masculine fills by creating meaning. In the consulting room the
struggle for acceptance of that which is, is often palpable. To listen
to a dream and hear its message, and to accept whatever that message is, and to acknowledge and accept the emptiness that exists at
the perimeter of our understanding, are developmental achievements
attained with difficulty.

The creativity of the scientist is one that orders the chaos and
finds ways of understanding what is, but it cannot reach into the
realms of darkness, or not very far. Perhaps these ways of knowing
are equivalent to knowledge versus wisdom. In the Holy Bible it is
stated that wisdom was there from the beginning. Wisdom cries out:
"I was set up from everlasting, from the beginning, or ever the earth
was." (Proverbs 8 verse 23) Wisdom was a companion to God: "The
Lord possessed me in the beginning of his way, before his works
of old." (ibid. verse 22) In other words, wisdom was there from
before the creation. Wisdom, like the pleroma, embraces the opposites in itself, whereas knowledge, like the act of creation separates
out into what is now known, the creatura. What verse 22 suggests is
that wisdom should be the companion of knowledge, the defining
creator.

In Blake's engraving entitled The Ancient of Days, we see the
Ancient crouching in a womb-like space. From behind a central disc
of red, shafts of white light radiate outwards; the light of consciousness perhaps. Almost enclosing them are red-tinged dark clouds
and the Ancient protrudes one hand, holding a "compass" or what
we would call a "divider", through the opening at the base of that
cloud womb. The divider is open, prepared to start measuring the
enormous darkness beyond what we might call the "clouds of
knowing". And it seems a wishful endeavour.

> For, as Tennyson writes,
>   knowledge is the swallow on the lake
> That sees and stirs the surface shadow there
> But never yet hath dipt into the abysm,
> The abysm of all abysms, beneath, within
> The blue of sky and sea, the green of earth,
> And in the million-millionth of a grain

Which cleft and cleft again for evermore,
And ever vanishing, never vanishes . . .

(*The Ancient Sage*, lines 37–44
in Buckley, 1958, p. 499)

Scientific knowledge scratches the surface of the Nameless and leads into larger and larger abysses whether it seeks in outer space or within the atom. The artist's creativity on the other hand, adds something new, opening wider our doors of perception and adding to the created universe. It does not, like logical science may, diminish the mysterious, but expands or extends the ineffable, reaching into areas of emptiness and containing them in its visionary acceptance.

The Symbolist artists are particularly adept at portraying the ineffable, taking one deep into the mists of ambiguity, healing the rifts that divide what is from what is not in the rational universe and they do it through characterizations of the feminine. There is an overwhelming preponderance of female figures in Symbolist art, and when masculine figures are present, they are usually being seduced by the feminine (*The Kiss* by Edvard Munch, Boe, 1989; or *The Kiss of the Sphinx* by Franz von Stuck, Gibson, 1999), or are at the point of drowning (*Hylas and the Water Nymphs* by John William Waterhouse) or of entering the underworld (*The Isle of the Dead* by Arnold Böcklin). (Gibson, 1999) But occasionally they are entering a higher more spiritual place where they may embrace a new vision of God. (e.g. in the illustrations to Dante's *Divine Comedy* collected by Taylor & Finley, 1997) And this new vision will be of a place beyond the "Cloud of Unknowing".

Of course what tends to happen, particularly in the male world, is that this newly discovered world is first colonized and then reordered. Warningly, Sister Wendy Beckett writes, in her notes to *The Ancient of Days*, "This God is not establishing order, he is circumscribing the imagination." (Beckett, 1999, p. 40)

My own preparation of the material for this book, my creation, initially came about because of a sense of there being something missing in Jungian writings. The more material I looked at, the more chaotic things became, until the work became driven by my desire to order the chaos of details. Nietsche's statement that "one must experience chaos" (one could also say "emptiness") "within oneself in order to give birth to a dancing star", reflects that same thing.

A lack or a super-abundance drives an impulse to order, or at least to find some principle that embraces, and that results in the birth of a new order of being.

Jung seemed more concerned with chaos than with emptiness. "Getting lost in chaos is the sine qua non of any regeneration of the spirit and personality but we must not underestimate the devastating effect of that," he writes. (Jung, *CW 12*, p. 74) He speaks of consciousness being flooded by the chaos or fullness of the unconscious rather than consciousness leaking away into the emptiness or void of the unconscious; into that space where the unconscious, or our connection with it, should be. But others express their dread of the emptiness that is lapped by the undifferentiated waters on the one side of it and has the void on the other side. Moving in one direction leads to the imaginal realm and moving in the other to an absence of all.

Conclusion

These marvellous stories all capture some of the aspects of the psychological reality of the void. They are universal stories reminding us of the archetypal ground of our being that when explored further and further backwards in time take us to abysmal depths or the empty reaches of space. They portray the solitude, the dark, the unawakened, and the undefined, but lead us forward into the jubilance of a freshly created world with all its *creatura*, including humankind itself. This aspect of them does mitigate the sense of terror and loss with which we tend to approach any re-experience of the void and allows us to view change as part of a slow unfolding, or the sloughing-off of the old skin of Atum-as-snake at the end of time. The skin will re-grow, the cosmos re-form, it will be painful but that is "Just So".

CHAPTER ELEVEN

Dimitri's void

Man faces the existential crisis of being a solitary and mortal conscious ego thrown into an ultimately meaningless and unknowable universe.

(Richard Tamos)

A friend, Dimitri, following a bad depression expressed the following. "[It felt] that I'd died and was still wandering about wondering why I was still here. That, too, my story now occupied those blank pages at the end of a novel that come after 'The End'."

He is describing that feeling of entering the void at the end of a life in which there no longer seems to be hope for a future. The Buddhist creed of emptiness ends "Gone, gone, totally gone, totally and completely gone, enlightened, so be it." (Moore, 2003, p. 33) Dimitri's creed might simply have ended "Gone, gone, totally gone."

When newly alone in a foreign country and waiting for someone to meet him, an image had seeded itself in his mind. It germinated there for about twenty years before he was finally able to describe it, and I quote verbatim from his written piece, a piece that he at one time envisioned acting. "The picture is of a man in a glass box in which he is able to move (i.e. roll over, turn around on all fours, etc.) but not much. He is lying in about three inches of what is effectively something like very thick, dark, gelatinous, smeary sump oil. He has his back to the viewer and is lying completely still. The light, from directly above, is large, overpowering, a blaze, an inferno of brightness. Nothing else. Then he starts to move, awkwardly, painfully, incessantly, feeling around him as if blind but with wide-open eyes. As he moves he speaks and as he speaks and moves, his contact with the glass smears it with what he is lying in."

What was it that he spoke? Dimitri wondered. It took many years for the words to come to him and they eventually presented themselves as a reply to a half-question: "What is it that persuades us that there is a need to move——?"

What to do. Here now. What to do. There is above, below, in front, behind, and elsewhere. What to do. I start here. Not there. Not elsewhere. Strange. What to do. Wherever I go I remain where I am. Above, below, behind, in front, elsewhere. What to do. Not do not possible. Disallowed by design. What to do. No answer. No question. No reply. Nobody to answer. What to do. Opacity reigns. Transparency is illusion. What to do. There is from here. My here. Your here. Their here. Our here. No here. What, ever. What to do. When front known, behind unknown. Vice versa. Also elsewhere. Many elsewheres. What to do. We cry. We scream. We laugh too. What is heard. My crying is elsewhere—to you. As my scream. As my laughter. What to do. I listen too, to my tears. And yours. All elsewhere. What to do. When inside, necessarily outside. Being inside inside not possible. Must be outside to see inside. A necessary distance. What distance. What necessity. Of the design. What to do. Further difficulties. Then. Now. And now what next. Sublime. We are forever now. Then is only pictures. We must wait for what's to come. It comes/it goes. Continuous, immediate, instant loss. What to do. Now is straightways then. Ungraspable. So we only have that which is not: only pictures. My pictures aren't yours. You can't see anything I have. It's then, in pictures you can't see. What to do. Despite difficulties we appear to be here. It would not matter if not. Not here no matter. Strange. What to do. Not here does matter. True. Here does not matter. True. What to do. Build a box. Not a box. No matter. Also we stop being here. There. Elsewhere. Anywhere. Nowhere. There is then nowhere to go. Nothing to do. Yet we are here. Stuck. Then unstuck. No release. Is. Is not. No resolution. No matter. What to do. Have stories. Perhaps not. Necessary fictions. Well OK perhaps not. If you wish. All understandings fictions. We have only the truth we are capable of. What is here is also not here. Can't be bothered. Story. No story. Nothing changes. What to do. Ask questions. Fail to ask questions. Still here. No change. What to do. Freedom. No freedom. Nothing. Nothing changes everything. Nothing changes anything. Nothing changes. We are here. What to do. Nothing to do. Then not. Over.

This spoken part was imagined to start in an almost inaudible whisper and to gradually increase in volume until it was unintelligibly loud. I think of the man's name as being Adam.

Disconnection

Written by a man who patently has more than a nodding acquaintance with the void, from his felt experience rather than from a theoretical point of view, this short painful piece highlights aspects of the void experience. The protagonist is unaware of the existence of others, of the observers, but we can see him clearly, under the inferno of light, and he is blinded with wide eyes staring as if into impenetrable darkness. So he is disconnected from "the other"; not only from those in the outside world but also from deeper aspects of himself.

The emptiness is both inside and outside and it arises from the felt absence of something or someone that should be there. There is a sense of sequestration or encapsulation, the "here" of me is apart from the "here" of you, others may exist somewhere in their own reality but not in a universe that is accessible to me, so that the felt aloneness is acute. It exists alongside the possibility of it ending, somewhere is another, and that makes it more difficult to come to terms with. Nothing we do can touch another, whether we laugh or scream, even if that is heard, will not move another.

That the protagonist should be in a glass box is apt. Glass separates, keeps away. We often come across dreams where the dreamer stands behind glass looking at some event that should move or touch him emotionally, but does not.

For example, a young woman dreamed of storm waves washing towards a building, she was too high up and well protected by Safety-glass doors, to be affected. And a male analysand dreamed of a forlorn crone wailing at him and beckoning from below. He stood dispassionately behind a plate-glass window while she threw pebbles at it to attract his attention. The dreamer observes, although he or she does not yet fully connect. Nevertheless, this observation may be the first stage of the healing process, the beginning of a connection.

Another analysand, in the midst of a regression following the loss of a relationship, felt as if she were encased in thick glass that prevented any contact, except for visual contact, with those outside it; she could only see others walking away from her. This disturbing experience was reminiscent of her early relationship with her mother who had "disappeared" into a psychosis when she was a child.

I've mentioned elsewhere the Sand Tray image of a young child who threw a handful of glass marbles into the sand where they settled, chillingly apart, until he proceeded to link them with bits of organic-like "vegetation". In Dimitri's vision there are no links, only presence and absence, here or not here, now or its vanishing. "Continuous, immediate instant loss" as the un-graspable "now" recedes into the misty world of forgetting or the mistrusted world of memory. Without links to others, or to various parts of our current selves, our "memories, dreams, and reflections", we remain drifting in space and time, and the flow of time, the ebbing away of the present, feels like a continuous depletion of ourselves, with the feared result an ongoing emptiness, "the empty pages at the end of a novel".

This is very different from the filling up of the emptiness that occurs via the constant accretion of new substance through the experience and memory of life's events, the writing of one's own story. This "filling up" can be thought of as the main work of healthy ego development that occurs in the first half of life. It is different from the formation of the false-self or of the persona that implies a mask donned to feel accepted and, often, a repression of those aspects that do not fit with our view of how we should appear to others.

Charles, in her paper on *Images of Emptiness in Men* (Charles, 2000b), describes the case of a man she calls Aron who had been born with visible deformities possibly as a result of Thalidomide. He was adopted by a woman who was psychotically depressed and frequently hospitalized, and her husband, a physician who worked long hours. Acknowledgement of Aron's physical differences or limitations had been tacitly forbidden during his growing-up and Charles notes that her mention of them in relation to his childhood was very distressing to Aron. "It was as though I had failed a very basic test, in which people who care about him do not see those parts of him, nor their absence." (*ibid.*, p. 130) Aron had thus never had the experience of being truly seen by his parents, and he lived perpetually in a state of yearning to be known and yet being terrified of being seen; looking for the "gleam" of recognition and being ashamed of being looked at.

The initial anxiety of the parents about reflecting the true nature of their son resulted in an emptiness felt within him. Charles describes Aron's yearning for her words in their sessions but, also, how he excluded her "by talking over my words, or ending a silence just as I move to speak". In a passage suggestive of Dimitri's writing she describes how her "words, as connecting links, appear to combust spontaneously within the toxicity of the atmosphere". "Even when he hears my words they tend to dissipate quickly; he often cannot recollect them seconds after their trace has left the air. This experience is accompanied by an inevitable sense of loss". (*ibid.*, p. 131) This is probably an example of what Bion calls "minus K" where the individual attacks meaning or awareness, consciousness in fact, leaving emptiness in its place. Meaning does often seem to fill the void.

From a Jungian perspective it is as if any manifestation of Aron's true self is attacked and destroyed out of his fear of his totality. This is different from the loss of meaning and identity that inevitably attends mid-life. A person such as Aron would have to develop a less defensive sense of self before he could reach a state in which his ego could resign itself to its discovery of an expanded identity in the individuation process.

What to do

What to do. Not even a question mark follows this oft-repeated sentence, suggesting the immense inertia of the protagonist. To choose what to do seems impossible, to do nothing is impossible too, it is not part of the design. It has been said that it is a man's function to do, that a man feels most alive or fulfilled when he feels effective, when his efforts are rewarded by results. Adam, in his glass box, in his slow unceasing exploration, effects almost nothing; he feels that nothing he can do, e.g. crying, screaming, laughing, moving, will change anything, because there is no contact or connection. He has his imagination, and that is working hard, but its products are "only" pictures that may not be transmittable to someone else and which seem to dissolve as quickly as they form.

Particularly in working with some creative individuals, the problem is not a lack of imagination but too many images. The issue becomes how to coagulate those images so that they do not simply disperse before they help the person to some new understanding or insight. In other words, how to help the individual be moved by his imagination. Some would phrase that as "How to embody the images?"

The only observable effect of Adam's moving about is that the glass of his box becomes more opaque, smeared with the dark oil. In effect this symbolizes his situation better than the clean glass did through which he could be clearly seen. The harder he tries the more alienated he becomes.

There is nothing organically womb-like about the box in which Adam is trapped; it is a sterile masculine rather than a fecund female space. I imagine that he is lying in a foetal position and his movements are like the exploratory efforts of a baby in an as yet unknown environment. What is chilling is the absence of the experience of a mother or mother equivalent, she who could witness her son. Worse still is that, in spite of his escalating efforts, his doing, Adam is unable to conjure her and this leads to his final return to the void state of not-being. Winnicott has expressed the idea that the infant in need hallucinates the mother, and that the responsive-enough mother is often-enough present in the space where she has been conjured for a clear image of the "good-enough" mother to form in the child's mind. For Adam there is no internalized good mother or any other to whom he can feel connected.

On knowing what is

Oil suggests the first matter out of which anything can arise; it is full of potential. Oil and its smearing are associated with anointing or consecrating. Then too there is light and movement. But nothing develops in spite of the hopefulness of these symbols.

This is to do with Adam's not letting go; you can only feel the supportive arms if you have begun to fall. By not abandoning hope he is constantly betrayed. You should only feel betrayed once by a particular set of circumstances or else you have not learned. (Thus says James Hillman, in an article on *Betrayal*.) A young woman with a severe narcissistic disturbance had been severely let down by her parents when a child, and still is, whenever she has contact with them. She somehow maintains the illusion that they will be the parents that she desires if only she behaves better. Each letdown by them is experienced as a new betrayal rather than as an acknowledgement of what she knows, an affirmation of herself, and of her previous experience. By refusing to know the truth about her parents she remains "empty of herself".

The writhing figure in Dimitri's piece eventually makes his impassioned cries so loudly that he becomes unintelligible. He is blinded by his terror and drowned in his own noise, feels unseen and unheard, is unmirrored and unechoed, all of which escalate his fear. That fear originates in the burgeoning realization of his inability to control and organize his world in a way that would make it seem safe for him. It is as though he has built a wall to ward off what he does not wish to know about and that wall separates him from himself, increasing his aloneness.

One could ask what it is that prevents Adam from seeing himself, from attending sufficiently to himself; in other words what stops him being an observer of himself. I think it is his refusal to accept "what is", and his own ineffectuality. He has a need to ask "What to do," which implies "what am I to do?" If that phrase is deleted from the piece how differently it reads. A quiet descends on the reader, a sense of peace and of acceptance and affirmation. This is the feminine aspect, the vessel, the womb, the container of opposites.

"What to do" suggests an either/or that excludes paradox, "I must do this or that." Michael Owen, in his book *Jung and the Native American Moon Cycles*, writes, "In using their free will to choose, humans are always birthing twins—the road we take and the road we do not take." (Owen, 2002, p. 262) Accepting these twins, accepting things as they are, accepts their paradoxical nature too and allows them and the subject of the thoughts, the thinker, to exist in amity.

It has been said that fiction is the only truth that is possible when representing the past. (Attributed to Gwen Conradie) This is one of those paradoxes that can further acceptance of the transitoriness and elusiveness of human experience. That our histories and under-standings, products of imperfect memory and blinding complexes, are fictions, are story, and are necessarily so, is a truth. Our being here and our not being here both matter and do not matter. To build a box or not build a box matters and does not matter. Even to ask questions or not ask questions matters and does not matter; a dif-ferent set of outcomes will emerge with each course chosen or not chosen, a different pattern result, with the configurations contracting or expanding depending.

By whom?

Perhaps the mattering or not mattering depend on the perspective from which the event is being observed. All these choices matter, to the ego, but not to the all-embracing other by whom all is given and into whom all is taken. For She who presides over the "Continuous, immediate, instant loss" is also She who eternally produces the new instant from the vastness of unfolding time.

We do not meet this "Other" as equals and our experience of her may be benign or malignant. If benign, we will experience the world as a safe place imbued with meaning, and if malignant, our experience may be either of being intrusively impinged on or of being abandoned to the void. What is outside of the box of rationality is the void, or more properly, chaos, as it is that which is as yet undif-ferentiated, and it is the walling off of that space or of ourselves from that space that generates the subjective experience of being in a void. In Dimitri's drama it is being boxed in, under the over-bright light of rational consciousness that blinds Adam's full imagination, that prevents him from seeing or taking in that which simply is.

To keep one's eyes fixed open in terror, to not let oneself fall, to be too defended against the void, is to remain in a walled-off place devoid of connection or the possibility of transformation or rebirth, a non-fecund womb, a dead end. For William Blake that was the world of rationality and religion. He abhorred rationality and exalted imagination, and he knew that the world of the imagination was both frightening and potentially generative. When we dive into the imagination we plunge into something darkly unknown. There is the possibility of a new birth but the risk of death.

A solid mandala

The building of a box would mean constructing a container, it has an inside and an outside, so it differentiates and organizes, it suggests the making of cosmos out of chaos and it could be called a "solid mandala". In Patrick White's (1966) novel *The Solid Mandala*, the mandala is a glass marble, spherical therefore, and it held a particular fascination for his hero and supported him in threatening times, it is clearly a Self symbol. My understanding is that squares, and by extension cubes, symbolize conscious wholeness, something achieved but not eternal, and thus to be let go of at some other stage. So some times the box should be built and at other times it can be destroyed.

Like White's solid mandala Dimitri's box is of glass, it is transparent which grants the illusion of clarity, it suggests "he can be known." But knowing is an illusion and a limitation; like Tennyson's "swallow on the lake" which dips only into the "surface shadow" but knows nothing of the dark "abysm" below. It is apparent that knowing fills the emptiness, in that way it obliterates the void. It illuminates the darkness and that brings us comfort, but the comfort is temporary because we soon realize that knowledge forecloses. We can see and know the interior of the box but what of that which is outside it? Like our blue-sheathed spaceship earth that seems so well circumscribed during the daytime, but switch the light off, our hot sun, and the unknowable reaches of outer space expand to thirteen billion light years away; and on the other side of that?

And so with Adam's images of being inside versus being outside. The pain of being inside is too much to bear, it suggests a state of non-differentiation, the dissolution of the ego within the Self. There is no one outside to witness me and I, if immersed, cannot witness anyone, even myself. I "must be outside to see inside". This necessary distancing or standing back must obtain for individuality to accrete. In alchemical terms, to rise out of the diffuse waters of the *solutio*, a solidifying or *coagulatio* must take place, that, or a greater distancing in the form of an elevation or *sublimatio*. But again, there will come a time when the new form must, for growth or change, be dissolved again.

Acceptance

There is so much that must be accepted, all these paradoxes, fate, our ineffectuality, and our humanness as opposed to godlike-ness. A short poem by D.H. Lawrence, *Basta!* says some of it.

When a man can love no more
and feel no more
and desire has failed
and the heart is numb

then all he can do
is to say: It is so!
I've got to put up with it
and wait.
This is a pause, how long a pause I know not,
in my very being.

(Lawrence, 1950, p. 154)

Then a rebirth perhaps, or, at the least, a continuation, life resumed.

The whole piece of Dimitri's can be seen as a description of this rebirth, the first movements towards an awakening, towards a connection with the outside. Adam can see the light and his marks are visible to the outside world; he is starting to delineate his world and to articulate it, and that gives it meaning. What begins as a paean to meaninglessness and despair about that, could, when viewed from another standpoint, become imbued with the light of significance, acceptance, and hope. Simply by describing what is, as it is, and not with the expressed (or unexpressed) desire for it to be something else, the emptiness is filled. *Can tell stories or not.* Yes. *Here now then not.* That is right. *Not here no matter.* No. *You can't ever see anything I have.* That is correct.

In Dante's *Divine Comedy*, having suffered through the ascent of purgatory, the souls are plunged into the river Lethe (forgetfulness), and with what blessed relief all memories are washed away, but the good with the bad. There then takes place a second immersion, this time into the river Eunous (good/sound mind) and all memory returns but without the affective component. They just are! How wonderful it is to experience the history without the judgments. Thus may end the "pause in my being", and the further ascent to the different levels of paradise can begin.

Dimitri describes elsewhere (private communication) that this piece of writing contains "the logic of our futility" and, further, "that if you put two individuals in the same situation with the same outcome the one will emerge feeling desperate and the other with a renewed determination to try yet again." Their difference is to do with the one denying the reality and the other one accepting it. Perhaps it will be the pessimist who finally emerges from this situation with a "renewed determination" rather than the optimist. For it is the pessimist who is more likely to see things as they are whereas the optimist tries to see things as they "should" be and thus will be betrayed, time and again, by life; until he cannot rise again. Life does not match the ideal.

This ties in with what Bion expresses with regard to "memory" and "desire" and their relationship to ultimate reality. "The abandonment of a protective shell of familiar ideas will expose the person or group who abandons it to the disruptive (even if creative) force of the 'contained' idea. Therefore memory is kept in constant repair as a defensive barrier." (Bion, 1967, p. 150) He seems to be suggesting that we manufacture or "hallucinate" memories as a defensive operation, and that we are capable of *not* remembering what *has* happened through the operation of "desire" and of *remembering* what has *not* happened "through the operation of the same agency". "In this situation desire would have the same value as memory." (*ibid.*, p. 144) By "eschewing" memory and desire we are more likely to see and accept things as they are, to make the "atonement with ultimate reality, or O, (which) is essential to harmonious mental growth." (*ibid.*, p. 145, my brackets) Atonement here suggests the reconciliation of God and man, or the becoming one with God. I think of this as a process and not an attainable end-point.

In Jungian terms it would mean an acceptance of the Objective Psyche and of the pettiness of the ego in relation to it. And in the terms of this paper it means an acknowledgement of the void, which, in the process, will (probably) start to fill with substantial meaning.

Conclusion

What I have been trying to articulate in this chapter is the idea that the void, in its negative sense, may be a subjective space generated by our desires not to see the world as it really is. By denying that which "is", because it does not fit in with our preconceptions or our desires, we separate ourselves from reality, alienate ourselves, become alone. In bemoaning that which "is", judging life from an idealized ego position, we see things one-sidedly and life feels futile. By accepting life as it presents itself, empty or full, with its paradoxes, its pains, and its joys, we connect with something greater. We are not that thing which we connect with but neither are we alone and in a void.

I end the chapter with another quote from *The Ancient Sage,* the first verse is the voice of an ego-bound young man oppressed by his sense of the meaninglessness of existence:

> For all that laugh, and all that weep
> And all that breathe, are one
> Slight ripple on the boundless deep
> That moves, and all is gone.

To which the sage, steeped in the wisdom of the ancients and his own long life experience, replies:

> But that one ripple on the boundless deep
> Feels that the deep is boundless, and itself
> For ever changing form, but evermore
> One with the boundless motion of the deep.
>
> (in Buckley, 1958)

By accepting life as it is we become one with it.

CHAPTER TWELVE

The King's sacrifice

I see the loneliness be like maybe the rain forget to come. And those grasses and those trees they waiting for nothing.

(from *Skyline*, Schonstein Pinnock, 2002)

Another idea of a black hole comes from a Southern African story about a nineteenth-century Xhosa King and his warriors. They had been defeated and had taken flight after a prolonged struggle with the British army. Their story is retold in a short play, *The Sacrifice of Kreli* (1976), by Cape Town playwright Fatima Dike.

When his army had been cut down to only 500 men, Kreli, the King, accompanied by his warriors and also a praise singer and a diviner, sought refuge in a mountainous area of the country. Protected by precipitous kranses behind, where the noise of stones slipping down the steep slopes would alert them, and a slow flowing river in front, wherein the sounds of men walking would also be clearly heard, the king and his remaining men hid in a "deep hole" and stayed there for seven long years.

The "hole" was more of a psychological hole than a physical one for it is described as being so many miles long and so many wide and it obviously contained enough to cater for the physical needs of the people who had exiled themselves to it. But the men were cut off from their families and, it turns out, from their ancestors too. In psychological terms, they have, in the long course of withstanding a repressive regime, fallen into the dark hole of depression and become alienated from their emotional and spiritual selves.

After seven long years, wanting to go forth into the world again but fearing that the British were waiting for them to appear, they decided to ask the ancestors for advice on how to leave this "deep hole". The ancestors in the Xhosa tradition can be equated with the lesser gods of Western mythologies and they act as intermediaries between the Great God Qamatha, who cannot be approached directly, and man. It is the diviner who acts as a medium between these ancestor gods and individual persons. The diviner has been chosen by the ancestors and, often with great personal reluctance, submits to their will.

A popular theme of Renaissance art is the depiction of the annunciation that focused on the Virgin Mary being informed by the Angel Gabriel that she is to be the mother of God. In many of these works Mary looks as though she has received news of a huge burden that she must bear and she seems to flinch away from it but yet submit to the inevitable.

In the present day I saw a middle-aged Xhosa woman from a long line of diviners who was receiving dreams that clearly indicated that she herself was being called. She simply refused to hear the call, which would have meant going against her modernity, and her immediate struggle to make a living and raise a family, and having to enter an arduous and expensive training.

The diviner must enter a rigorous training and purification period; in fact, to function well, he (or she) must maintain his (her) purity, through ritual, throughout life. The personal sacrifice involves even giving up ownership of the body, which, the diviner begins to realize, belongs now to "us" rather than to "me", in other words it belongs to the particular incarnated ancestor or god as well as the diviner in his or her personal capacity. This is akin to the relativization, or bringing down to size, of the ego in relation to the archetypes of the Collective Unconscious as discussed in Jungian psychology.

To return to our story; the diviner is requested to ask the ancestors how they can get out of their predicament and, more specifically, whether the British are still watching for them. But there is a split in the camp between the King and his diviner, on the one side, and the praise singer and warriors on the other. It feels like the split between the Self and the ego. To accept the will of the ancestors, like accepting the reality of the autonomous psyche, means to submit to fate and this is something the warriors, like most young heroes, are reluctant to do.

The diviner returns with an answer that the ancestors have no idea where the king and his people are as they had moved from the places they had been known to inhabit without informing the ancestors, via appropriate rituals, where they were going or where they were now. A proper ritual is thus needed to reconnect them and this is to take the form of a sacrifice, the first of the sacrifices from the title of the play.

The first sacrifice

This initial sacrifice is of a strong black and white bull that has ancestral links with the king and his progenitors. As part of the ritual, an old woman, a keeper of ritual knowledge, and two youths and three maidens, symbols of innocence and purity, are brought to the hole. While the knowledge of the process is carried by the old woman, the sacrifice or actual killing of the bull is the work of the warriors. The function of the youths and maidens, first checked to ensure their virginity and then washed or cleansed repeatedly to ensure their purity, is to present the sacrifice to the ancestors.

Soon after the beast is slaughtered, green willow twigs are gathered which must be taken to the mountain by the children under the guidance of the diviner. The willow is a tree of blessings and healing that is used medicinally to cleanse both body and spirit. The green twigs when set alight should smoulder and smoke, linking the world of men with that of the spirits. But something happens to obstruct that process.

The rejection

The king becomes distracted when a white journalist, in the company of three Xhosa men, who would these days be described as "sell-outs" as they had embraced the "White-man's" God and professions, come to visit the king. Although technically still at war, Kreli is unable or unwilling to send these visitors away. Perhaps it is his curiosity, perhaps his desire to follow custom by offering some form of hospitality to them, perhaps it is his pride, it is him they want to interview after all. Whatever the reason, the continuation of the ritual is delayed. When at last the diviner and the children make their offering by burning the twigs at the top of the mountain, instead of smouldering, they burn quickly to nothing. This is interpreted as meaning that the ancestors refuse the sacrifice.

The authority of the king and of the diviner now starts to be questioned, as is the very existence of the ancestors, the belief in whom underlies the whole sense of meaning of the protagonists. The subliminal text queries whether the failed sacrifice was due to the absence of the ancestors, the failure of the diviner, or the fault of the king or his warriors.

The warriors make ready to go their own ways and as they do so they reminisce about the destruction wrought on the Xhosa nation through its blind following of the prophecies of a young girl some years previously. The diviner is now out of favour, the men further dislocated from their original beliefs, deeper in the hole of their own making.

The king's masterful but tragic solution captures the essential flavour of many Greek tragedies where man's bowing to his fate and the reality and power of the transpersonal world of the Gods is often the issue.

The second sacrifice

What he does, is order that the diviner, his friend and companion since childhood, should be sewn up within the skin of the slaughtered bull, and that this macabre cocoon be left exposed to the elements. Each of the warriors becomes complicit in this new sacrifice, one must bring the skin, another sew it up, and others guard it or watch over it.

After three long days and nights within this shrinking suffocating straitjacket which, strangely, does not dry out, the presumed-dead diviner is released. Even the vultures, circling overhead, are taken in and the warriors can not understand why the king does not bury his friend. He does not breathe and his heartbeat is impalpable; yet his body remains warm.

A day later the body croaks a request for the king's presence. To everyone's surprise, except the king's perhaps, the diviner is precariously alive and, when the king appears, he proclaims through cracked lips: "The ancestors are alive. I'm from them. They say our survival is guaranteed." His last words.

The king sends out the children with messages to the "people to plough their burnt fields and build their fallen walls", for "our sun is rising", "we will work and grow" and "defend our honour". And the chorus proclaims:

The cloud of death has been lifted
Giving way to the light of life.
We will walk into our future fearless,
Showered by the blessings our ancestors have given us.
(Fatima Dike, *The Sacrifice of Kreli*, Act 2, Scene 10)

The connection with the ancestors, the two-way connection, has been restored, and the prospect of a generative life, out of the darkness, has been returned to them. The king and his people are free to leave the hole but at this great cost to the king, the sacrifice of the one closest to himself.

Near the end of the play is a wonderful section when the diviner has been released from his cocoon and the play drifts into time-lessness. Dawn, night, midday all collapse into each other and we are uncertain if we are waiting for death or a new birth. "This wonder has no beginning and it has no end!" it is said, and the feeling is that we have entered the dream world.

There is a resonance here with the crucifixion story, another story of the sacrifice of an innocent that leads to both death and rebirth with a three-day wait in between. And, as in the crucifixion story, we are uncertain who has ordained the sacrifice, man or God.

Submission or atonement

The point the play makes is that there are certain things that must be done to keep intact the connection with the "other" realm, that of the gods or ancestors, or the unconscious or autonomous psyche. That axis, the ego–Self axis in psychological terms, must be serviced to be kept in good working order and the individual ego must submit to what is required of it. In certain cultures that servicing may be through the doing of defined rituals that often involve some sacrifice on the part of the doer, an individual activity that also links the individual with the community and their ancestry. In others it may be taking part in a communal activity such as a church service and in yet others it may be a much more personal or individual process such as meditation, active imagination or paying attention to one's dreams. If this connection with the "other" is not maintained we lose a sense of meaning and it may be as though we are lost in a dark hole where not even the gods can find us.

The king and his men had neglected their rituals, and their connection with the gods had been severed. It is more than submission that is now required. What is needed is atonement and for that a much greater sacrifice is demanded. The bull of the first sacrifice suggests power and fertility, it connects back in time to the clan and thence to the ancestors, it is both earth-bound and godlike, and, also in its colouring, is symbolic of wholeness. It should have been enough, but it wasn't. Why wasn't it?

Primarily it was to do with the king's attitude. This attitude placed the visitors before the ancestors, people before the gods. Being a hospitable host was more important to him at that moment than being true to what he should have known was more imperative. Psychologically, we would call that a persona driven attitude. Identifying with the persona or mask necessarily prevents a deeper connection, we can't look outwards and inwards at the same time, and seeking that inner connection, the connection to the Self or to the divine was what was required at that moment. Outer connection proceeds from inner connection and not necessarily the other way round. In being a good host to the visitors and abandoning or delaying the ritual, King Kreli distanced himself from the gods.

The word atonement suggests an act of expiation or reparation that will result in an at-one-ness or harmony between gods and man. Is this a return to paradise before the fall, a return to the conditions that obtained before the eating of the fruit of the tree of the knowledge of good and evil? Or is it the re-gaining of heaven having suffered that knowledge? This second implies access to the other great tree in the Garden of Eden, the tree of everlasting life. (Hodson Public lecture, 1997) There is an emptiness that obtains in the first scenario and a fullness in the second. What is missing from paradise-before-the-fall is consciousness and what is absent from paradise-lost is God. They are both void states, the one empty of aware-man, the conscious ego, and the other empty of God or the Self. Atonement suggests paradise-regained, a coming together of God and man, the Self with the ego.

Interconnections and submission

The image of the early mother–child interaction, as witnessed by infant observation, can be seen not only as a precursor but also as a paradigm for the Self–ego connection. Winnicott states "there is no infant without a mother" and Enid Balint retorts "there is no mother without an infant". Both statements are true and refer to the dialectic that occurs between mother and child, a dance of interactions and responses to responses, out of which the child discovers not only who she is but the identity of her mother too. It is not only the gleaming reflection of herself that the infant sees in her mother's eye, but she witnesses her mother too. And so it is with the ego and the Self.

The poet Selima Hill states: "Whenever a child is born a woman is wasted. We do not quite belong to ourselves." (Hill, 1989, p. 20) Thus, she suggests that the mother's role is very different from that of a woman and a woman will need a profound readjustment to attain it. She may also be referring there to the idea of woman as individual ego who has felt able to deny or transcend the demands of her body up to this point. Once a child is born she can no longer distance herself from the complex calls of both psyche and soma that force her willy-nilly into the being of "mother". "Bidden or unbidden the gods will enter." She may fight against those gods but almost inevitably will have to submit to them. (It is apparent that Post Natal Depression is commoner amongst older women and especially those who have been immersed in their careers, those who are more identified with external roles and less in touch with their "true" selves, less able to submit to their new functions.)

I see it as something like this. That, in the first stages of life, for the ego to develop it needs an external source, the "good-enough mother", who, without too much intrusion or too much neglect fosters the growth of the "I-ness" of the child without dislocating it from its embeddedness in its archetypal ground. As humans we come out of that rich archetypal ground, our roots are in it, but without the illuminating power of our consciousness it remains darkly inaccessible. Similarly, without the fecundating power of the dark matter, our egos, as regents of the realms of consciousness, hold sway over an impoverished kingdom. Just as our mothers, the conscious aspects of them, shone a light for us, were a beacon and a mirror for us, discovered us and showed us to ourselves, invited us into and showed us the New World, and were delighted and enriched and appalled and changed by us for ever, so we enter a similar relationship to the unconscious, showing it to itself and discovering it for ourselves and changing not only ourselves but the whole collective consciousness irrevocably. But without continuing interconnection and mutual feeding, stagnation occurs, and we end up stunted and empty, and in a dark hole.

The interplay between conscious and unconscious is one of connecting back as well as of looking forward. The psyche is both conservative and creative. In the play, the old woman, suggestive of the store of tribal wisdom, is as necessary as the children are, signifiers of the future. But when matters are really stuck these two elements are not enough and something more cruelly radical is needed to shift and rejuvenate things; death is required for new life. One senses that if the warriors had simply left the hole without the blessing of the ancestors, theirs would have been a hollow life. On the other hand, without their rebellious energy the king would not have been forced to make his radical move and they would all have remained in the dark of their no-where place.

Trauma and sacrifice

The dark hole of the play represents one of the void states, that state of alienation that prevails when the ego is cut off from its connection with the objective psyche, consciousness from the unconscious. This is like a loss of faith in a religious context and there are different causes of it. The origin of the predicament that King Kreli and his men find themselves in is given as the war. Clearly, prolonged or severe trauma can give rise to a state of deadness or psychic numbing leading to the psychiatric disorder known as Post Traumatic Stress Disorder or PTSD. One of the features of this condition is that it seems to block symbolic thought or playfulness, particularly around areas associated with the trauma, and also that it may lead to a feeling that life is foreclosed. It may give rise too to feelings of being outside of the realm of communicable experience, "No one, not even myself, can understand what I have experienced."

To break through this state, to link with the symbolic realm, some sacrifice is necessary. The word sacrifice, translated literally, means to make sacred but it also means to give up something for a higher good. Perhaps its most profound meaning is that of a sacramental meal at which the communicants are a deity and his worshippers. (Macdonald, 1967) This suggests an event where the god, or gods, and (wo)men communicate with each other, connect with each other, become known to each other, and, finally, become one with each other. In psychological terms that implies an intactness of the ego/Self axis the pathway along which communications can be sent from the God-image, or Self, to the realm of the mortals, personified as the ego, and back again.

It is a two-way process and the communications along this axis are largely in non-verbal symbolic form. The furthest development of this process would be the individuated self, that, in the *mysterium coniunctionis*, becomes one with the all. When less advanced it would be experienced as being in touch with one's creativity or imagination, or simply the sense that one's feelings have an internal and external validity, or that one is not alone.

After particularly traumatic events an impasse is often reached, where the remembrance of the trauma seems needed to validate the person's experience and yet the remembrance of the trauma is itself re-traumatizing. The therapist feels as though she is either blundering into the wound, or else that she is colluding with the patient in not addressing the trauma. Probably an attitude of patient expectation that he will speak, or communicate in some other way, when able to, is the most helpful one. That the therapist keeps the trauma from falling through the cracks in her own mind, and is mentally as ready as possible to hear it spoken aloud, will create the right ambience for its eventual release into the light. Somehow, and mostly unconsciously, the available therapist metabolizes the unthinkable thoughts (Bion) so that they can be thought consciously and thus move out of the realm of the nameless dread which is so close to the bottomless pit, or "the abysm of all abysms". (Tennyson)

Making sacred, giving up, and communion

More directly, sacrifice is called for and the analyst can be like the officiating priest whose role is to help connect the supplicant with the divinity. For this the first meaning of sacrifice is the key; that is to make sacred, to honour the work and the individual's struggles, her memories and her reactions to them. The supplicant is someone who has been violated and her therapist should treat her as though sacred and thus inviolable.

The second meaning of sacrifice is to give up something for a higher good. In the language of analytical psychology this would suggest giving up a one-sided ego or persona attitude by embracing new or previously unconscious knowledge or awareness. This is notoriously hard to do. Often our whole psychic outlook will have to change. However this will lead to a broadening and strengthening of the ego, and, further, to the third meaning of the word, that is, the communion with God or the gods through which the ego–Self axis will be enhanced.

Mary's story

A woman, in her early twenties when she entered therapy, was the daughter of a couple who belonged to a fundamentalist Christian sect. She had been physically, emotionally, and sexually abused by her parents and later by a pastor. In effect, they had stolen her core from her and left her with the shell of an identity that required regular patching. At the start of her therapy she was unable to lock a door between herself and her parents. In spite of feeling the threat of intrusion by them, to be totally separate from them felt annihilating. After many years of therapy she left home and bought her own apartment, achieved more and more highly at work, and made closer and more numerous friendships. Yet it was as though she lived in two worlds, the world where she felt full-of-herself and the other world where she felt empty-of-herself, the world in which her identity had been sucked out of her.

She was aware that when she was away from the parental home and planning how she would furnish her apartment or entertain her friends, for example, or when she was at work, she took on some substance as an individual. This was particularly felt when she was doing something creative around her therapy, painting or writing or taking photographs. On the other hand, when she visited her parents or invited them over, her experience was invariably one of feeling her self, her person-hood, ebb away. At these times, she felt that she belonged to her mother, and she lost any sense of internal solidity, and relied instead on the fickle goodwill of her mother to support the shell of her being. Enid Balint (see above) aptly terms this the void in the presence of the mother.

In spite of experiencing her parental home as an excruciating and depleting place, she was unable to stay away from the allure of "my mother". She was magnetized by the idea of "mother", of what a mother ought to be to her daughter, and she felt herself betrayed and let down time and again. The sacrifice that she needed to make was to acknowledge that her mother was incapable of being the mother she wanted and needed, and that her father too, in spite of what she desired, was a weak, severely narcissistic old man who would never have her best interests at heart. (Nor could she have accepted his beneficence should he have demonstrated some.)

She is surprised each time a memory surfaces, or a dream image slides under her defences, which reminds her or reinforms her of the reality of her truth. She mistrusts herself, at least in part because she wants to believe differently. She wants to have a mother who remembers her infancy with warmth and love, not one who, when asked about her birth, tells her "All I can remember is that they gave me an enema and it was horrible." She does not wish to feel equated with faeces in her mother's eyes.

As temple priest during her long struggle, I felt that my initial duties were to honour not only the "God" that she was attempting to connect to, but also the empty shell that she presented. Her increasingly differentiated experience of her memories and feelings would start to fill the "physical" emptiness, while the products of her imagination, her fantasies, drawings, and dreams, would start to bridge the gap between her and the Self.

During this long process of taking her seriously, giving value to what she was, as well as being open to what she could become or to what was moving beneath the fractured surface, I felt that I had to show her that in this space she was inviolable, especially when she herself invited violation, as Mary sometimes did. This meant dealing with countertransference feelings of both an abandoning and an intruding nature. I had to become aware of my desire to give up on her, to turn my back on her and her struggles, as well as of my impulse to fill her up with penetrating ideas and insights that I felt at times were a distortion of an erotic countertransference. Or perhaps, it is that emptiness or a void within a patient which constellates a desire within the analyst to fill it, and that desire may be felt or expressed in a physical, sexual, spiritual or intellectual way.

It felt to me at that time that I should make a special effort to counter those penetrating impulses and I consciously tried to even sit in a way that I considered receptive; that is with legs apart, open hands in my lap, gaze not too direct, etc., and to let my interpretations, such as they were, demonstrate acceptance rather than sharp insight. I had in my mind, I now realize, the model of the good-enough mother, present but not intrusive, who demonstrates the axiom "acceptance cannot reject." (Blum, *Conversations with the Wise Old Dog*)

Another part of the making sacred was to stand against her self-harming tendency and the attitude of abandonment that she evidenced towards the infantile aspects of herself. In her early therapy she would dream of an infant whimpering in the forest. It needed Mary's help, yet she turned her back on it and heard the cries falter and die. In terms of more direct self harm, she would cut herself, or binge and starve in rotation, and later, when she started to express her thoughts and feelings on paper by writing or drawing, she would almost invariably tear the papers up in a fit of vengeful rage. At times like these I attempted to help her understand her impulse but also stood up for the part of herself that she was attacking. After many years she has incorporated that attitude of inviolability towards herself.

Now that she has learned to feel herself as sacred, at least at times, the second meaning of sacrifice can come into play, that of giving up for a greater good. In the context of analysis this giving up is two-fold. The one is to let go of a one-sided view of oneself, "I am not the sweet saint that I thought I was," or "I am not as stupid and ugly as I always thought." The other is that of standing against a damaging impulse. The impulse may be self-injurious, such as cutting herself, bingeing on food or alcohol, or entering a destructive relationship, or it may simply be growth inhibiting, such as retaining an old pattern of relationship that feeds on some degree of self-abnegation.

The first of these is actually to do with the taking on of Shadow aspects with the consequent broadening of the personality or sense of self and it occurs through being confronted, in dreams or in life, by "other" aspects of oneself with which one can learn, painfully, to identify. To begin to know, "this too is me." The second, the standing against an impulse, helps to differentiate that impulse out from the darkness of unknowing. By thinking about a feeling rather than acting it out we become more aware of it and of ourselves, we rescue ourselves from the void, and, in the process, expand ourselves. Also, we throw more light onto our surrounds which would otherwise be forever darkened by our projections. It is difficult to become a true saint if you have not first been a sinner, and yet how easy it is to remain a simple sinner by blindly acting out our desires. The "greater good" that we should aspire to is that of our own expansion, our individuation.

One of the impulses that Mary had to stand against was that of connecting with her family members. For various reasons she felt drawn to see them and yet seeing them, as described above, was dangerous for her, it resulted in a loss of her sense of self. A visit from her brother would leave her feeling vulnerable and ashamed. She admired her brother and wanted to be loved or at least noticed by him. Yet time and again he made inappropriate comments to her, invaded her physical space by pinching or "playfully" punching her, or else he simply ignored or failed to contact her or return her messages. If he should visit on a whim of his own she feared that he might make sexual advances towards her and that she would be unable to rebuff them.

Over time, circumstance revealed one or another of his negative aspects and each time it was as if Mary was betrayed anew; somehow she managed to keep repairing the image of the brother that she longed for. And that is what she had to sacrifice, she had to let go of that idealized view of him, in effect, to lose him. Or more accurately she had to be prepared to give up her fantasy, what she wished were true, and trust and embrace the reality, what she knew was true, and in that process grieve for what she had lost. And the resultant self-knowledge, or self-realization, is where the final phase of the sacrifice comes in, the communion with herself.

One of the fears of someone like Mary is that the emptiness within, already intolerable, will increase in this process, the hole will never be filled. There is a sense that whatever is given up will be a subtraction and will lead to an increasing alienation, an expanding void within and without. But what actually seems to be true is that whatever is meaningfully felt starts to fill that internal cavity. It is not necessary that it be a "positive" feeling like love or warmth but it should be a real feeling, i.e. connected with something genuine rather than with something just wished for. So in the nature of things it is more often a "negative" emotion such as grief that slowly fills the emptiness.

Very primitive or raw emotions do not seem to work in this way. "Nameless dread" does not fill the emptiness but may extend it rather, and this was true of much of Mary's early expressed emotion which she spoke of in terms of a dark red, symbolizing her raw rage and pain, or else dead black, that described her experience of the cheerless dark. These red and black emotions happened to Mary, they were not hers, rather she was a victim of them. For the emotions to function as void fillers they must be part of differentiated experience, they must be metabolized in some way.

Metabolism

Edvard Munch, the Norwegian artist of the late nineteenth and early twentieth centuries, created a number of works entitled *Metabolism*. In a small lithograph of 1916, the sun shines down on a pregnant woman leaning with her back against a tree. In the distance children play in a field, while at her feet sits another child. Green leaves are visible on the tree and we can see that its roots are entwined in the skeletal remains of a human form. One of the picture's messages is clear, that a combination of suffering or death, and consciousness, in the form of the sun, leads to a filling out of the feminine; pregnancy and a new life. The woman is pregnant with feeling and productive of new growth.

His 1899 painting with the same title is on the theme of Adam and Eve. They stand naked on either side of the Tree of the Knowledge of Good and Evil looking robustly healthy, a foetus is faintly visible within the trunk of the tree. As in the later *Metabolism* lithograph, the tree's roots are visible. They are embedded in the soil and penetrate a human and what seems to be a reptilian skull. On the frame above the tree is painted a view of a city. This has a biblical feel but is also thought to represent the energetic life of a modern city in contradistinction to the dead matter from which the tree draws its sustenance. (Boe, 1989, p. 19)

In the picture Adam is imbued with light and Eve comes out of the darkness and they are both separated from and connected to each other by the tree. The picture affirms the idea of the metabolism of suffering in the creation of something new and, for me, suggests that the splitting apart that occurs with the knowledge of good and evil can be healed or reunited by the conscious awareness of that knowledge. Primitive consciousness splits, a higher or more developed consciousness joins together. In Mary's case, through becoming aware of her parents' negative aspects, i.e. through sacrificing the perfect parent fantasy, can come the de-idealization of them, and the possibility of giving up expectations that they will fulfil some nurturing function in the outer world. The loss of the expectation that they will be "all good" if only Mary behaves properly, frees both Mary and her parents. Who they are is no longer dependent on how good she is, which frees her, and letting go of her expectations of perfection or even of adequacy from them, frees them to be human. It is out of their sacrificial "death", and her grief, that new life for Mary can be metabolized.

Conclusion

Linking back to the play, the sacrifice that King Kreli makes is slightly different. He has submitted completely to the will of the Gods, allowing them to decide whether the diviner should live or die. The loss to him is of his friend and companion of many years, but what he gains is the reconnection both with the divine and with his people. Through that reconnection all are rescued from the dark hole in which they have been imprisoned and their lives are once more imbued with meaning. Through the sacrifice of his friend a communion has taken place with the gods, and the separation from them, the void, has been obliterated.

CHAPTER THIRTEEN

The "Birthday Present"

Because something is happening here
But you don't know what it is
Do you, Mister Jones?
                    (From *Ballad of a Thin Man*, Bob Dylan)

Paradise?

I n a collection of erotica called *The Gates of Paradise* (Manguel, 1993) is a wry story by Eric McCormack entitled simply *Birthday Present*. It opens with the middle-aged birthday-boy driving down a narrowing road through a snow-covered landscape. The description of him is shadowy, what he encounters old-fashioned and dulled, and he relates to nothing with any passion. Even when he stops at "High Point Lookout" the experience just seems "so familiar".

It is a wonderful description of a man in the midst of a midlife stagnation, nothing is new or exciting, and the patterns that have developed over half a life have lost their meaningfulness and simply carry a stale sense of familiarity. He is on his way to meet a woman and that is his expected "High Point", but he, and we, are given this scarcely veiled warning, "Lookout!"

The assignation is to take place in a motel, symbol of anonymous collectivity. A flaking totem pole stands outside, suggesting that such an assignation at such a place may have had some meaning in the past but that meaning has since decayed. The im-, or perhaps trans-, personal receptionist does not look at him, but, like one of the Fates, impassively continues her knitting and refers him to room thirteen, number of the lunar months, changing luck, and instability. Once in the presence of the smiling naked woman there, he is overcome by a nostalgic sadness; he should know this vaguely familiar woman. He wants to speak to her but she adjures him not to and instead strips off his clothes (where had they come from anyway? whose choice had they been?) and with them his sadness.

His desire, if that is not too strong a word, is to spill himself quickly into her and return to where he belonged. He had no wish to change or to fully experience the thudding in his chest that might presage its splitting apart and giving birth to feeling or at least to something new.

In tender silence she positions herself, supine, with spread legs on either side of his prone body. Gently, and very slowly, she inserts the toes of his right foot into her and gradually the whole foot disappears inside her spread warmth. The story describes in slow detail how first the one foot then the other, then both legs up to the buttocks and with a supreme effort those too are sucked inexorably into her by a type of reverse peristalsis. The description conjures up the image of a huge reptile swallowing its prey, except that our subject, in a passively ecstatic way, embraces (and is embraced by) his fate. He instinctively presses both arms to his sides to facilitate the entry of his torso and all goes well again until from the despair heard in her groans he realises that his head is too massive for her. He stops ascending and slips out a little. He too is filled with despair, as to enter her is the only desire left to him. Urgently, lovingly, she asks for his help.

He "wished and wished and wished. She shuddered and miraculously her muscles took hold again, the sucking resumed." A little later "a wall of slow sweet flesh covered his lips, flattened his nose. As he closed his eyes, he heard her utter one last great shriek of effort, or triumph, or love." (Or loss, we might add.)

Then darkness as he shoots along a brief tunnel and spills out into a balloon of soft pink light and opaque waters; great throbbing surrounds him. He tries to express his rapture but finds he has "cast himself off from all words". This is where the story ends, wordless inside the womb, conjoined with the mother in unconscious rapture, a wonderful reversal of the Miraculous Birth. It seems like a return to Wordsworth's "God who is our home" from which our birth has separated us. Except that here one senses a deepening unconsciousness, a falling back into the dark womb from which a prescient birth will be impossible, in fact a falling into an undifferentiated void.

"The Great Mother"

In *The Great Mother* (1963), Neumann vividly describes how "hell and the underworld as vessels of death are forms of the negative death-bringing belly-vessel" of the Great (M)other. "The opening of this vessel of doom is the womb, the gate, the gullet, which actively swallows, devours, rends and kills. Its sucking power is mythologically symbolised by its lure and attraction for man, for life and consciousness and the individual male, who can evade it only if he is a hero, and even then not always." (Neumann, 1963, p. 171) This passage comes from the chapter entitled *The Negative Elementary Character* and captures the feeling of loss that our story engenders, and the sense of return to a space that can entrap you forever.

But what is forever in the unconscious? It may not be very long before enantiodromia sets in and what had seemed a place of death, in that dark "death-bringing belly-vessel" of the mother, switches into its opposite, a place of renewal that leads to rebirth.

In his chapter on spiritual transformation, Neumann asserts that

> the spiritual aspect of the feminine transformative character leads through suffering and death, sacrifice and annihilation, to renewal, rebirth and immortality. But such transformation is possible only when what is to be transformed enters wholly into the feminine principle; that is to say, dies in returning to the Mother Vessel, whether it be earth, water, underworld, urn, coffin, cave, mountain, ship or magic cauldron.
>
> (*ibid.*)

All of which symbols are themselves "encompassed in . . . the womb of night or of the unconscious." (*ibid.*, p. 291sq)

Neumann reminds us that in every case, renewal is possible only through the death of the old personality, and it occurs in the dark, in the feminine.

"There must be some way out of here" (Bob Dylan)

This description could have emanated from Campbell's detailing of the Hero's journey and hints at the connection between the transformative feminine and that journey. There are two main routes out of the "belly of the mother". One is via the heroic masculine; through the strong-enough father who is able to stand against the power of the elementary maternal using his intellect, like Daedalus, or his physical power, like Heracles. The other is via the transformative feminine, the positive anima or negative witch who promises change, something new. In these days of *The Sibling Society* (Robert Bly) and *Man's Fear of Women* (Wolfgang Lederer) the path of the heroic masculine is often not open to us, except in the empty form of "Macho Man". Hence the transformative feminine has become more important. The transformative feminine, either in her positive aspect of spiritual guide or muse, or in her negative aspect as witch or Lilith; transformation is offered via inspiration or dissolution.

Unfortunately, in modern times, being projected in a distorted, saccharinized form often depotentiates the potential muse; she has become the sweet woman who adores. Experienced in fantasy as a figure who will admire rather than transform, she has lost her power to bring about deep change. What could have been a positive, life-enhancing impulse, the attraction to someone who sees one's potential and is able to show that to one and force one to live it out, has become perverted and addictive and now leads directly into the elementary maternal embrace where no change is desirable. In this other compartment of the void, a place of stagnation, the individual is firmly swaddled in the admiring glances of his (usually) youthful "muse". (The *anima* usually connects upwards to spirit but also down again into the flesh leading to a painful expansion of the personality through deeper knowledge of oneself. The adoring woman suggests that one is perfect the way one is and thus no change is necessary.)

There are numerous Fairy tales and myths that testify to the psychological truth of what Neumann asserts, i.e. "that transformation is possible only when what is to be transformed enters wholly into the feminine principle." For example, the dumbling who falls into a hole in the ground, in the forest, at night, undergoing his final transformation while lying passively asleep in a cave. Or Sleeping Beauty, for whom life stands still for so many years, in her castle surrounded by containing vegetation, or the hero myths, such as the night sea journey of Heracles in his cauldron of change or Hiawatha's struggle within the belly of the Great Salmon. These images are all of the Great Mother and of the archetypal unconscious.

Active or passive

In most of these stories, apart from the purely passive "returning to the Mother Vessel", there is an active and a passive element. The dumbling has served his mistress for three long years and done things contrary to his known nature, before he falls asleep; the sleeping beauty enters her period in the unconscious by going against the admonitions of her mother; and, in the case of the hero stories, it is heroic action as well as some contrariness to the established way which is to the fore.

Sometimes the passivity is dominant, as when the old king allows his dismemberment in the cauldron of rejuvenation, or when Jonah is in the belly of the whale and simply waits to be disgorged. And sometimes the action is dominant, as when Hiawatha battles the great fish, or the young child stomps and dances inside the belly of the All-Devourer until he gets released into the outside world. One can also think of these as being attitudes, either of submission to, or of fighting against, for release from, the Mother.

At different times different attitudes are necessary. At the start of the story of *The Birthday Present*, one could imagine that either attitude might have been helpful, struggling against the "perilous sameness" of his life, or submitting to fate. Either could have been a way out of our less-than-hero's stuckness and brought him from the sterility of his existence into some form of relatedness to the Mother as the unconscious.

Actually, both attitudes are probably necessary; the tension is about being in contact with, or in relation to, the Mother, without being drowned within her, so submission and assertion are both required. The danger in this story is that the mysterious woman, who first appears as an anima figure, is highly contaminated with the Great Mother archetype in her negative elementary character. In real-life situations this constellation can lead to an impasse; death rather than change. For the elementary feminine has little time for man as a hero, just as the transformative character has little time for man as a baby.

We do not know how this story will eventually end. As with those caught up in a midlife depression where some will battle through unchanged, except for a stiffening of their muscular ego-defences, whereas others will submit, regress, gain in wisdom through experiencing previously impermissible aspects of themselves, and be reborn into a changed world.

An image that captures the active–passive combination is from the story *The Bath Badgerad* from Marie Louise Van Franz's (1990) book *Individuation in Fairy Tales*. In this story Hatim has been sent to explore the Bath Badgerad by his queen and has reached the barren surrounds of the Castle of Nothingness. He is surrounded by statues of previous heroes who have failed in their quest and been turned to stone, and it is in this bleak landscape that Hatim must perform his task. This task is to shoot down a specific parrot in only three attempts or be turned to stone himself.

Armed with a golden bow and a silver arrow, his determination and hard-won prowess as an archer, and, of course, his great courage, he carefully aims, looses his arrow, and misses. With his legs turned to stone he tries again with even greater concentration and misses again. Realizing that he has reached the limits of his own abilities, and two-thirds paralysed, he calls upon Allah ("The Magnificent!"), closes his eyes, and lets loose his last arrow. The parrot drops, the heroes are liberated, and the illusory castle disappears. In its place lies an enormous diamond; a symbol of the Self replaces nothingness. This precious stone is to be taken back to the Queen. The Queen, in this story, is a good example of the transformative feminine who sends her subject away from safety and into the most dire situations wherein he fully experiences himself, both his power and his limitation.

In the therapeutic vessel

The barren space, the locked-in womb, the belly of the All Devourer, the Castle of Nothingness, all places shrouded in emptiness or darkness or meaninglessness, must be met at times with action and at other times with resignation. Sometimes it is the outer ear of the ego that must be used to inform us and sometimes we need to tap into the deep resources of the unconscious to discover transformative energies and wisdom there. When a patient says, "I can't go on anymore my life is in such chaos," or an attentive therapist admits, "I have no idea what this dream is about," these are admissions that the conscious ego has reached its limit. There is suddenly the opportunity for another centre of intelligence to become operative and be listened to and evoke change. Nietzsche has said: "One must feel chaos in oneself in order to give birth to a dancing star." C.G. Jung quoted this passage and discussed it in a lecture on June 13, 1934. (Jung, 1968, p. 51–53.) I would say "one must experience emptiness within oneself in order to give birth to a new idea."

But to do that as an analyst, to admit defeat, to allow oneself to enter the "clouds of unknowing", is like experiencing death and it is usually defended against. Following all these hours and years of study and analysis, after all this thinking and feeling, we should be becoming experts after all, and we are, and yet, paradoxically, we seem to become increasingly aware of our limitations, of our "unknowing". This is one of the more excruciating aspects of this work and the way we are tempted to deal with it is through treating symbol as sign, limiting meaning by becoming more linear and rationalistic in our thinking, and circumscribing the whole truth within walls of reason. For, to paraphrase an autistic child's statement, "when the walls fall down there is chaos", and we do not like chaos because it feels like a defeat.

I'm often comforted by the explanation of a teacher who spoke of consciousness as being like an island rising up from the ocean of the unconscious, the bigger the island gets the greater is its shoreline. The area of contact between consciousness and the unconscious is forever increasing, the more we know the more we realize that we don't know and thus we feel that the void or the chaos is increasing. Sometimes that experience is terrifying and at others it is strangely comforting and it can rapidly shift from one feeling to the other.

Real-life pathologies

Back to our big-headed gentleman, warmly ensconced in the throbbing womb, with no words any more, no logos. How does this space relate to real-life events? The most obvious way is to addictions of all sorts, whether to drugs, alcohol, sex, work, exercise or dependence on others' appreciation; the "noble" addictions as well as the "decadent" ones. The sublimated and regressed addictions lead to a similar place psychologically, a place of limitation and constraint, within another compartment of the void where the patient may be gently embalmed or else sequestered inside his or her own thin shell of tightly circumscribed "meaning". The regressed addictions seem close to Tustin's idea of "autistic shapes", enfolding and comforting and eventually suffocating, whereas the sublimated ones I liken to "autistic objects"; with their brittle hardness they ward off pain, emptiness, and/or meaninglessness.

And which is the worst sort of pain? Physical suffering or mental anguish? The pain of loss or of emptiness or of meaninglessness? The artist-of-pain, Freda Khalo, who often painted pictures depicting her physical distress, demonstrated that for her the void was even more awful than her physical suffering. In her picture, *The Tree of Hope* (Milner, 1995), she depicts herself on a cracked earth landscape with vegetation behind and her body scarred and entangled with surgical paraphernalia. The earth on which she sits comes to an abrupt end just before the margin of the picture, one can see the roots of the vegetation holding the clods in place and forward of that, nothing. The viewer wonders whether she is sitting on the side of a crack in the earth, or a chasm, or right on the edge of nothingness. It is her own terror of the void that Khalo has articulated. If she were to slip a little forward she would disappear from view and fall endlessly into oblivion.

For her, the void was constellated by a severe accident she suffered when she was a young woman, and also through her felt disconnection from herself and others, which perhaps preceded that accident. This disjunction was objectified by the multiple betrayals that she endured at the hands of Diego Riviera, her lover, husband, lover again, husband again, and life-long friend and deceiver. Racked by her emotional pain, and the physical pain from her initial trauma and innumerable operations, Freda became an alcoholic. She died aged 47 leaving behind an impressive body of powerful work. It is difficult to say whether she was redeemed by her regressive acts or delivered into the arms of death.

A common midlife experience, perhaps particularly for men, is that of realizing how implacable the universe is. There comes a sense that all our earthly endeavours take place within "the belly of the Mother", our reaching for the stars is like crawling from sequin to sequin on her carelessly draped shawl. There is no way out of her, no way to conquer her except within the fantasies of our patriarchal mythologies. We strive after deeper knowledge and better skills, extending the limits of our lives and capabilities, through training techniques, drugs or medications, technology and science, but always, if we are conscious, we come up against our limitations, whether it be in sport or in science or in the fuzzy world of trying to be a good parent.

Reaching for the pinnacle of perfection is always away from the earth, and away from the possibility of broadening our bases, extending our boundaries, enlarging our island and increasing its shoreline. Instead, it takes us to the sharp tip of a brilliantly illuminated point; one more step and we fall into nothingness. The light is comforting but what it has to show us quickly grows stale. What is outside of the light's range seems empty and yet it is not, for in the dark, if we have the courage, our imaginations may soar without restraint.

There was an old diagnostic category called "rejection sensitive dysphoric" that captured the exquisite sensitivity that some people have to rejection or loss of relationship. For them, not to be in a relationship is catastrophic because their sense of identity is so tied up with being seen by another or having another on whom to project aspects of themselves. This implies that they have no felt connections within, no relationship to the inner world as a place of comfort through meaning.

A young student, when asked to describe herself, said, "I am my boyfriend's girlfriend." Without her boyfriend she felt she would cease to exist. Another patient, whose husband had deserted her, experienced herself as a leafless tree. Like Osiris she was immured in the trunk. She initially felt quite empty but slowly her deep structure affirmed itself. The loss of her family as shapers of her identity enabled her to at last experience herself from within.

The fates

In the last years of the Second World War, Henry Moore made a number of drawings (Neumann, 1959: figures 44–46) that were characterized by evocative female figures statically enclosed in a sort of industrial or gallery space. Actually "enclosed" is too warm a word, for these figures are more "imprisoned" within bare walls that have no openings to the exterior, and they have a feeling of segregation from each other. There are shelf-like areas on the walls that look as though they should be windows, but they are simply indentations and their presence serves to underscore the closedness of the space. Small protrusions like wall fragments, and the way the figures stand in complete disregard of or non-relation to each other, complete the sense of isolation that the pictures portray.

After the war Moore drew another in the same series that has a completely different feel, although obviously connected with the previous works. (*ibid.*: figure 48) What has changed is that a wall now has a large opening in it, and through that opening can be glimpsed the ocean extending to a distant horizon. Infinite possibility is sensed. The eye, instead of being enclosed by walls, is free to travel to the ends of the earth and beyond, taking the imagination with it. It is as though a door has slid open onto the universe and the Fates are extending an invitation to visit.

What makes this new place not void-like, in spite of the huge spaces implied, is a sense of connection between the figures and the surroundings and between the figures themselves. The figures in the first, *Figures in a Setting*, drawings are unrelated to each other, whereas in the later one they stand in a group, they are in "communion". There is something sacred about them, and they stand as keepers of the gate or hostesses even of the world beyond.

This is such a different feel from the invitation to the interior that the *Birthday Present* offers. In Moore what is offered is space for the individual to continue to grow in relation to herself and others. In the *Birthday Present* it is a regression that is offered, a return to the womb.

That return to the womb may be the precursor of a new birth, but the loss of identity that the return implies, the giving over, causes a rent in the psychic envelope which may give rise to one of two sets of potentially traumatic experiences. In the first, the rent may be one through which the contents of the collective unconscious can pour. That is, that the fullness of things, or chaos, could invade the psyche leading to inflation or insanity. In the other, it may feel as if the individual psyche is spilling away, leaking into nothingness, or, in the idiom of the story, merging with the mother. Only time will make clear whether the flooding, or the dissolution within the mother, will result in the gift of a new birth or eternal loss.

As therapists we can only stand and watch because we do not know whether a particular regression will end in entrapment or liberation. Whether the regression is a much-needed rest on the journey, or a return home to the womb or death. The ego cannot plan or even know what the ultimate outcome will be and perhaps that is of no significance. In our story, what we know is that the hero is enwombed again, by his choice and hers, but we do not know whether that means he will be entombed forever or not.

CHAPTER FOURTEEN

The dark night of the soul

Oh my God
Am I here all alone?

(From *Ballad of a Thin Man*, Bob Dylan)

Eloi, Eloi, lema sabachthani?

"My God, my God, why have you forsaken me?" Christ's cry from the cross of his crucifixion epitomizes the suffering of the lost soul. At that moment Christ could have had no expectation of release, or of his imminent resurrection. This despairing cry, from a son to the father who has abandoned him, has echoed down the centuries.

The way it is phrased as a question rather than a statement suggests the difficulty with which we approach God's negativity, his dark side. Man does not want to see his abandonment as a betrayal; he does not state "My God, God, You have forsaken me!" He wants to give God the benefit of the doubt. In one interpretation of that cry, it is even seen as a cry of rejoicing; any death, no matter how painful, is welcomed because it will lead to a union with God. (Edinger, 1985) Confronting God would be to confirm our separateness from him.

In Psalm 22, in the Old Testament, David is expressing his distress and he begins with the same words.

My God, My God, why have you forsaken me? Why are you so far from helping me, from the words of my groaning? . . . I cry by day, but you do not answer; and by night, but find no rest.

(Psalms 22 verses 1 to 2)

In a determined effort to be heard, David then flatters God, calling God holy and praiseworthy and helpful to the peoples of the past, and reminding God of God's good deeds; he affirms God's good side. But receiving no response from God, he falls back on the common reaction of the abused child and takes the responsibility for God's neglect onto himself. "But I am a worm, and not human; scorned by others, and despised by the people." (Psalms 22 verse 6)

There follows a vivid description of what it is like to feel abandoned, lost in the void.

> I am poured out like water, and all my bones are out of joint; my heart is like wax; it is melted within my breast; my mouth is dried up like a potsherd; and my tongue sticks to my jaws; you lay me in the dust of death.
>
> (Psalms 22 verses 14 to 15)

Redoubling his efforts to be heard, the psalmist then promises to praise and glorify the Lord loudly and suggests that to be satisfied with their lot, whatever it is, is the right path for humankind. We need God, (we need to connect with the God-image within, the Self) we need to maintain a connection with God in the hope that we will be sustained through any eventuality; even if it means denying ourselves (our egos) or prostrating ourselves in front of a perhaps indifferent Lord.

God turning his back on us is what is so hurtful in these images. Like the mother who has been there from birth and before, and given life and hope with the milk from her breasts, the presence of her body, the gleam in her eye, and who has now left. Swallowed up in a depression or other life event she is no longer available to respond to her child's needs, and the emptiness where she once was is enormous. There is the idea here of that which is taken away being more traumatic than that which never was, and also of the wilfulness of the God who deliberately turns away. God is omnipotent after all and could choose not to. In the human realm the question, "How can my mother desert me?" is often coupled with "It must be my fault" and the rage that is natural, becomes turned on oneself or pushed far away, split off and disowned.

The psalm that follows the above is the well-known Psalm 23 wherein the vision of God is one of loving kindness, the giver of sustenance.

The Lord is my shepherd, I shall not want. He makes me lie down in green pastures; he leads me beside still waters; he restores my soul . . . Even though I walk through the darkest valley, I fear no evil; for you are with me; your rod and your staff—they comfort me. You prepare a table before me . . . my cup overflows. Surely goodness and mercy shall follow me all the days of my life, and I shall dwell in the house of the Lord my whole life long.

(Psalms 23 verses 1 to 6)

As the opposite of the void, of absence, here is an attentive God who has us, and our well-being, always in mind. This psalm is a rhapsody, the previous one a lament. And they are to the same "Lord".

As in the psalms, we see this fluctuating presence and absence of God or the Self regularly in the consulting room. With the right attitude on the part of the analysand, the work proceeds apace, driven or guided by some watching other that stresses this aspect, then its opposite, highlights this strength, that weakness, showers the person with meaning-filled dreams and significant synchronies, gladdens her heart with a new or deeper relationship, and then, all of a sudden, the work seems to stop. The leader has gone, the guide galloped away in the night, leaving the pilgrim stranded; alone and forgotten in the dust of a foreign country. "Poured out like water . . . bones out of joint . . . mouth dried up . . . la(id) in the dust of death." All that supports her is the presence of the analyst and his wan hopefulness. Trust, at moments, or hours, like these is too strong a word, it denies the person's experience of abandonment and implies a knowing that things will improve. And they may not, and knowing they may not but hoping for her sake, and his own too, that they will is all that is possible.

On being seen

Psalm 139 is a poem about being known by something bigger than oneself and finding that comforting. It suggests the insufficiency of the ego and hints that the psalmist has reached the limits of his capacities, the capacities of the "I", and that these don't compare to those of God.

"O Lord, you have searched me and known me" it begins. "You know when I sit down and when I rise up: you discern my thoughts from far away." (Psalms 139 verses 1 to 2) Whatever I say, wherever

I go, God is there before me, there is no escape from him. "If I take the wings of the morning and settle at the farthest limits of the sea, even there your hand shall lead me, and your right hand shall hold me fast." (Psalms 139 verses 9 to 10) I have been known, since being in my mother's womb, and, although I am imperfect, the image of my wholeness resides as it always has done in "your book", in God's knowledge of me. This is one of the sources of the attraction to a omniscient Godhead, the feeling that one can be known, in one's fullness of being, by another, and that other can only be God.

But being known by God may be unendurable and the psalmist writes, "Where can I go from your spirit? Or where can I flee from your presence?" (Psalms 139 verse 7) This suggests that he had had thoughts of trying to get away. Samuel Beckett wrote a short screen-play describing a figure in flight from an outside observer, portrayed as a camera, that pursued him down the city streets and into a room, just watching him. Beckett's character demonstrates the anguish of being perceived from the outside, and, later, the inescapability of self-perception, being looked at from within. It is not always comforting to be known by another, even if the knowing or being-seen is a knowing of the true.

There seem to be two ways of being seen which Kenneth Wright in his book *Vision and Separation* (1991) thinks of as masculine and feminine or paternal and maternal ways, and which he distinguishes as being looked at and being seen. Being seen in the maternal way is to be embraced by the warmth of the maternal vision with a feeling of acceptance by, and connectedness with, the mother; it is an undifferentiated "being seen". Being looked at by the father, on the other hand, is more critical or judgmental and serves to help the growing child separate from his oneness with his mother and family, and move into his own life. Instead of being "just fine as you are", the elementary maternal attitude (Neumann), it brings in an aspect of the transformative element or differentiating consciousness and asks further "is *this* how you want to be?"

God and Job

In the Book of Job, God turns his face away from Job, or, an extension of that, turns a malignant face towards him. Job feels misunderstood and abandoned by God and brings his powerful ego to bear in a long argument with God. Job is like the too-bright kid in the class who has to find some way of telling an authoritarian teacher that they are wrong, it is very shaky ground to be on and while Job does get through it, it is at no small risk to himself. By this stage he has lost everything that he valued: health, possessions, status, children, and friends. He is not God, he may have been valuable to God, but he is not God, and, in chapter 38, God lets him know that by describing the differences between them. God details much of what God has accomplished, challenging Job to match this with his understanding.

What God describes are a series of differentiations that God has wrought. God has set doors and gates to contain the waters and separated death from life and darkness from the light. God asks if Job knows where the darkness springs from as though darkness was not simply the absence of light but a thing in itself. In fact, what God is describing are the limits of, or boundedness of, the created world and God's embracing of the differentiated universe, now a step removed from the pleroma, the oneness of all. God is detailing opposites and suggesting that God made them.

But this creating of the *creatura* out of the pleroma is actually the domain of a splitting consciousness, usually thought of as the rational ego. In *Answer to Job* (Jung, 1969) Jung suggests that a main theme of the Book of Job is that God needs Job in order that God become conscious and especially self-conscious. Job forces God to know himself better, he confronts God's dark side, and God does not like it one bit and so God's tirade against Job is defensively self-righteousness.

The ego too suffers from becoming increasingly conscious of its archetypal ground through the Self's capacity for compensation. Jung reminds us that the experience of the Self is always a defeat for the ego, implying that the ego has to stand against the Self and risk being defeated by the Self's greater power and pervasiveness. "(B)ecause of its all-encompassing nature it is brighter and darker than the ego, and accordingly confronts it with problems which it would like to avoid." (Jung, 1963, p. 545–546)

In Chapter 38 and the following chapters of the Book of Job, God demonstrates to Job the depths of Job's unknowing and his lack of understanding, his smallness in the light of what God knows and has made. It is at the moment when Job admits his lack of knowing that God relents and once more turns God's face towards him. God blesses Job and rewards him with a fullness of things, described in terms of gold, children, land, and livestock, symbolic of the wealth that comes from a deep connection with the Self.

It is through submission to God's greatness that more of God can be experienced; the archetypal description of this submission is the incarnation of God himself as Christ and his subsequent immolation and death. God turns God's face away from God's incarnated aspect; the father abandons his son, as is expressed in that cry with which this chapter began. The story of Job is a precursor to that of the incarnation.

Kenosis

The word that is used to describe the renunciation of divinity as occurs with Christ in the incarnation is kenosis. It comes from the Greek word meaning emptying, which connects it with the void, and implies the relinquishing of God-likeness and indeed even the knowledge of God. For one who has felt glorious in the presence and knowledge of God it is experienced as a collapsing down into an abyss of despair, the pain of separation from God, the Dark Night of the Soul.

In the traditions of Christian mysticism, the mystic is initially sustained in these dark times by the trappings of his religion and by blind faith, but finally even these must be relinquished if the unknowable is to be experienced. This is what the emptying refers to. It is always an excruciating experience accompanied by a loss of meaning and direction. In Christianity, kenosis has also come to imply the reverse process, a reconnection, but with a new vision of God. Thus, there is a belief that the dark night will be followed by a new light, a new dawn.

Is that belief an article of faith or is it born out of hope? Whichever it is, I think it is a bar to the deepest experience of the void. A theologian suggested that hope is a component of faith (Denise Ackermann, personal communication) but T.S. Elliott reminds us that "hope would be hope for the wrong thing". (Elliott, 1974, p. 200) In fact longing, or hope, for anything is central to the experience but still may be "hope for the wrong thing", as it implies a picture of that which is hoped for. If we desire to experience God in His/Her/Its fullness we must be imageless, or else expect that the image we hold will be demolished.

Darkness and light

The yearning after the light comes from our deepest parts, and the experience of light after an experience of darkness is usually numinous. A simple, human event, such as stumbling through the dark of the bush, not necessarily lost but just overtaken by the dark, and coming to a known shelter in which a candle or small lamp is burning, will send the spirits soaring; a feeling of well-being pervades one. We feel contained by that small circle of light and the walls that it illuminates which shut out the darkness of the endless unknown. We wrap ourselves tightly within its circumference so as not to feel the enormity of the "other", to avoid what William Johnston calls "the ultimate archetype: emptiness, nothingness". (Johnston, 1993, p. 254) Whether that nothingness is the absence of God, "a dark vision of God" (ibid.) or a vision of a dark God, it has the sense of an unstructured emptiness containing all.

As I write this I sit on the half-enclosed stoep of a remote farmhouse facing the blank loom of a dark mountain. Storm clouds remaining from the night's meteorological activities shut out the usual starlight, but, as dawn approaches, the area above a dip in the mountains becomes suffused with a reddish glow which abruptly shifts to a pale cold grey with the faintest touch of blue in it. Dawn's rosy fingers, the sky of the new day, the vault of heaven; I am filled with a sense of awe and, yet, a feeling of containment. All is right with the world as I know it, the storm abated, the night ended, and I don't have to change my belief in the universe as an ultimately benevolent place. I feel settled in what Hopkins refers to as "Wild air, world mothering air, Nestling me everywhere". (Gardner, 1953, p. 54)

At night, in a small boat far from land, under thick cloud cover where no light is to be seen on the boat or off it, and the wind has dropped after some weather, one rapidly loses all sense of orientation. The horizon has been obliterated, the boat rolls and lurches from the irregular waves, where is up or down, north or south? Blinded by the dark one must make use of one's proprioception rather than vision to help one, but even that is rendered ineffectual by the constant randomness of the boat's behaviour. The harder you try the worse it gets until the best course seems to be to relinquish all trying and jam yourself into some soft corner until dawn breaks. But it is hard to keep the fearful demons of the night and of aloneness subdued.

Again, it is "the rosy fingers of the dawn" that renew hope and soothe us with a sense of "now we can see what is going on". Wind-filled sails, a clear horizon, and a visible compass complete the picture of purposeful movement that is under control, i.e. "my" control, again. And we can forget that we play in this small corner of the ocean by kind favour of the gods, or, perhaps, because of their indifference.

Separation from (good) God

The young mystic Thérèse of Lisieux described her "night of faith" like this:

> Then suddenly the fog which surrounds me becomes more dense; it penetrates my soul and envelops it in such a way that it is impossible to discover within it the sweet image of my fatherland; everything has disappeared! When I want to rest my heart fatigued by the darkness which surrounds it by the memory of the luminous country after which I aspire, my torment redoubles; it seems to me that the darkness, borrowing the voice of sinners, says mockingly to me: "You are dreaming about the light, about a fatherland embalmed in the sweetest perfumes; you are dreaming about the eternal possession of the creator of all these marvels: you believe that one day you will walk out of this fog which surrounds you! Advance, advance; rejoice in the death which will give you not what you hope for but a night still more profound, the night of nothingness."
>
> (Quoted in Johnston, 1993, p. 253)

Note the word "rejoice" which resonates with Edinger's interpretation of Christ's cry from the cross as mentioned above.

What has started as "the cloud of unknowing" through which the English Mystic suggests we seek glimpses of God, has become impenetrable darkness. The young Thérèse has entered that space where the contemplative should seek God, that is, between the clouds of "unknowing" and the clouds of "forgetting". The space appears dark and hopeless with no hint of the longed-for God on the far side or remembrance of God on the near and Thérèse is in despair. (As a note: The English Mystic was the anonymous fourteenth-century author of *The Cloud of Unknowing* and *The Book of Privy Counselling*, works about the spiritual quest.)

William Johnston suggests three possible reasons for the depth of Thérèse's despair. "First, that the very love which in the early stages creates a warm sense of presence eventually creates a gnawing sense of absence."(*ibid.*, p. 254) I take this to mean that through the contemplative's initial experience or glimpse of God she becomes aware, not only of God's grandeur, but of her own smallness or meanness. There is an illumination of both God and self, or, what in psychological terms we would call Self and ego.

What follows is a realization of separateness from God. By knowing that I am human, I know, my ego knows, I am not God, I am apart from God, I am apart from the Self. And at that moment there is nothing I can do about it, it is as though God has turned his face from me and I am plunged into darkness.

This is part of the experience that Wordsworth must have been referring to in the poem *Composed upon an Evening of Extraordinary Splendour and Beauty*; the loss of or distancing from God that is so inexorable. But Wordsworth also has a sense of the possibility that makes life and striving worthwhile. "My soul," he says, "though yet confined to earth, Rejoices in a second birth!" (Smith, 1921, p. 132) The void experience occurs more acutely in those who have lost what has been present, a spouse perhaps, or a child, and in this case God. The loss of what was had even briefly can lead to "a gaping wound, the wound of love". (Johnston, 1993, p. 255)

Separateness creates the emptiness in which consciousness can emerge and consciousness is the organ with which we perceive separateness. In psychoanalytic theory, the realization that the breast is not under our control, that we are not omnipotent is what opens the punctate or linear ideogram into a triangular structure that encloses space, the space in which we can play and thus symbolize. (Winnicott, Waddell, Britton)

That capacity for symbolization increases the capacity for imagination and for a richer, deeper form of consciousness. Increasing consciousness leads to an increased awareness of our separateness from God or others (in the sense of being different from them) but it also leads to a deeper connection with our own interiors, our selves, and thus to the God-image within. By being more separate, by de-identifying with the Self, we can connect more deeply to it.

We have now re-entered the terrain of psalms 23 and 22, God as presence and God as absence. Johnston takes it another step further by saying re. Thérèse: "But, alas, she was unable to understand that the blackness was a dark vision of God." (Johnston, 1993, p. 254). He seems to be hinting here at something more than the absence of God, that is the dark or evil side of God. We know that the absence of a parent is liable to activate a negative or abusive parental archetype, Kali for example, and the same may be true on this divine scale; the absent God is experienced as an evil God.

Thérèse was ecstatic to know God as "good" and her experience of God as evil was intolerable to her. Perhaps the Christian mystics have a more difficult path to follow than do mystics from other traditions because of the problem of their traditional split between good and evil as God and the Devil which leads to a one-sidedness in their experience of God. Spirit should be thought of as the spirit of truth not only as the spirit of good. In this way the experience of the "Spirit of God" becomes an experience of wholeness, the "perfect balance of the two great forces in the universe" expressed by the Chinese in the yin-yang symbol. (Cooper, 1978, p. 196) For the initiate, Thérèse, that was not yet possible.

Loss of the known

Also, "the symbols which formerly nourished her life fell to pieces . . . And *with the loss of symbol came the loss of meaning*: she no longer saw meaning in the great (Christian) story on which she had built her life." (Johnston, 1993, p. 254) This loss of meaning, one of the afflictions of modern man, is the result of an increase in the differentiation of consciousness. What had seemed a living truth becomes nothing but a fairy tale. Ken Wilber (1991), in his book *Grace and Grit*, suggests that the rise of rationality has dealt a deathblow to the mythic phase of psycho-spiritual development, and that this is a necessity if we are to journey further along the path of enlightenment. This is one of the ways that thought, or the development of consciousness, leads to emptiness; myths become meaningless. And yet a new way of seeing, a new vision, may take their place.

It is paradoxical that meditation should lead to a similar place to where thinking leads, for most meditation techniques require an emptying of thought. This emptying can be done in a number of ways such as focusing the attention on a picture, e.g. a mandala, or a word or sound, or by a process of letting-go of any thoughts that enter the mind, a paradoxical focusing on no-thought. As the English Mystic makes clear, with his stress on "the cloud of unknowing", all pictures that we start with must be relinquished, they are not God. For Thérèse, who was dead by the age of 24, her childish images of life after death could not match her spiritual growth; they had to be let go of but they left images of darkness and emptiness in their place.

Johnston also suggests that Thérèse suffered a sort of double depression, where "the (dark) night of the senses and the (dark) night of the spirit came together". She had exhibited some neurotic tendencies in childhood and "in her last months of agony" was frightened by suicidal desires. (ibid.) She seems to have suffered from the mediaeval affliction that Lyn Cowan refers to as acedie or "(m)onastic melancholy". (Cowan, 2004, p. 138)

Meditation does not cure neurosis; it may help us accept and live with our neurosis, but a lowering of the repression barrier usually takes place during meditation with the consequent invasion of consciousness by previously repressed shadow material. This may be intolerable to the ego and incommensurate with our sense of self. (Wilber) The English Mystic puts it like this: "The first time a man looks on this Nothingness and Nowhere the sins of his whole life rise up before him." (Johnston, 1973, p. 137) And further, "this whole wretched lump called sin is none other than yourself . . . and you understand now that it is part and parcel of your very being and something that separates you from God." (ibid., p. 102) That is the double darkness, a consciousness of our own evil and the awareness of our separation from "the light of the world", that with which we would most connect.

Johnston describes the emptiness, the space between the cloud of forgetting and the cloud of unknowing, as an "imageless, supraconceptual void". (ibid., p. 16) In this void we remain suspended or, more likely, we fall, because there is nothing to hold us, no previously useful container of myth or magic or rationality even. They have all been swallowed by the cloud of forgetting and there is nothing visible through the cloud of unknowing to take their place. And there may never be. It seems to me that this space is outside of faith, if faith sustains you here it means you have not yet let go. As noted previously, hopefulness has been described as the necessary background to the journey and hope, defined as "faith on tiptoe" (John Freeth, personal communication) still implies a tentative belief. But I think despair is the most authentic response, as it suggests a complete giving up or letting go.

As Jung says, the Self, the internal God image, is essentially amoral, and, I would say, non-ethical; it is one of the functions of the ego to take an ethical stance, to attempt to disidentify with collective consciousness or collective values or with a one-sided complex driven position with an archetype at its core. Although archetypes have a bipolar structure, only one of the poles is usually available to consciousness at any one time. Complexes flick from one pole to the other through the process that Jung called enantiodromia. It is up to the ego to seek for the opposite pole, often available to it through the unconscious' capacity for complementarity that continually attempts to correct the one-sidedness of the conscious attitude. The ego must reflect on the issues and engage with them with both feeling and rationality. In this way it connects the complementary aspects together. By this I mean to highlight the idea that rational thought splits, whether in science or metaphysics, so that one-sidedness is born but that that one-sidedness can be healed both through feeling and by groping for the opposites in any situation.

Knowing and not-knowing, individuation and beyond

What has this to do with the dark night of the soul? The growth of consciousness is very broadly the move from "rotunditie to rotunditie", from unconscious wholeness to conscious wholeness. From non-differentiation, through differentiation, which makes the opposites conscious, to the (re)union of and thus the obliteration of opposites, which occurs by means of the transcendent function. The archetype of the Self, with its ultimately non-dual character, transcends the opposites and is greater than the products of creation. The Self is not composed of the sum of created fragments, rather the totality of created fragments originate in the one-ness of the Self. The Jungian concept of individuation, the conscious realization of the Self, takes us into the realm of the ultimately unattainable.

In his complex book, *Mysterium Coniunctionis*, Jung attempts to describe this process using alchemical images. By their very nature these images are difficult to grasp hold of, like the often-mentioned

Mercurius or Mercury. Jung explains how, in a process beyond that of individuation, the individual psyche becomes subsumed into the *unus mundus* as an individual part of the 'one world' or whole. In this state some form of consciousness seems to exist but it is experienced as separate from and not identified with personal consciousness.

As a prerequisite for this process a so-called *unio mentalis* must first take place. This is the union of spirit and soul, reason and feeling, or intellect and eros and this is what is usually called the individuation process. As Jung puts it: "The goal of the procedure is the *unio mentalis,* the attainment of full knowledge of the heights and depths of one's character." (Jung, 1963, p. 474) The *unio mentalis* results in a psychic equilibration of opposites "in the overcoming of the body", a state of equanimity beyond the body's affectivity and instinctuality.

But this position is not enough; it is too removed from the body, home of the instincts, and so a further connection between the *unio mentalis* and body must take place. In this connected state it becomes possible for an individual to "rein in the soul" so to speak and gain the capacity to reflect (a spirit activity) on an affect (an expression of soul) without necessarily acting it out (through body action).

The final stage of the *mysterium coniunctionis* is a further step, to do with the union of the individual with the collective unconscious or world soul or *unus mundus.* He or she thus becomes a grain of individuality in the Universal oneness, aware of but not identified with either that oneness or the "I-ness" of the individual. In the East this may be thought of as Atman, an individual part of Brahman, the universal whole, and in Wilber's terminology as reaching the causal level of the psychic worldview.

In the psychic worldview as a whole:

> I begin to sense a single Divinity lying behind the surface appearances of manifestation, and I commune with that Divinity—not as a mythic belief but (as) an interior experience. . . . This is the subtle worldview—that there is a soul, there is a transpersonal God, but the two are subtly divorced . . . At the causal level that divorce breaks down, and the supreme reality is realised. Pure nondual Spirit.
>
> (Wilber, 1991, p. 200)

In the mystic traditions, this experience is empirical and reached through the "experiment" of meditation. The experiment leads to an experience rather than a new theory or idea and it is remarkable how similar are the experiences that individuals from different times and different cultures have had.

Dorn, a sixteenth-century alchemist, calls the *unus mundus* the One and Simple. "The third and highest degree of conjunction was the union of the whole man with the *unus mundus*, . . . the potential world of the first day of creation, when nothing was 'in actu', i.e. divided into two or many, but was still one." (Jung, 1963, p. 534) Thus, the highest development takes us back to the beginning, back to the pleroma before any-thing came into being.

Jung also describes Philo Judaeus' ideas: "(He) says that the Creator made in the intelligible world an incorporeal heaven, an invisible earth, and the idea of the air and the void." (*ibid.*) "(T)he relation of the creator to the *mundus intelligibilis* is the "imago" or "archetypus" of the relation of the mind to the body." (*ibid.*) The idea comes first, the idea is archetypal, the idea precedes that which is created.

In the next few pages Jung wrestles with these very difficult concepts.

> That even the psychic world, which is so extraordinarily different from the physical world, does not have its roots outside the one cosmos is evident from the undeniable fact that causal connections exist between the psyche and the body which point to their underlying unitary nature.
>
> (*ibid.*, p. 538)

Our powers of thought and language do not permit us to conceive of this unitary Being, but we

> do know beyond all doubt, that empirical reality has a transcendental background. . . . The common background of micro-physics and depth psychology is as much physical as psychic and therefore neither, but rather a third thing, a neutral nature which can at most be grasped in hints since in essence it is transcendental.
>
> (*ibid.*, p. 538)

In my thesis, this transcendental background that is common to both depth psychology and microphysics, and also to what is sought by the mystics of various disciplines, is the void. Out of infinite nothingness, arises emptiness, which suggests idea not yet realized, or energy perhaps, out of which appears matter in increasingly differentiated forms. This matter is imaged, in alchemy and in Jung's psychology, as the philosopher's stone or *lapis,* with its multitude of meanings ranging from the *prima materia* to the *spiritus mundi* made visible. It is difficult to say how much of this enormity coincides with the Self; both the void and the Self have been called the ultimate archetype. As mentioned elsewhere there is a Hindu myth of creation that suggests that the void is primary and eternal. It is contiguous with "emptiness", which links for me with Dorn's *mundus intelligibilis* where nothing is *in actu,* and that emptiness is contiguous with ocean, the *prima materia* or original matter, out of which all "things" are given substance.

Active imagination

Techniques of active imagination help connect the Self with the ego, enhancing thus the ego–Self axis. They bring consciousness to bear on the unconscious, allowing the Self to speak through image and symbol to the conscious parts of ourselves, and demonstrating our conscious availability to listen. They are indispensable adjuncts to the "talking cure", especially as far as the stage of individuation, the *unio mentalis,* and the union of *unio mentalis* with body, are concerned. The level of consciousness at which Active Imagination works coincides with what Wilber terms the humanistic-existential worldview. After this stage the various levels of the psychic world-view are reached and to explore these realms, relating to the *unus mundus,* some form of meditation, spiritual path, or non-verbal technique is required, to "(melt) down opposites and distinctions". (Fox, 1980, p. 193)

I am aware that this sounds like a contradiction because the last phases of the *Mysterium coniunctionis* do coincide with Wilber's psychic worldview. Perhaps the paradox is understandable when one realizes that the journey is not a linear unidirectional one. There must be an immersion in and return from "the one". (Dourley, 2004) Meditation helps the immersion, Active Imagination aids the return.

Rationalism leads to a splitting up and, therefore, loss of the sense of the *unus mundus,* or unitary reality, that underlies this psychic worldview, and, I suspect, so do words used in a linear rather than poetic form. Words used as symbols connect, and it is here that the difference between the reductionistic and synthetic or symbolic approaches to depth psychology is most obvious.

Active imagination is a purposeful but not a goal-directed activity. Like meditation it involves a listening but, contrary to meditation which implies a stilling of the ego, it actively involves the ego. One can ask whether active imagination is "better" than mysticism or meditation, or is the mystical experience, the return to a unitary state, the ultimate experience? Many aspire to it but it is an opposite to the state of differentiation that consciousness creates. The melting into unitary reality implies a loss of ego whereas individuation implies a conscious involvement by the ego in a relationship with the Self.

Wilber expresses an irritation both with those who consider mystical experience a sublimation and with those who see it as a regression, both ego defences. The spiritual quest may seem at some times like a rising above the confines of the flesh and at other times like a dissolving into the mother. The question for me is how do we keep our balance on that perilous membrane that separates the one from the other; how do we keep in touch without falling into? The void is sometimes to be embraced and at other times shunned.

God and the void

Mysticism is the attempt to attain direct spiritual communion with God and yet mysticism can be equated with entering the void, which can be described in terms of unknowing, emptiness, darkness or nothingness. William Johnston clearly disagrees with some people's view that

> the void or the cloud means blotting out all images, getting rid of thought, making one's mind a blank—becoming a zombie! . . . *The void is constituted by detachment, nonattachment, nonclinging—not by blotting things out.* In the void I do not cling to thought; but I may think. I do not cling to words but I may use words; I do not cling to pictures; but I may have mental pictures.

He states that one can enter the void through prayer, or a mantra, or "while listening to the sound of a waterfall or watching peach blossom fall . . . or attending to one's breath." "The void is no mere negation (even though it is often described in negative terms) but a state of <u>consciousness</u> full of spiritual wealth." (Johnston, 1993, p. 289, my underlining)

This area is full of paradox. Are there not two different void experiences that he is conflating here? The one that one could term "the dark night of the soul", a separation from God or the Self, a loss of meaning, etc., and the other "full of spiritual wealth" which implies the experience of God or the Self as a numinous but undifferentiated reality of whom or of which I am a part. The symbolism of the first is of darkness and of the second is light. The "dark" void, arising sometimes by design, e.g. through meditation, or via fate, e.g. through trauma or loss, is a place of emptiness or lostness. It may fill at some time or another with "spiritual wealth", in fact the emptiness is a prerequisite for that filling, but equally it may not be filled or the filling may be of a tantalizingly short duration.

We seek God and the ecstatic experience that that might bring and we find the desolation of the void. Within the desolation of the void we may find God. Or perhaps God seeks us, and, as we empty ourselves, become void, God may find a place to enter into. Allowing ourselves "not to know" creates a space that can be filled by the wisdom of the Self. The Self, at some level, desires to become known. It wills contact with the conscious ego. When the ego allows itself to melt into the Self, when it is lost in the oneness, it loses its capacity to know and it feels to itself to be dying.

In another paradox, that "nothing", which may be experienced as the absence of anything, including God, can be thought of in the sense that Meister Eckhart, a fourteenth-century mystic, spoke of it. This is a direct opposite, in that "nothing", for him, was the presence of God. When Paul arose from the ground, blind after his conversion, according to Meister Eckhart he "saw nothing, and this nothingness was God". In another context Eckhart talks of God as having "his changeless existence and his nameless nothingness" and that God can only be approached through unknowing, "if you know something about him, he is nothing of that which you think you know."

This is the *via negativa*: "you should love (God) as he is, a not-God, not-mind, not-person, not-image—even more, as he is, a pure clear One, separate from all twoness. And we should sink eternally from something to nothing into this One." (Sermon 12 in Fox, 1980) We should sink into nothingness, into the void, and thus we sink into God.

Consciousness or not

In his commentary on Sermon 17, Fox writes about letting go of knowledge and will, becoming empty, so that God will fill the vacuum. He quotes from the sermon where Eckhart says "He is not further off than the door of your heart; there he stands and tarries and waits to find someone ready to open up to him and let him in ... He is a thousand times more eager for you than you for him." (*ibid.*) This reinforces Jung's expressed idea that the unconscious needs the ego to become conscious. Consciousness is necessary.

Fox further suggests that "Letting go and letting be allow letting in to occur", and he elaborates on this theme with another quote from Eckhart: That if a cask "is to contain wine, one must necessarily pour out the water; the cask must be bare and empty. Therefore, if you would receive divine joy and God, it is necessary for you to pour out the creatures." (*ibid.*, p. 247) By "creatures" I think he is referring to what Jung, in *The Seven Sermons*, calls *creatura*, in contrast to the *increatum* or pleroma, which is the undifferentiated oneness or allness. The *creatura* are roughly equivalent to the contents of the conscious ego. We must empty ourselves of consciousness.

In Sermon 13 Eckhart says, "Outside God there is absolutely nothing but nothing. Therefore it is impossible that any change or transformation would be able to affect God. God is one." (*ibid.*, p. 193) That is, God is a unity that cannot be reduced or increased. And yet Jung, Neumann, and Edinger would all say that any change in any of the parts affects the whole and that that is the purpose of the work. It is only through the unitedness of consciousness and the unconscious that change is possible. Jung suggests that psyche is a constellation not a unity. (Jung, 1963, p. para. 502)

"Unity is the negation of negation" Eckhart continues, and, "all creatures carry a negation in themselves; one denies that it is the other." (Fox, 1980, p. 193) Perhaps in the latter part of the sentence he is referring to the personal psyche; man, the created, is not unity but differentiation. And the Self or God is not differentiation but unity. As Fox writes: "Nothing can exist outside of God: therefore everything is already united in God. It is the removal of all separation, the melting down of opposites and of distinctions. God is not separations but unity." (*ibid.*)

At the end of the chapter, Fox discourses on the difference between what he calls dualistic and dialectical consciousness and this discourse helps resolve the paradox about consciousness being both necessary and to be avoided. He asserts that dualistic consciousness leads to an either/or sort of knowing, knowledge that divides and excludes, splits up in effect, whereas dialectical consciousness is a both and/or "true" knowing. "It is the way we know things and respect their differences, but all within the truth of the panentheistic interrelatedness of all that is." (*ibid.*, p. 197) That nice phrase "within the truth of the panentheistic interrelatedness of all that is" suggests a state just this side of the pleroma where the opposites have not cancelled each other out. Where the ten thousand things exist in relationship and within God, and where there is some consciousness.

I would like to refer back to the book *Vision and Separation* mentioned at the beginning of the chapter, which differentiates between being looked at and being seen. Being looked at is the more masculine way that separates in a judging or critical fashion, saying "You are this not that", whereas being seen is more feminine or maternal, enfolding the object of observation in the embrace of acceptance. Being looked at separates us both from ourselves and from our doting mothers and from what the doting mother symbolizes, the *prima materia* or the unconscious. Dualistic consciousness is masculine consciousness and dialectical consciousness a sort of combined masculine and feminine consciousness. Not the unconditional-positive-regard type of non-seeing, but the way we know things and respect their differences, but yet transcend those differences.

Potjie-kos

There is a South African barbecue speciality, called potjie, where a stew is cooked in a three-legged pot over an open fire. There are as many ingredients as your imagination can embrace and they all go in at once. During the cooking process, custom prohibits the lifting of the lid or the stirring of the potjie. You are allowed to listen to it to make sure that it is gently bubbling! The challenge is to cook the whole potjie so that all the ingredients, from tough stewing mutton to fresh-from-the-garden peas are all cooked, tender or al dente, keep their discrete forms and yet impart their individual flavours to the whole dish.

I think of the individuated psyche as being something like that, differentiated but interrelated, unique but balanced. This is about as far as my consciousness can reach. A higher "mystical" consciousness is necessary to embrace the vision of a unity that is not simply sludge. Not like an overcooked potjie, where the ingredients blend together in an undifferentiated mush (which may still be delicious), but a supra-ordinate state where difference is obliterated by union, a union of both this and its opposite, which cancel each other out, a state beyond *creatura*.

In the Jungian framework we value consciousness, the differentiation of opposites and the holding of them apart as the source of psychic energy, and yet, the main thrust of the individuation process is the push towards wholeness or unity through the transcendent function. This is the function that brings together the seemingly irreconcilable and it is very different from ego-consciousness. Yet the transcendent function arises out of ego consciousness' capacity to be crucified on the cross of the realized opposites, a crucifixion that results in the death of what is known and the sense of loss or abandonment and the cry that forever resounds: "My God! My God! Why have you forsaken me?"

TREATMENT

Rather than words comes the thought of high windows:
The sun-comprehending glass,
And beyond it, the deep blue air, that shows
Nothing and is nowhere, and is endless.

(Phillip Larkin)

Introducing the management
of void states

This kind of emptiness, confident but never certain, gives us the
room to be flexible and self-aware.

(Thomas Moore, 2003)

In general there are two aspects to the management of void states.
The first is concerned with helping to build an ego strong enough
to resist the fragmentation that threatens when a person feels
too close to the void. There are various ways of solidifying psychic
structures, e.g. through enabling connections, form, and meaning,
so that experiencing emptiness does not feel catastrophic. This is
more to do with trying to obliterate the sense of the impending
void and is more appropriate to early life or damaged psyches. The
second aspect is concerned with enabling a creative position that
requires the void for its functioning, it fosters a connection with the
void rather than trying to avoid it. Here the void is like an open
container of the imagination, an emptiness into which new thoughts
can expand and where the Self can manifest.

In different chapters of this book different aspects of treatment
appear. Most of these are part of what analysts are trained to do,
they are the usual aspects of psychoanalytic work, but some are more
specific with regard to dealing with the void experience itself. In
general the therapeutic aim is to help the individual feel connected
to her own interior and this is done through the fostering of
relationships in the interior world of the therapy itself and, by
extension, relationships in the outside world too. This is primarily

achieved through the transference relationship, where "transference" is considered in its widest meaning to refer to both conscious and unconscious aspects of the felt relationship between analyst and analysand. The inner connection may be initiated or enhanced, not only through the "talking cure", but especially through those activities that fall under the rubric of Active Imagination.

Many patients who feel overwhelmed by emptiness have sustained injuries at the pre-verbal level of development and thus they have no words for their experiences or for their emotions. (Joyce McDougall, 1986, explores this "alexithymia" in some depth.) Body memories may be released and psychic connection with soma improved through the encouragement of some type of movement. This is aimed at "listening" to how the body can express some aspect of itself that is non-verbal. When a patient reaches a point in the analysis where "there are no words", I do not usually wait for long before I offer some other medium such as chunky crayons and a large sheet of paper, access to other images in card form or to a sand-tray, or an invitation to take up a posture, or mime a movement, that evokes or depicts the unnameable.

There are a few ideas that I find helpful to myself in being with void-visiting patients. The first is that the analyst does not have to "do" anything to remove the analysand from the void, in fact, by staying in the void, the void begins to become defined, and in this way it loses some of its distressing characteristics. Then the idea of "enantiodromia", a word coined by Jung to refer to that process whereby the opposite of whatever it is that you have been working on or with suddenly becomes true. Linked to this idea is that of time passing and the achievement of distance, these ideas remind one that life is a process and the most important thing is not to foreclose on that process, not to think that because a person is in a terrible state now that that is where she will stay.

It is a bit like that children's game "pass-the-parcel" in which a heavily wrapped parcel is sent round a circle of participants and halted randomly by stopping the accompanying music. Whoever has the parcel in her hands when the music stops must unwrap one layer. In the deep centre is an unknown treasure. Everyone wants the treasure but also they want the excitement of unwrapping a layer, even though they know that the unwrapping will not reveal the treasure until the last. Stopping too early, all one has is a bundle of wrapping paper. At the end of the game, only one person gets the prize (will it be a booby prize?). However, in life it is as though another parcel has already by then begun its rounds. We have to keep going even though we know that what we find may not be what we sought, neither will it be what we can see in front of us; it may be nothing or it may be more than we could have dreamt of. But we have to keep on unwrapping.

In this fuzzy world where we find what we do not seek, articulated so beautifully in dreams and fairy tales, the topsy-turvy world where things change so rapidly that the outcome is unpredictable, the analyst's attitude has to be one of the awake companion who has been there before but has never been here before. He must be guided as much as he guides, follow as much as he leads, be taught as much as he teaches, contain without boxing in, and let loose without abandoning. She will try and do it as well as she can and yet it may be her biggest mistakes that lead to the greatest growth in her clients. And she may never know what helped until much later, if at all! No wonder it has been called "the impossible profession".

The aspects of treatment that have been raised in the book so far are many and include the following:

1. Helping the analysand with the acknowledgement and acceptance of limitation and of shared reality (including the reality of the void) is written about in the chapter on Tustin's work, *The Void in Psychogenic Autism*, and in *The King's Sacrifice*, *The "Birthday Present"*, and *Dimitri's Void*.
2. Linked with that is the idea of submission (and what may be its opposite, self-assertion) which is expanded on in *The "Birthday Present"*, *Trauma as a Void Experience*, and *The Dark Night of the Soul*.
3. Making sacred is amplified in *Primary or Secondary?* and in *The King's Sacrifice*.
4. The ambiguous value of regression has been discussed in *The "Birthday Present"* and *The Dark Night of the Soul*, and will be revisited in *On Active Imagination*
5. Aspects of the analytic attitude, including witnessing, mirroring or echoing, and not invading or filling the empty patient with the therapist's self are discussed in the chapters *Another "Black Hole"* and *Empty of Oneself*.

6. The ambiguous nature of "frames", as containers or as closed boxes that inhibit growth, is explored in *Dimitri's Void, The Void in Psychogenic Autism,* and *Primary or Secondary?*
7. Dealing with absence and return is dealt with concretely in *Memory within the Borderline Condition* and more symbolically elsewhere.

The following three chapters develop some of these themes further.

CHAPTER FIFTEEN

Aspects in the treatment of void states

If you want to go anywhere, the map is absolutely necessary.

(C.S. Lewis)

If you don't know where you're going, I guess you can't get lost.

(J. Lair)

If you follow the map too closely, you will never reach any place new.

(PA)

Connecting with emptiness

A disconnection from aspects of one's own experience, a disconnection from one's Memories, Dreams, and Reflections, precipitates the void. The moment one starts to engage with an aspect of that felt emptiness, the emptiness begins to become bounded; one can start to differentiate what is and what is not part of the void and that sets limits to it.

One of my analysands, Gert, described how thinking about approaching his father was like climbing steps up to a doorway in a castle wall. On knocking at the door it opened and he found himself standing on the edge of a chasm. Where his father should have been was nothing, a vacuity void of his father. In a recent one of her dauntless shows, Oprah Winfrey interviewed daughters and the fathers from whom they felt disconnected. One of them described herself as having "an emptiness inside that has the shape of my father".

Once, when working in a Child and Family Unit in Cape Town, I saw an adolescent male who was like a walking emptiness, defined by absence rather than presence. After an interview with him, in which he spoke in platitudes rather than his own words, I found it difficult to articulate what I felt about him. Being in a unit where one expected people to paint, I decided to paint my impressions and what spontaneously emerged was a picture of a room that extended up to his outline and then . . . nothing. It was not so much that he was invisible but that he was completely empty.

There are three different grades of emptiness, a chasmic lack, an absence, and an empty presence. Engaging with images such as these starts to change them; first a definition of boundedness takes place. Like a footprint that demonstrates an absence but also gives some idea of the object that is absent, or an empty room that one can peer into. In spite of being empty it has some parameters. Those outside parameters are like a bite out of the void, a bite that can begin to fill with substance.

In an essay on Henry Moore, Neumann (1959) describes how the absence of something can constellate its presence in the observer. He was referring to one of Henry Moore's sculptures of women where various parts are missing, for example a breast or the face, or there is a hole in the middle of the abdomen. In some of these images it is the lack or the emptiness that strikes you but in others the emptiness just gives rise to a feeling not of loss but of a sense that one is looking through or even into the missing part, experiencing it in a new or deeper way. Paradoxically, through its absence it becomes more present, better known.

A similar thing starts to happen when you really look into the void where, for example, the father ought to have been; you may start to experience someone in place of that father who never was or who had withdrawn himself. This new figure is archetypally based, and thus is undifferentiated. Not adequately humanized by contact with a real person, it may take the one-sided form of a negative, or, sometimes, an idealized father. Sometimes the father image is something generated by the Self as something that is needed by the individual for his or her development. By this I mean that its origin is from more than just the lack itself, it is what-is-needed that gives its shape to the new form.

Three weeks or so after the event of experiencing his father as a void, Gert woke after a bad dream to find himself hugging himself and crooning "its going to be alright, you're going to be alright", and having the subjective sense that that was true. He realized that he was fathering himself, and felt further, that he could transmit that fathering to his sons, and others in his circle as well.

Defining the lack

In Gert's case, his healing engagement with the experience of emptiness was quite spontaneous, but for those for whom that is not the case they may be helped towards a deeper connection by being invited to explore the resonance of the void image within them. What does the lack of the father feel like? How does it affect you? How could it be different? What could be worse and what more ideal? This allows for a double process to take place, the uncovering of what is there but has been hidden, and also the structuring of something across the emptiness, a thought skeleton or framework that can later be covered with the warm flesh of feeling. Both of these processes result in a filling of the void space through the direct involvement of the conscious ego.

On being known

Parts of us are known not through the ego but through the dim perceptions of other autonomous aspects of the psyche and this "being known" by those others may be reassuring. That experience of "being known" comes via dreams or active imagination or through the direct experience of Psychotherapy and the therapist as an observing other. In *Mysterium Coniunctionis*, Jung states, "For everything that is only is because it is directly or indirectly known, and moreover this 'known-ness' is sometimes represented in a way which the subject himself does not know, just as if he were being observed from another planet, now with benevolent and now with sardonic gaze." (Jung, 1963, p. para. 501)

I wrote, "may be reassuring", but would add that being known can also be intolerable. Being known in a way that is different from the way I know myself is painful. For example, given the sort of parenting that Balint discusses (*Empty of Oneself*), being known by another can conjure up the "void in the presence of the mother" sort of experience; the other's view of one has been wrong before and is expected to be wrong again, and thus threatening to one's view of oneself. Dreams, and the view of one that they demonstrate, may be untenable for a person like this. I am thinking of a woman who had been in therapy with different analysts for over fifteen years who asked me one day whether dreams were important. After an initial explosion of disbelief, I explained some of what I considered to be the significance of dreams in the analytic encounter.

After some months she let me know that she was capturing some of her dreams in a dream-diary and some time later she started bringing her dream-diary to sessions, but it was many months before she was able to actually share dreams with me as a routine part of her therapy. Her fears were manifold, most basic were a lack of trust that being known could be self-enhancing and also her expectation of being known in the wrong way, but, in addition, she feared that the dream may tell the truth; that she could be seen correctly, as she really was; that the letter to herself and the analyst, which was uncensorable because she did not yet know how to interpret dreams, may tell something about her that she did not want known. If the knowledge that the dreams had of her had come into consciousness it would have been a more severe blow to her sense of self than she felt she could survive.

This not-telling of the dreams is quite common and may be a defence against the void experience that is precipitated by experiencing "I am not this" when there is not yet the possibility of accepting "but I am that". My impression is that it occurs more commonly in women than in men and this perhaps relates to the fact, noted by Balint, that the "void in the presence of the mother" sort of experience is more common in women than in men. In general, men seem to seek identity and want to be known by the dreaming self, whereas women are trying not to be known as their mothers have "known" them.

The covering of the pit

This is different, again, from what could be called the Erebus experience. Erebus is translated by Graves (1955) as "the covered

[pit]" and in mythology is often synonymous with the underworld, the place of shadows and mysteries; it has the connotation of having a lid on things and we walk about gingerly on that lid for fear of falling through and into the abyss beneath. A middle-aged female client dreamt that she was descending onto the flat interior of a dormant volcano, one that she had visited in her waking life. As she descended, the ground became abruptly steeper and she sensed that the covering of the abyss had gone. She feared that she might fall into nothingness. She cried out to warn her children and woke up. In an active imagination she allowed herself to fall and continued and continued falling, passing verdant trees in her descent. It felt to her as though she was "falling" forever; gradually her fear left her.

We may fear that the lid will open and too much will become uncovered and escape, like the contents of Pandora's box. I recently had an interview with a rage-full child whose father had abandoned the family to live with a girlfriend in another country. When I asked about his feelings about that; "It's fine", he said, and simply shrugged.

Lifting the lid on his feelings was too frightening for him to contemplate; would he drown in that undifferentiated confusion? Yet the fear generated by the threat of this uncovering is probably not as bad as the fear of falling forever into the void. Here the falling is into a space that one may not want to be in but at least it does have limits. In it one may encounter one's shadow and the possibility of transformation, but not the nothingness of the void proper. The beginning space of Dante's Divine Comedy is such a space.

> I found myself obscured in a great forest,
> Bewildered, and I knew I had lost the way.
>> (Alighieri, 1993, *The Inferno*: canto 1, lines 2–3)

Later, Dante and his guide Virgil arrive at the gateway of the infernal regions. On it is written:

> Through me you go into the city of weeping;
> Through me you go into eternal pain;
> Through me you go among the lost people.
>> (*ibid.*: canto iii, lines 1–3)

His journey begins in the outer-worldly darkness of the forest and then continues in the deepening dark of the underworld.

The suggestion for me is that, armed with the knowledge that you have a good guide, and knowing that your Beatrice has you in mind, it is possible to allow yourself to start to uncover the infernal regions of your own psyche, and to begin your journey through them. It will be hell but there is the chance that you will get to heaven in the end.

Dante's Inferno is reserved for those who have not acknowledged the existence of God or experienced a sense of responsibility for those things they did while on earth. These are the "lost people", and they are, according to Dante, irredeemable. For the others, even those who committed grave sins, if only they acknowledge God there is the possibility of redemption through enduring the fires of Purgatory. Being unable to acknowledge God or the Self makes the journey well-nigh impossible and the result is that the "pilgrim" stays lost forever; eternally separated from the possibility of achieving the sort of self-knowledge that brings us closer to our own wholeness of being.

What is there?

The sort of example I have in mind is one of a young woman, Megan, who early in her childhood had decided that she would lead a "good" life. This entailed expunging those parts of herself that she felt her father disapproved of (the cheeky, messy, fun-loving aspects), and not excelling too much at school or University, as that was deemed unfeminine. She felt she should make herself available to look after members of the "weaker sex" (her father's words for women) who would need her care. She had covered over the pit or core of her being and she slid imperceptibly into a deep depression and state of confusion, with patches of paralysing emotionality and inhibited sexuality.

Falling in love with a caring man, who really seemed to have her interests at heart, started to dislodge the lid of the pit and, in the abysmal zone beneath, all manner of shadows made themselves known to her: rage, envy, lust, and irreverence, to name a few, but also her liveliness and intelligent capability. Their presence filled in the empty shell of her being into which she could now dare to fall and more fully discover herself.

But to experience these aspects of her wholeness was traumatic for her. For that involved a reawakening of parts of herself and a realization that "this too is me". This brought with it a fear that this new young woman would not meet the approval of her father, who might then turn away from her leaving her adrift. She had always relied heavily on her narcissistic father for her sense of identity, because her mother was one of those too accepting mothers whose totally "unconditional positive regard" was so encompassing that it did not foster any sense of individuality or separateness.

The Erebus aspect implies both the lid and the fear of the emptiness below it. Uncovering the joyous impulse to find oneself may expose the dread of losing one's nurturant objects. Even if those nurturant objects had only nurtured a part of a person, that part may have felt like her one link to life.

Yearning, mourning, and acceptance

Experiencing the void often leads to yearning for fullness or connection. If this yearning can be lived without hope but simply contained between analyst and patient, something new may happen. A sense of mourning may arise for all that never was and never can be, and a new dawn begin to break after the interminable seeming "night of the soul". (cf. D.H. Lawrence's wonderfully evocative poem about that night, called *The Ship Of Death*, 1950)

The mental holding of both the yearning and the hopelessness is extremely difficult not only for the analysand but for the analyst as well. He may often be tempted to act out in some way that will relieve the tension. Paradoxically, the joint experiencing, i.e. by analyst and analysand, of the analysand's yearning and hopelessness will forge a connection between analyst and patient. Looking emptiness squarely in the face results in acceptance, an acceptance that starts to fill the emptiness.

As we engage with the void we begin to differentiate some of its aspects and that starts to lay down strands of linking across it. Although the void is an individually felt, internal experience, we think that what we require is outside of ourselves, there must be a saviour somewhere. "My mother will see me today", "my husband will never be unfaithful again", "my therapist will surely remember what I said last week", etc., "and then the feeling of emptiness will lift". The seductive or addictive part of it is that it will lift but only momentarily, because the damage is more in the past than in the present. Hope that it will be different, even if it does become different, can never undo the past. To deal with the past, and the constant betrayals of the present, acknowledgement and mourning are required. Mourning not only the other who we feel could change and make things better for us, but also our impotence with regard to healing that other. (Charles, 2000a)

It can be especially difficult when a parent changes during the life of their child, as of course most of them (or us) do. The thoughtfully sweet old man who cherishes his son and grandchildren may be the same man who terrorized his son many years previously. It is difficult to come to terms, in the therapy, with the childhood monster, when confronted by the saint of the present.

In therapy, in his middle years, Sammy gradually acknowledged the dark and shameful aspects of his childhood, for example that his father had been imprisoned for embezzlement, and this acknowledgement led to a deeper sense of substantiality. This quite suddenly allowed a connection with positive memories from his childhood that had not previously surfaced in the therapy. In defending against the bad memories he had been separated from the good ones as well; allowing the bad in allowed the good ones to flood back too, bringing with them a feeling of reconnection with himself and a fuller range of felt experiences. He articulated how that increased feeling for himself led to the deepening of an adult sense of "returning home".

Sage advice re: complexes and connections

The English Mystic, in writing about meditation, gives good advice to those struggling with what we would call complexes. He suggests that, when thoughts or feelings intrude and come between you and God, you should "look over their shoulder". This is a nice idea about not identifying with a complex. Further, he suggests that if they do engulf us we should admit defeat, not contend with them any longer, but fall down like a captive or coward and commend ourselves to God. (Johnston, 1973) Appeal to the Self rather than the complex, to the greater rather than the lesser deity.

It has been said that the right brain is "the biological substrate of the human unconscious". (Schore, 2004: 16) Certainly, the right-brain is where awe is experienced, and reverence, and patterning, and God, and Art, and, more clinically, "the right hemisphere specialises in the unconscious process of social and emotional information, the regulation of bodily states, and attachment functions." (*ibid.*) Via the left-brain, seat of rational consciousness, verbal reasoning, logic, and verbal language we experience and express the false-self (Winnicott) and the conscious sense of identity that is an ego function. Freud's *Id* makes its presence felt, via instincts and affects, through subcortical structures. By conscious submission to that which is, left-brain connects more fully with right-brain while experiencing instinctual impulses from below. That whole amalgam is close to the Jungian concept of the Self.

"In the beginning was the Word" (The Gospels John Chapter 1 verse 1), or logos, or mind. But that is only the conscious beginning of egohood; the formation of the *creatura* by differentiation out of the pleroma through the Word. The world becomes through language; and language becomes deified. "The word was (i.e. became) God", it becomes masculine and the ultimate effectiveness. "Without Him was not anything made that was made." (*ibid.* verse 3) The Word is the most highly prized but it is only a part; without the Word we are not; with it we are separated from our wholeness.

The puzzle is how to connect the part with the whole, above with below, the left with the right, the god that is the ego with God who is the Self. Dreams, active imagination, art, (form) drawing, music, poetry, fairy story, spirituality as opposed to religiosity, are all expressions of or ways to connect with the Self.

The burgeoning number of complementary therapies suggests that modern man is desperate for some way of rejoining the split-off parts of himself. Aroma-therapy and the many different massage therapies may foster an experience of the emergent self (Stern, 1985) through olfaction, which is intimately involved with the limbic system, and give rise to a feeling of personal boundedness through the deep and surface sensations engendered by the massage.

Exercise, sport, and the movement therapies lead to a felt affirmation of the core self, and an enhancement of sensory-motor experience. Games also enhance affective attunement that fosters emotional expression both inter- and intra-personally.

The linking of the emotional with the verbal self is particularly the field of the psychotherapies, and depth psychotherapies, especially analytical psychology, can encourage the development of the spiritual in man. The mystic traditions and meditation are more non-verbal ways of furthering spiritual development, particularly in their fostering of the sense of awe and wonder that accompanies the realization of "ultimate unknowable reality" and the limitation of the thinking ego. Like the alchemists we are seeking to unite above with below, inside with outside, and to find, within the ordinary, the jewel without price.

"Acceptance cannot reject"

In the video, *Appointment with the Wise Old Dog: Dream Images at a Time of Crisis*, which is a documentary about the painted dreams of the musician David Blum, Blum quotes words of wisdom expressed by Papageno, the Wise Old Dog, in some of his dreams. Papageno always speaks in a solemn resounding voice. At one point he intones, "Acceptance cannot reject!" This affirms one aspect of the right analytic attitude, to value all parts of the individual and stand against the "oughts" and "shoulds" and the one-sidedness that diminishes her. It is an enormous step forward when a patient can learn to continue with that attitude of accepting what is in her nature. I am not suggesting that any action is a "right" action, ethically that is just not so. Accepting that "this desire too is mine" is different from unconditionally accepting that any action is permissible, and it can painfully lead to an attitude of felt responsibility that is grounded in self knowledge.

The analyst attempts to connect with his analysand but later accept her disillusion. He should allow the transference projections which request, "This is who I want/need you to be", before he eventually demonstrates "but I am not that". Accepting both the negative and the positive transferences and later giving them up can be an extremely difficult thing to permit. For some there is a temptation to identify with the positive transference, "Yes I really am as wise as she thinks," for others it is the negative transference that seems "true".

Witnessing

Being a witness means to see what is and it implies being awake and open. The pupil of the eye comes from the Latin word *pupus*, meaning a boy or child, and it refers to the little figure visible on looking into another's eye. To a certain extent we learn who we are through seeing our reflection in the eye of another. Another of the therapeutic roles is thus to reflect to the analysand how they come across. Some difficulties in this process are discussed above in the chapter *Another "Black Hole"*.

In the quote mentioned above about "being observed from another planet" (Jung, 1963: para. 501), Jung is writing about "being seen" by an aspect of one's own psyche. However, I think it could also refer to the way that one's psyche feels seen by another, given shape and substance through "external luminaries". When a child has not been adequately reflected within the family she may nevertheless be deeply transformed by a seemingly small contact with another, outside of the family. As though she needed and has waited to be recognized by this external other.

That recognizing need not be a conscious knowing and usually is not; rather it is by a part of the observer that also "cometh from afar". In fact, it is closer to what Bion calls reverie and involves free-floating attention, a trying-to-know that opens possibility rather than forecloses it. It results in "a new amalgam of a more comprehensive nature which has taken into itself the influences of the other planets." (*ibid.*: para. 504) An apt image is one of cupped hands that form a container (a chalice?) open to the skies, rather than a vessel closed by our knowledge that allows no distant influences to affect it.

In analysis we should be looking out for those patterns that bind our clients or ourselves too rigidly to one-sidedness, but, too, the analytic attitude should be able to encompass different life and religious philosophies. In helping to develop the potential of an individual embedded in a particular culture, the analyst does not have to extricate that individual from that culture but it may be helpful in bringing to consciousness the conflicts inherent in a particular situation. It is not a question of "you shouldn't be generous and caring toward your brother's son" for example, but "the depletion that you feel after being so generous and caring to your nephew may have something to do with the subjugation of your own needs." Not making judgments either way but elucidating conflicts and splits within the personality is what is important.

Religious counselling tends to focus on "you should do such and such" or, more often, "you should not do x, y, or z". As a few of my clients have pointed out to me, the religious experience, especially in the more fundamentalist churches, is suppressed by dogma. The would-be soaring soul is bound to earth by the chains of dogma or submerged in the underworld by the weight of sin. The relation to the church may be more of a social connection, one that fosters identification, on the outside, with the collective, and on the inside, with the persona or "false self".

The relationship with God is more individual than this and implies a connection with the true self. In this model God can be approached through awareness of desire, through sin even. As William Blake asserts, those who do not give in to their desires have simply not experienced desires strongly enough. Paradoxically, the sinless life is a Godless life which may connect you with the church, whereas the sinful life or more aptly, the sin-felt life, is far from the church and the persona but may be close to God and the Self. The differentiation between God and the church, between spirituality and religiosity, and between the Self and the persona, are all important.

Affective not effective

Most crucial in the treatment of most void states is the idea of really feeling that feeling, even if it is a feeling of emptiness, loneliness, or being in the dark; half the battle is won when that can be done. Once there can be an expression, in word or image, of "my void experience", "everything seems meaningless, has no point, I feel disconnected, my life is as dry as sand, etc."—the process of delineating and engaging with the void has begun. When you are doing that, your emptiness is bounded and has begun to be filled with meaning; it is no longer empty.

The often heard lament of "Why?", which is close in tone to "What have I done wrong?", takes the energy away from engagement "with", makes it into a rational, judgmental experience and furthers pathological guilt and shame. "I am so blessed with these things in my life, so why do I feel so empty? I should not. I'm bad, I'm worthless, I'm nothing!" The void expands at worst, and at best, the analysand escapes into his head, distances himself and remains disconnected from his own experience. Asking "Why?" splits one from one's self, whereas observation of "that", initiates a connection with that self.

But it is a strong temptation for the analyst to follow the quest for the "Why?" We have so many theories and it is lovely to have an opportunity to expound, bring our clear intellects to bear. Listening to one's own voice fills one's own abysmal silence but may not fill the patient's emptiness. This is not to decry words, the naming of parts, the differentiation of the members of the family that makes up the individual. The naming of those members gives them a right to exist, an authenticity. Primarily words are signifiers, with a discriminating splitting function, but words are also symbols and the more symbolically they are used, the wider meaning they may come to possess and thus the more they can hold together.

The more any experience can be analysed (not the "why" of it but the "what" of it), the wider its meaning extends and the fuller it becomes. This refers to the void experience as well. We can discern its colour, shape, texture, what is missing, what could be there, and what the significance of its absence for the individual may be, even what images describe it.

For example in Rothko's "Seagram" murals, in the Tate Modern gallery, he uses a deep tertiary-red palette and some vertical strips of black that bar the way for the viewer. He seems to be describing the enclosed emptiness of the time before birth. In late works in the Rothko Chapel in Houston, the brownish-purples have the depth of the infinite in them, inviting the eye to travel unopposed— forever. Both of these works are empty of detail, void-like in that regard, but yet they describe very different imaginal landscapes. It is that sort of difference that can be elucidated through exploration, lightly bridging the emptiness of not-knowing, while retaining the unsaturated space that enables continued growth.

Using words there is always a danger of cluttering the space rather than exploring it and helping it be tolerated. Because language has both shared and individual meanings, it both connects and separates. The therapist both understands and does not understand. In sharing his experience with his analyst, the analysand builds a bridge to the outside world and feels a connection with it. By not "knowing it all", by acknowledging "O", the analyst does not close off the roadways or wall off the new city but ensures it has the space in which to expand. There must remain space for paradox. Jung, when over 80, is quoted as having said, "Life is—or has—meaning and meaninglessness. I cherish the anxious hope that meaning will preponderate and win the battle." (Jung, 1967: 393)

We somehow work to transform our feeling of fate (that which is done to us) into a sense of destiny (the fullness of our individual lives), the individually meaningless into the meaningful. We do not wish the void behind us to become the void ahead. But once we have known the connections in the safe world, once we have experienced meaning, we can enter the dark labyrinth to meet the demons there, and then, by following Ariadne's golden thread, return once more to that surface safety. Ariadne's connecting thread does not lead the way but it allows us to return again and again to the light, seeing it anew with each return, for we have been changed with each descent. Having survived each submersion we are emboldened to try again, to allow ourselves the plunge.

Tolerating separation

There are many ways in which we experience desolation: it is part of the ordinary pain of living. Doubt, anxiety, melancholy, and deflation, are all part of both the mystical and psychoanalytic journeys. Johnston (1993) calls this desolation the dark night of the senses and encourages us to stay within this darkness, as, for him, God is more present in darkness than in the light. Perhaps, also, this is because we try to see harder when we are in the dark or perhaps because God, being the ultimately unknowable, is more at home in the dark. Jungians analyse the shadow and stay close to felt experience and desire in their attempt to further individuation, intuiting that this will bring us closer to the God image, the Self. Either way, as we grow we experience a loss of meaning, our old symbols no longer speak to us and we may react to that defensively, by attempting to discover new ones, building another cosmos, or, with courageous openness, accept the new emptiness as "O".

In his Sermon 12, Meister Eckhart exhorts us to "sink eternally from something to nothing into this one." (Fox, 1980) It is only by being free of the illusion of certainty that we can uninhibitedly explore the mysteries that make up life (Moore, 2003), by trying to be a certain way we separate ourselves from life. Like the Self and God, by being nowhere we are everywhere, by being nothing we are everything. Why should a man feel sorrow in realizing not only

"What he is", but even "That he is"? Because if he exists he is not God, or the Self, or the Pleroma, he is outside of the Oneness. Our being separates us from God.

The mystics renounce the body's senses because they give us knowledge of the material world and not of the inner realities of the spirit. For the mystic, everything known is not-God. But artists such as Bill Viola feel that sensation, perception, and experience are all avenues to self-knowledge; for them, everything known is God. (Tate Modern exhibition notes on *Angels for the New Millennium*, 2003.)

How can we reconcile these paradoxical views? Perhaps by adding the word "towards".

Starting in the darkness of meaninglessness and non-differentiation, we slowly expand our knowledge of the world and ourselves through the conscious experience of the previously unknown. We are moving towards an experience of the all, coagulating that which had been *in potentia* and making it visible. The Self is becoming more conscious. And yet, that is not the Self, the Self is both less and more. More, in the sense of stretching ever outward (and inward), less, in that in the ground of its being there is no-thing. It is both knowable and yet unknowable. The artist and scientist look towards "the things" (the knowable) while the mystic looks beyond and into the no-thing (the unknowable) and there may find God. The analyst tries to look both ways.

Denial or renunciation

My remarks are particularly about Western man who has been split from himself by the concept of sin for centuries. It is one thing being told that you should not kill or steal or fornicate with your neighbour's spouse, reasonable rules which society might develop to protect its members, but it is quite another to be told that you should not even desire to do any of these things. To deny whatever it is that you feel leads to a state of emptiness, but to experience fully your desire fills you with self-awareness. This is especially true where the consummation of that desire is prevented.

In Dante's description of the punishments meted out in *Purgatorio* this aspect stands out, the gluttonous see food just out of reach, the drunkards cannot reach the wine, the lustful see the objects of their lust but cannot satisfy themselves. They are not separated from their cravings but experience them magnified a thousand-fold. They burn in the fires of their desires and only thereafter may they progress toward Paradise.

The idea of the Kundalini is of an unfolding through different levels of awareness, one stage is experienced fully before another can be reached. Ken Wilber's ideas of consciousness have a similar flavour. If we view this process as a developmental one, it becomes easier to understand and more acceptable to our puritanical minds. We have to experience our sexuality, and our sensuality, our attachment to the ten thousand things, before we can move beyond our need of them.

It is a truism that we become addicted to those things that are not filling the emptiness that we are using them to fill, and the opposite is also true, that we do not become addicted to those things that we really require. If I use food to fill my "love cavity", I will end up obese and empty. If I eat because I am physically hungry, my hunger will be satisfied when I have had enough and I will stop eating. If I am totally unaware of my hunger I may smugly starve, or explode in unconscious nocturnal binges, or suffer, like the she-wolf at the start of Dante's *Inferno* "which seemed in her leanness, gorged with all cravings." (Klonsky, 1980: 25)

Another of the tasks of the therapist is thus to help his client differentiate between these different ways of feeling or not feeling. Is there no felt hunger because the hunger has been repressed or because the individual is replete? Is she filling her life with relationships because they are meaningful to her? Or is she using them to avoid the emptiness within, in spite of their being essentially meaningless? Is this man faithful in his marriage because he has not allowed himself to feel attraction to another or because he has made a testing personal decision not to act out his desires for that other?

As a middle-aged man discovered, even a basic act like masturbation may have a direct link to God, it reveals aspects of one's self. One supervisor of mine used to tell clients who were troubled by their child's masturbation that the Inuit Indians would recognize a future shaman in a child found to be masturbating excessively. Perhaps it was that child's contact with his own desires that was important or perhaps it was that an "excessive" masturbator (how many times is that?) is dimly aware of another sort of emptiness that they are trying to fill in this way, and that is their valuable attribute. The creative fires underneath addictions of all sorts may be a result of an awareness of emptiness, an awareness that there is something missing, that there should be something more.

In summary

I have tried in this chapter to articulate some of the many ways in which the analytic attitude may be useful in dealing with the void experience but also to indicate that the analytic approach is not the only route that is of use and that it does have its own limitations. There are many compartments of the void and the light offered by depth analysis will illuminate only some of them. However, the attitude that offers acceptance of what is and acknowledgement of limitation will go a long way towards healing, because, *inter alia*, it gives permission to explore other routes and does not foreclose. By healing, I mean the development of the capacity to endure and accept the feelings of emptiness that are the natural concomitants of an openly experienced life.

CHAPTER SIXTEEN

Connections, walls, and windows

Neither God? nor the Void? should be penned in by a full-stop.

(P.A.)

Contained by rhythm

Rhythm is a vital part of the healing rituals of Sangomas or traditional healers. (Helen Anderson, a Cape Town Music therapist) From our earliest beginnings we are surrounded by rhythm. My mother had a repetitive song, a wordless lullaby with which she would soothe a fractious child. It pulsed out at about 80 beats a minute and went something like this: "Addjew, addjew, addjewww, ... wwooshna wooshna wooshna." It was immensely soothing, and later, singing it to my own children, I would feel my own calm returning and have to stifle my yawns to keep on singing. I have come to think about it as a discovered replication of the early *in utero* sounds, the continual "lub dup" of the heartbeat and the swooshing of blood through the uterine arteries and placental circulation.

I wonder if the infant *in utero* would have been aware of his own faint heartbeat pulsing away at double the rate of his mother's? Certainly he could have sensed the periodicity of things, like activity and rest periods, light and dark, and fluctuating noise levels emanating from the outside world and over which he had no control. Already, here are the seeds of a trusting acceptance of the imposed rhythms of life, as well as the vagaries of the unexpected, coughs and sneezes and shouts, and the irregular murmur of borborygmi.

Movements of the foetus tend to be stimulated by high frequency sounds and inhibited by low frequencies. After birth, a mother will tend to preferentially place her baby on her left breast where it can hear her heart beat and be soothed by it. Pre-term infants show EEG changes in response to light, and repeated flashing of light will soothe babies. A foetus can touch parts of his body, the placenta, the cord, and the uterine wall, with his hands and feet and be touched by the umbilical cord all over his body. Twins can explore each other *in utero*, and be explored. In early pregnancy the response to touch is withdrawal, but later on the foetus moves towards what she touches. A rooting reflex develops so that the foetus may suck her own thumb. (Valman & Pearson, 1980; Piontelli, 1989) From early on the foetus is both active and passive, a recipient of stimuli and an initiator of action.

We experience order and chaos from our earliest beginnings, and both are important, one implies stability and the other the possibility of change. This flux in our first environment teaches us not to experience change as a catastrophe that must be prevented at all costs and that we must wall ourselves off from. And this is important because it may be the wall behind which we shelter that breaks the connection with the other and gives rise to at least some of the void experiences. The felt absence of the other constellates the void and connection with an-other if not the other helps obliterate it.

Order implies a going-on-being in the rhythm of life that extends from the cradle to the grave. From intra-uterine times, through birth and life to death, rhythm is experienced. From early childhood onwards, yearly events, birthdays, and festivals such as Christmas or Pesach or Ramadan punctuate the flow of life. Great movements are made by the growing child, from inside to outside of the family, from home to pre-school to "big" school to high school and beyond. And within those movements are the rhythms of the seasons and the terms and within those, the rhythms of the weeks and of each day, the study periods, the intervals, the work, the play; each has its rhythm within another rhythm within another rhythm.

Rudolph Steiner had an acute awareness of the importance of rhythm in the developing child and in the Steiner schools a special festival is incorporated in each term of the school year to mark connections to events within the natural environment by means of a school activity. So, for example, the Winter solstice may be celebrated at the end of the winter term with a Festival of Light. This reminds us on a psychological level of the light that may emerge out of the deepest dark. The festival connects the occurrence of an external event, such as the Winter Solstice, with something closer to the child, e.g. the school terms, and also with something deeply internal, the symbolic world connected to through story. This can all be internalized by the child, and link his cognitive with his symbolic worlds.

Stern suggests that one can interact with an infant through "affective attunement" across different modalities of experience, for example sound, movement, and touch. Affective attunement gives rise to a dialogue and sense of connection between mother and child, an emotional connection. This affirms to the infant not only that he is witnessed by his mother but also that he has an effect on her, that things he does modulate or modify her behaviour. (Stern, 1985)

Eurythmy is an activity taught in the Steiner schools that also connects across modalities. Music is translated into movement, and structural forms too, originally experienced on paper, are translated into a pattern existing over time and space through music and movement. Sounds and emotions are expressed in posture and rhythm.

In the same way that affective attunement takes place trans-modally within the mother–infant pair, so can the infant's, or even the adult's, self-experience occur trans-modally. This linking across modalities is a connection that fosters the sense of being "all-in-one-piece" or "all-of-a-piece", a complete individual with no parts missing. Feeling united in oneself is likely to result in a felt sense of connection with others too.

Rhythmicity that swings

Of interest to me is how one can foster, either as prevention or as cure, this sense of connection, and particularly the sense of being connected to an alive other. There is an especial aliveness in the Irish way of speaking that is most alluring, and the word that conjures that is "lilt". The word "lilt" suggests singing or playing merrily or gaily and with a rhythmical swing, melodious modulation, or a springy movement, etc. (Chamber's Dictionary) That covers most of what is needed in development, a rhythmicity that swings, that varies, unlike a metronome or the dully accurate beat of an electronic keyboard, a rhythmicity that is not foreclosed but is open to change. This has the openness of play and the gaiety of acceptance and is responsive to what it encounters; it modulates its melody accordingly.

Lilt is thus a perfect word to describe the alert interaction that can occur between mother and child and on a good day between an analyst and her analysand. I recall reading a description of an infantile memory of a young woman who had later been an abused child. She remembers being wheeled outside in her pram and left under the trees. Watching them sway and sway and sway became a stultifying nightmare. One can intuit how at first the swaying branches would have had a soothing effect, hit upon by her caregiver as a good way to calm her down, but that later they became associated with something outside of her control. Their movement was unavoidable, unless she closed her eyes or turned her head to focus on the indifferent interior of her pram. My father had a definition of hell that was "being forced to do all the time what you love to do sometimes".

A rhythm may at one time be soothing and at another time oppressive. Giving oneself over to watching the waves roll in, in their repetitious changefulness, is often experienced as a stilling meditation, but if that is all there is and you have to watch them, they become a nightmare. There was a machine on the market in which you could place your child and it would be automatically rocked, thus freeing your arms and mind for some "more important" task than being with your baby.

I remember watching, with increasing claustrophobia, the stunned expression on the face of the infant daughter of a friend stuck in one of these devices. She suffered from what was called "low muscle tone" but looking back on it I would say that she was in a sort of anaclitic depression with no sense that she could effectively modulate her world. Another rocker of the same period was a simple sprung device that the baby could lie back in and learn to set in motion through some movement of her own; she could start it autonomously and could stop it by lying still. She had some control over her world.

One way of thinking about the soft autistic shapes that Tustin describes (see above) is that they are under the child's omnipotent control, they can be switched on at will so that the child becomes cocooned in their soft rhythms. An adult patient who had some autistic defences could not bear to let herself be rocked in one of the chairs in my consulting room, it felt as though the chair was doing the rocking to her and that was intolerable. When she rocked in the privacy of her home, it was a movement that demonstrated her omnipotence, she would thrust against something in her environment in a forceful manner that defined her on her own terms.

Another young woman with severe self pathology could set up a self-cohering rhythm in increasingly subtle ways whenever she became distraught, was threatened with an impending disintegration, or needed to ward off a strong emotion. To be aware of it I had to learn to watch her big toe clenching inside her shoe and sense the movement extending throughout her body. The "rocking" served to wall her off, both from her internal emotions and from the outside world, i.e. her connection with me, her therapist. Making her aware of it would bring about a flood of emotion from her and a deepening in my feeling of connection to her.

Pattern, structure, and rhythm then, can either ward off or produce the void and which they do is dependent on the developmental stage of the individual involved and their flexibility. Playing some easily fragmented person the sort of open spiritual music that Arvo Pärt composes is likely to lead to a breakdown as she drifts into space without her space-suit; she needs the armour that can be supplied by the regimented rhythms of Disco or Rave music. For another, the latter rhythms could bring on a compressive suffocating type of void experience, whereas the former may lead to the experience of wide spaces into which she could safely and expansively travel.

The form and patterning of music are processed by the right brain. Song being words and music suggests a synthesis by left and right brain. The modern habit of having translated surtitles at operatic performances, so that the audience can understand what the performers are singing, tends to seduce the brain away from its direct feeling experience of the music and into the left-sided knowledge of its "meaning".

Books on accessing one's creativity, such as *Drawing on the Right Side of Your Brain* (Betty Edwards), confirm that language, especially the written and read word, seems to block the right brain connection that is required for drawing or painting. Many artists listen to music while they create and will describe how, when they are in that creative vein, time seems to disappear or lose its usual feeling of continuous unfolding. Words on the other hand seem to limit creativity, douse the imaginal fires, and fix one in time.

Poetry is different, here rhyme and rhythm give a structured three-dimensional frame to the words that is lacking in pure (linear) prose. Even when a poem is about nothingness, or loss, or absence, as in an elegy, the structure contains, and imparts shape and meaning. (Stephen Watson, public lecture) Most of the early written stories are written in verse; Homer's works, for example, the old Icelandic sagas, and epic works such as Beowulf. Or there is a mixture of language forms, a movement from prose to poetry and back again, usually related to the need to express a greater or lesser degree of emotional arousal.

An excellent example is in Thomas Mann's *The Holy Sinner*, when Gregorius' lone battle outside the city gates is described by another character, M. Poitevin. Poitevin's monologue imperceptibly changes its inner structure so that it becomes highly rhythmical, galloping along in a way that matches the action he is describing, and becoming filled with rhymes or "jingles" that the speaker seems unable to prevent. (Mann, 1952: 110–111) This is a nice literary illustration of affective attunement.

When scientists listen to outer space in the hope of receiving a message from other intelligent life, what they listen for is structure or pattern that suggests an ordering mind. Bursts of order against the background static or noise of the "void and formless infinite". But they are not just listening for something fixed, but for something that can also change or develop, it is that which demonstrates intelligence.

Order or structure *per se* can be limiting and inhuman, cutting us off from connection with those outside our frame of reference. It is easy for somewhat schizoid people to wall themselves up in an ivory tower of their own making where their only visitors can be like-minded individuals, those that speak the same language. We Jungians need to guard against that and continually search for new metaphors to express our concepts so that they do not become walls with no windows.

Some thoughts about music

To a music therapist sound is most primary, it is everywhere and has been from the beginning. (I am again indebted to Helen Anderson for many of the ideas expressed here.) Sound is equivalent to the Self, or perhaps to the archetypal feminine, and music, which is sound acted on by the ego, is closer conceptually to the mother. In general, the unconscious is expressed in sound and consciousness by music but the borders between these two are fluid, and music, through its use both of silence and of monotonous sound, can be used to express something of the intuition of the vastness of psyche; consciousness' apprehension of the unconscious. Musically this can be achieved, for example, by using the sound of a drone or repetitive notes whose pitch changes almost imperceptibly.

Like the anima, music connects one psychic state with another, e.g. body with spirit, and like the soul it is intangible and ineffable. It can soothe or stimulate, bring together or split apart. High-pitched sounds are associated by the infant with the human mother's voice and deep low sounds suggest the rhythm of the spheres, the rhythm that underlies our going-on-being.

Void states can be thought of as music-less states if not sound-less states. The white noise of some types of tinnitus obliterates patterned sound and black cacophonic noise suggests the state of chaos. Music contains rhythm, melody, and dynamics. It is transitory but infinitely variable and can resonate in our minds forever. It is relative but contains the absolute, and it can unite in harmony or split apart in discord. The different instruments evoke different aspects of the human psyche-soma. The strings are soul-like and link body and mind, woodwinds are closer to pure spirit, the extrovert brasses connect us with the world, and percussion resonates within our bodies. A full orchestra can affect all domains.

One of the great mysteries is how the eight tones of the octave bring a note back to itself, an endless repetition that reminds us of the uroborus and of God, of sameness and variability. It has been said that the interval of the fifth represents the incarnation, God becoming human. The new-born child's cry approximates that downward interval of the fifth, which "is THE most stable interval to the ear." (Henderson, 1995)

If we think of ego consciousness as that which separates the primary or pre-conceptual void from the secondary, post- or supraconceptual void, it leads to an idea that there may be some sorts of music that cohere the ego and other sorts that sunder it. Some music may be a defence against the void and other music a tool that helps enable us to enter the secondary void.

Some people with fragile personalities may need music that would give them an almost physically felt experience that consolidates ego structure. They are held more by the structure of the music than by its meaning. A rhythm of simple regularity will act as a sound object for them and can be internalized as an internal sense of stability, or it can be used as an autistic object to ward off threatening nothingness. When the ego is more intact, a more varied spiritual music can take one from ego-hood towards self-hood, towards a stilling or shrinking of the ego and its return to the greaterness of being. In this latter category is the music of Arvo Pärt which has been called "angel music" and that of Hildegard of Bingen who uses a drone to underpin the soaring voices of her singers. A 1984 Hyperion Records version of her music is titled *A Feather on the Breath of God*. The "high loveliness" (cover notes) of the voices rests always on the drone, perhaps that is the music of the spheres, the sound of God's breathing. (I would like to refer the reader too to Melinda Haas' outstanding paper on Mahler's Ninth Symphony published in the Proceedings of the 2004 IAAP Congress held in Barcelona.)

Connections without and within

Winnicott, in a 1958 paper, *The Capacity to be Alone* (in Winnicott, 1965), explores the idea of the mature capacity of an individual to experience "I am alone" as a healthy non-threatening state that is not a defence against relating to another nor filled with the anxiety of being in a void. He points out the paradox that the capacity to be alone begins with experiencing being alone while in someone else's presence, i.e. while being not completely alone. To be alone requires the development of a good internal object within the psychic reality of the individual and Winnicott suggests that it is through "good-enough mothering" that the child has the opportunity to internalize this good object and build up a belief in a benign environment. This implies a state of relative freedom from persecutory anxieties and also that these good internal objects will be available for projection, thus imbuing the external world with the aura of safe relatedness.

Winnicott further suggests that the capacity to be alone is crucial to the discovery of the personal impulse, "his own personal life". Only when alone in this way will the infant be able

> to become unintegrated, to flounder, to be in a state in which there is no orientation, to be able to exist for a time without being either a reactor to an external impingement or an active person with a direction of interest or movement ... In this setting a sensation or impulse, (an id-experience), will feel real and be truly a personal experience.
>
> (Winnicott, 1965: 34)

Drifting into the void allows one to experience oneself. "A large number of such experiences form the basis for a life that has reality in it instead of futility." (*ibid.*)

I see it as a spiralling process that starts with the good-enough mother who has helped the infant cohere. Being alone in her non-impinging presence both enables and encourages him to internalize her containing qualities that are both flexible and holding. Internalizing those qualities enables him to let go of his own ego-fixity, and experience impulses originating from the physical or instinctual realm, and perhaps from the spiritual realm too. Having been shown himself by his mother, he is now able to show himself to himself and in the process expand his capacity for experience that enhances his meaningful sense of self. The more this happens, the more receptive he will be to stimuli from within and without, without being simply a "reactor" to those stimuli or warding them off by action.

The infant, naturally, has an immature ego, which needs the ego-support of its mother. Without the presence of the mother or good object, an id-impulse is likely to disrupt the weak ego, to disintegrate it. With the support, but not impingement, of the mother, the id-impulse will strengthen the infant's ego. With an intrusive mother who attempts to force her view of life into the child, he will experience life either through his mother's eyes or in opposition to that. With a depressed mother the infant's impulse is to enliven her, so again he is driven by a need outside of his own needs; the focus is on his mother rather than on himself. There is then no practice in experiencing and engaging with impulses from within, and thus, when the infant is alone and uncontained, those impulses are experienced as dangerously disruptive and threatening; the void experience of falling apart or falling forever that may persist into adulthood.

One could say that in Jungian terms it is the connection with the objective psyche that is roughly equivalent to what Winnicott is writing about. To connect is to be in some sort of relationship with oneself and this may be via any of the four functions, namely thinking, feeling, sensation, and intuition. The acceptance of these modes of functioning and their products fills the void within and populates and furnishes the external world too.

A 50-year-old "thinking" woman whose husband had unexpectedly died a few years previously, had simply "forgotten" to pick up his ashes following his cremation, or to mourn him properly. There was just absence where he had been. She connected in her therapy with memories of his abusive, destructive aspects, which led her to remember her father's emotional abusiveness and her mother's envy of her.

Allowing the feelings that these memories evoked, led her to an interior space where she could suddenly experience her missing of her husband. She had warded off so much of her feeling world, because the feelings were so "negative", that she had become disconnected from herself. Re-establishing the connection with herself through the unpleasant memories enabled her to feel the missing; she could now connect with her grief, collect his ashes from the crematorium, and bury them, and in that engagement fill in further some of her emptiness.

Metaphorical walls

Possessing knowledge is like having a wall around oneself. We need enclosures but the walls need to be an adequate distance away. In a dream reported by Margot Waddell (1998) the dreamer is on a tennis court. It is open behind him but above him the ceiling is too close. This suggests that the dreamer is confined yet not contained. Walls may be built as a container that protects and sustains, but they may also become a prison, a closed castle complete with a moat and a raised drawbridge.

A middle-aged woman had been brought up in a chaotic, often violent, home. As a child she would take refuge in a garden cottage and the image of this sustained her into adulthood. She had the metaphorical key to its door, which gave into the garden, and this cottage fantasy became an inner object for her, more potent than her internalized parents. Within its walls she could let her guard down and experience her own playful imagination. Without them she would have had to construct other rigid defences to ensure her integrity.

An opposite image is of a 20-year-old male patient who had been brought up by parents who were obsessed by the idea of improving the family's financial situation through renovating houses. They did not live in one house and renovate another, they broke down and developed the house that they were living in at the time; fixing it up, not for themselves, but in order to sell it. The family moved sixteen times in eighteen years and my client felt that his parents' minds were always on the building and not on him. Order came to be experienced as that brief interlude that preceded, and was preceded by, chaos; that which presaged falling apart. I experienced him as being someone shapeless, not having a containing skin. He could not engage with another from his own separateness but was flooded or impinged on by internal or external stimuli.

Aspects of linking

At an early phase of his development, Henry Moore explored the use of string in the linking together of parts of a sculpture or of one figure with another. Starting with his already abstracted forms, with their holes and areas of emptiness, he added connecting strings. In this way the space where the infant's eyes might have been could be linked, for example, to the maternal face, thus giving the feeling of a returned gaze. Or the infant's mouth area became linked to the maternal breast region creating an image of an instinct and the object that will satisfy it.

Somehow these works are unsatisfactorily static and cluttered, they are foreclosed perhaps, we are told what to see. In later works, abandoning the strings, he captures both the experience of the unfulfilled desire, the yearning, but also the feeling of what it would be like to have that desire satisfied. He captures the opposites in one ambiguous image.

Balint describes how her very disturbed patient's pictures, which were like fragmentary self-portraits, started as drawings composed of unconnected lines and dots. Later, these became pictures of bits of the person, but nothing was complete or joined up with anything else until the last years of her patient's therapy. (Balint, 1993: 44–45)

As a trainee psychiatrist working in an admissions unit in a psychiatric hospital, I would often ask individuals to draw a person at various stages of their treatment. The initial drawings of very ill schizophrenic patients might be as Balint described, with tentative outlines composed of tiny lines giving the effect of a fragile porosity. The lines may or may not have connected up to make the shape of a human form. With treatment, primarily medication in that unit, the fragments came together but resulted often in simplified caricatures of the human form and only seldom in a flexible form that cohered.

In a forensic unit, it was clear that psychopathic patients were often adept at drawing stylized figures with hard, clear boundaries but with little feeling tone attached to them. They had strong walls but there was no possibility of an interaction across the barriers to the outside world and little sense of meaningful connection within either.

Antinomies

Antinomies are legion in the human condition. There is rhythm and its absence, order and chaos, structure and the lack of structure, meaningfulness and meaninglessness, form and void, connections and the absence of connections, light and dark, walls and the openings in those walls. When a patient dreams of the windows and doors in a closed house flying open and the winds (of change perhaps) blowing through, the analyst may breathe a sigh of relief.

The therapist's knowledge about the psyche and about a particular patient helps construct a containing wall around him, but her admission that she does not know will keep some apertures open in that wall. It is imperative that the therapist does not come between her client and his experience of or exploration of the void, and yet it is important too that the therapist is available as an alert and containing presence. This is like co-constructing a nest from which the fledgling may explore the large spaces about it. From this position an individual may experience his psyche, and the void, as that which is infinite yet finite, bounded but limitless.

Summary

In this chapter, I have tried to bring together my ideas about what may be helpful preventive or healing attitudes for developing individuals of all ages. I have used music as a metaphor, but I do also believe that actual music can be used as a medium that can link different aspects of a person to each other. Further than that, the idea I wanted to punt was that of rhythmicity in all aspects of a person's life, rhythm and the normal breaks in rhythm that must be accepted and tolerated for any meaningful growth to occur. Rhythm keeps us safe from the pre-conceptual void of meaninglessness, while, if we have experienced both its presence and its absence, we may feel supported in our reaching towards that state where all rhythm breaks down and only the sound, or its absence, of the deep drone that is God's voice, is audible.

CHAPTER SEVENTEEN

On active imagination

It is a fearful thing to fall into the hands of the living God.
But it is a much more fearful thing to fall out of them.
(D.H. Lawrence)

So when anyone falls the perfect sum is not lessened. Whoever
lets go in his fall, dives into the source and is healed.
(Rainer Maria Rilke)

The long fall

This chapter is centred on the experience of a late-middle-aged woman whom I'll call Wilma. Eighteen months into her therapy she described herself as having been like one of those signs marking the gender on the door of a public toilet; simply a silhouette that gave her the semblance of an identity, but demonstrated no internal features. Because she felt it had been created by her daughters' love, even that silhouette would disintegrate at times should she feel that they no longer loved her.

What substance she had resulted from the achievements of her children and those of her husband, and while she remained married to a successful man and the children were all at home and performing well, she felt she was "a something". However, her shape as a mother imploded when a daughter became addicted to drugs, and her identity as woman and wife collapsed when her husband lost his job and then left the family. She was left with nothing to sustain the image of herself, to fill in the details within her outline.

While in this state she had a dream of being on the roof of a tall building that was burning. As the flames came towards her, her only option seemed to be to jump. She could look down on other women who had gone before; some had survived the fall but one had broken her back. (My patient associated that image to a gruesome story from the early history of the then South-West Africa when soldiers broke the backs of tribesmen they had killed in order to symbolize their utter defeat.) The dream ended in an impasse where she felt too terrified to jump and yet the flames were encroaching.

When the dream resurfaced in the following session, I encouraged her to "dream the dream onward" and it was with considerable anxiety that she once more teetered on the edge. Feeling that there was some hope forward but none behind she let herself over the side of the building and began a long and frightening imaginal descent. I was aware of my own fear; what would it mean if she were crushed to a pulp or fractured her spine, or the opposite, that she sprouted wings and flew off to become a new star in the firmament? I was sustained by the idea that probably nothing was worse than being immured in the ashes of her previous life and also by the theory that it is only when falling that one can fully experience the containing "hands of the living God", in other words, the Self.

At last, her described descent had taken so long and slowed to such an extent that I suggested she might actually be able to reach out and touch the ground. She landed then with a soft bump, "on all fours like a cat" (that archetypally self-reliant animal) and realized that she was surrounded by women of different ages who had welcoming smiles on their faces.

She described later that after the session she had felt in love again, but this time "with myself". In Jungian terms she had had an experience of the objective other within, i.e. the Self, and this numinous experience was made possible through allowing herself to fall, even if unwillingly. Fear and courage are an important part of the equation; after all, if it seems easy there has not been enough letting go or giving over. Falling into perceived emptiness without hope is what may bring the discovery that there is something there after all.

Wilma demonstrated the common deep fear that when one falls one will not be caught. This may be archetypally based but will be exacerbated when the childhood experience has been that one was not safely held and could at any time fall through the cracks and into oblivion, or be thrust impotently out into the void. Neither the patient nor her analyst knows how the fall will end and it requires courage on the part of both not to foreclose the outcome of such a descent but to simply remain observant, if frightened, presences.

Into the unknown

For there is no way of knowing with *certainty* which way we are headed, whether it be into rebirth or into madness, whether we will be encircled by welcoming faces or lie dead with a broken back. As in *The "Birthday Present"* above, we are not certain whether ecstasy will lead to rebirth or to death. So the experience of fear is understandable and, in fact, a *sine qua non*. If we "know" what the outcome of something is going to be and that it is going to be positive, we have not opened ourselves to all possibilities.

I have been struck by the variety of ways that individuals approach deeper insight into themselves. Some seek it out diligently as if pushed from behind by some force. Others seem to calmly accept that which is shown to them, and yet others go kicking and screaming "into that dark night" fighting tooth and nail against the "pitch upon pitch of grief" that their psyches hurl at them. A middle-aged man who had been in analysis for some years as an active, dutiful analysand went through a painful week hounded by various aspects of his relationship with the negative feminine to which he reacted with an attitude of passive resignation. He told me of a dream in which his wife and a strange man had forced him into a flooding storm-water drain. He fought against them for as long as he was able and then knew he was going to be sucked under and would drown.

He had started the session telling me how positively he felt about life and the future, and of the enjoyment that he was experiencing, and at first I could not understand why his conscious attitude on this day was so buoyant. The dream seemed to suggest that a despondent attitude would have been more appropriate. Then, spontaneously, he volunteered what a profound feeling of relief he had felt when he realized in the dream that he could do no more. However hard he fought, he was doomed. The giving up, the submission to something greater than himself, brought the relief. If you are the biggest object around then who is there to protect you?

To give over may be an act of faith or the last desperate possibility but either way it may lead to feeling held in containing hands.

I am reminded of the work with trauma victims and how some will remain victims, wounded by their trauma and suffering from Post Traumatic Stress Disorder, whereas for others the trauma is like a door opening into a transformation process leading ultimately to a new-found wisdom. Perhaps the key is in the attitude of submission to fate, or evil or power, and knowing when to submit and when to stand against. PTSD is a state where, among other symptoms, the future is foreclosed, the victim cannot see further onward, and he cannot fully accept, or know, what is. It is as though the victim says, "I can see that this is how it is BUT it should not be." Wisdom suggests the possibility of a broader way of seeing; a more embracing way that does not exclude life's (or God's) dark side.

Alchemical view

Looking at Wilma's scenario alchemically we could say that initially she is in a sublimated state, what Edinger would call a *sublimatio* of the lesser kind, high up and disembodied. She is offered the choice of burning in the fire that threatens her from behind, a *calcinatio*, or of descending from her high but insubstantial position, a *coagulatio*. *Calcinatio* would lead to the conflagration of her old life; only a pile of ashes remaining but always with the possibility of a phoenix-like rebirth. But what *coagulatio* offers is incarnation, the taking on of substance or humanness. It implies a loss of divinity and the acceptance of mortality; being mortal you run the risk of death, but you may also be received into the company of other mortals and start a process of redemption. You may be linked once more to others and to yourself.

In *Mysterium Coniuctionis*, Jung's great book on the coming together of the opposites that either confront each other in enmity or attract one another in love, Jung (1963) writes about active imagination being the tool or process that we can use to achieve the second stage of this connection within ourselves that he refers to as the *coniunctio*. The first stage of the *coniunctio* is the process of individuation, which leads to what he calls the *unio mentalis*.

The starting point of this whole process he calls the *unio naturalis*. In this the soul is inextricably interwoven with the body making a "dark unity." The *unio naturalis* is the original half-animal state of unconsciousness, a state of non-differentiation or chaos known to the adepts as the *nigredo* or the *massa confusa*. Jung uses the term to describe both the union of psyche and soma, or of psyche and matter even, and also that natural state which consists in consciousness embedded in the unconscious. (Edinger, 1972, and Neumann, 1954, also articulate this.) We are reminded of Jung's assertion that individuation is an *opus contra naturam*, a work against this natural union, and actually a process of separation and differentiation.

The first or primary state (the *unio naturalis*) represents the "natural" state of unconsciousness as opposed to the "unnatural" state of consciousness attained in the *unio mentalis*. During the process of individuation the soul is "freed from its fetters in the things of sense" (meaning not those things that make sense but those things that are sensed physically) and it is this that results in the *unio mentalis*. This process of separation produces conscious and rational insight, but the soul takes flight from the influences of the body. (Jung, 1963: 488)

The *unio mentalis* is thus a removed or sublimated state, a disciplined distancing from the body and the world of the senses. This separation via consciousness, this disidentification from instinctual desires, has to occur, but it leads to an alienation from one's wholeness. This is similar to a schizoid position where the separation of consciousness from feeling aspects is achieved through building a wall of repression or by splitting off unwanted affect, but the difference lies in the depth of conscious awareness. The process involves a confrontation with the shadow wherein the very sense of identity becomes doubtful, so the alchemists also called this condition the *nigredo* or chaos.

To clarify; the first *nigredo*, that of the *unio naturalis*, is an objective state, visible from the outside only; the subject would not be aware of being in that state of "dark unity". It is an unconscious state of non-differentiation between self and object, consciousness and the unconscious. The *nigredo* of the process of individuation on the other hand is a subjectively experienced process brought about by the subject's painful, growing awareness of his shadow aspects. (*ibid.*: 497)

In this second *nigredo* there is a conscious withdrawal of projections, an assimilation of shadow, perhaps even a partial identification with it, that leads to a chaotic state of mind as in "I thought I was that but who is this then?" It is a state of confusion that stems from an awareness of dual aspects within that are intolerable to consciousness; one solution is to distance oneself from the affect. "If I can think about this impulse rather than act it out then I am not that." Or, "I am above the impurities of the flesh," say.

The alchemists referred to this sublimated state as the *albedo*, a state of felt wholeness and purity; but one that denies the dark. Although this union of spirit and soul means, psychologically, a "knowledge of oneself", it is only the first stage of the coming together that has resulted, as stated above, in the *unio mentalis*. (*ibid.*: 499) Edinger confirms in *The Mysterium Lectures*:

> the *unio mentalis* . . . unites the soul and the spirit, and at the same time separates them from the body. This amounts to a *mortificatio* and a death of the body at the same time as it brings about a *sublimatio* of the combined soul and spirit.
>
> (Edinger, 1995: 296)

The body is left behind and the soul/spirit ascends into the ether.

(There is a confusing array of terms used to describe aspects of what has been called the individuation process. In Chapter vi of Volume 14 of the *Collected Works*, Jung describes the individuation process as only the first stage of the *mysterium coniunctionis* and there is a rough equivalence, or at least an overlap, between it and the concepts of the *unio mentalis*, the *albedo,* and *sublimatio*.)

The second stage of the *coniunctio* involves the reconnection of the *unio mentalis* with body, a coming down to earth or *coagulatio*.

> This stage involves bringing the consciousness of wholeness, which in the first stage is a kind of abstract realisation, into full-blooded reality, so that one lives it out fully in everyday life. And this phase corresponds to the alchemical *rubedo*, also called reddening.
>
> (*ibid.*)

Jung's metaphor for this process is the waterfall because it connects that which is above with that which is below. The psychological method of achieving this connection is Active Imagination and

Jung describes this process in his chapter on *The Conjunction.* (Jung, 1963: 495) His point is that Active Imagination allows us to visualize and feel the greater psyche's reaction to the conscious attitude. "(I)n this way we get to know aspects of our nature which we would not allow anybody else to show us and which we ourselves would never have admitted." (*ibid.*: 496) Active Imagination helps us grasp emotionally what may have only been thought intellectually and vice versa.

The mortificatio

Being shown "that which we would never have admitted to our-selves", by ourselves, and with our consent and indeed participation, is experienced as a leap into the unknown. Every time we enter an Active Imagination, in fact, every time we write down a dream or bring that dream to our therapists, we submit ourselves to a *mortificatio*, we allow ourselves to fall into the unknown and undergo yet another little death. And yet, the opposite happens simul-taneously, that new life substance is laid down. "I now know that I am not only that, but realize that I am also this," and also "I now know that the other is not only as I thought but is also this."

In the metaphor of this paper, we start off the process of individuation unconscious or void of our individual natures, our "true" selves. So my client Wilma saw herself as a silhouette on a toilet door. As she withdrew her projections, she became empty of even that tenuous but previously known identity, "the person I thought I was", and more conscious of the void state that she was in. There was also a feeling of loss of what might have been.

The distressing emptiness is now about, "Who am I if I am not even that?" Wilma's reading of "self-help" psychology books enabled her to distance herself from a direct experience of her own emptiness by focusing on what she could or should do. This led to a state where, whilst seeming to address the issues, she was cut off from her feelings. "What should I do?" she questioned, "How should I act?" rather than acknowledging, with feeling, "So this is who I am!"

Through the therapy she had become more acutely conscious of her true nature and how damaging some aspects of that may have been for her children while growing up, and in fact still were in her present-day relationships. She was still emotionally distant from her new insights at the time of the dream mentioned above, and, faced by the dream with a choice of being consumed by their fire, or risking death in her fall from the heights, she took flight into wakefulness. In finally allowing her fall in the Active Imagination, she experienced the feeling of something or someone being there for her. Welcoming women surrounded her. This seems to be a direct experience of the Self made possible by her and her therapist's willingness to face the unknown.

And more

The individuation process involves many of these *sublimatio–coagulatio* cycles, which result in the fuller experience of the *unio mentalis* and its subsequent conscious union with body. But according to Dorn, the alchemist, and Jung, the psychologist, there is another, third stage to the *coniunctio* and this is the union of the whole man with the *unus mundus* or one world, "the potential world outside time". (Jung, 1963: 505) This is a rather difficult process to grasp, as it is a transcendental process and thus "can be expressed only as paradox". (*ibid.*: 502) Jung interprets Dorn's idea of the *unus mundus* as

> the potential world of the first day of creation, when nothing was yet "in actu", i.e., divided into two and many, but was still one. The creation of a unity meant the possibility of effecting a union with the world—not with the world of multiplicity as we see it but with a potential world, the eternal Ground of all empirical being, just as the (S)elf is the ground and origin of the individual personality past, present and future.
>
> (*ibid.*: 534)

Jung links this idea of the third degree of conjunction with ideas from eastern mystic traditions. He suggests that it is concerned with the relation, or identity, of the personal to the transpersonal. These ideas are not limited to eastern mysticism; all the mystic traditions speak of a union with the ultimately unknowable, some unity that exists outside of space and time. This is also suggested by the work of modern micro-physicists where causal connections exist between the psyche and the body which point to their underlying unitary nature . . . The common background of microphysics and depth-psychology is as much physical as psychic and therefore neither, but rather a third thing, a neutral nature which can at most be grasped in hints since in essence it is transcendental.

> (*ibid*.: 538) (Other references in Meier, 2001: e.g. 126; Stein, 1998: Chapter 7; and Jung, 1959)

The unitary ground idea ties in with the concept of the *increatum* or uncreated in western mysticism, and the pleroma in *Septem Sermones ad Mortuos* by Jung & Basilides (1916). The pleroma is a state of nothingness or fullness depending on how one looks at it. It is eternal and infinite and has no discernible qualities, for if qualities were discernible they would distinguish whatever has them from the pleroma. Whatever is distinguished or separate from the pleroma, i.e. whatever can be differentiated from the pleroma, are called *creatura*. The *creatura* are those things that have been created (by consciousness presumably) out of the Nothing or the All, i.e. the pleroma, in contrast to the uncreated or *increatum*.

As individuals we are *creatura* and our natural impulse is to stand against the "primeval perilous sameness" of the pleroma by seeking our distinctive individuality through the process of individuation. If we do not do this we are in danger of falling back into the pleroma, into a state of non-differentiation. Says Jung:

> If we do not distinguish (ourselves from the pleroma), we get beyond our own nature, away from creatura. We fall into indistinctiveness, which is the other quality of the pleroma. We fall into the pleroma itself and cease to be creatures. We are given over to dissolution in the nothingness. This is the death of the creature (i.e. of the conscious individual). Therefore we die in such measure as we do not distinguish.
>
> (Jung & Basilides, 1916: 10, my brackets)

Distinguishing or differentiating is an ego activity; it is a product of consciousness and also the *sine qua non* of consciousness. We come out of the oneness through differentiating and we fall back into it when we fail to differentiate, or re-enter it when we achieve a state that transcends differentiation. And when that happens it is experienced by the ego as a death or an entering of the void. The falling back occurs particularly in those regressed states such as with drug or alcohol abuse or, for example, the states that a borderline patient may enter when she feels abandoned. (Given a sense of identity by her partner in a relationship, her individuality implodes when that relationship breaks down.) But the re-entering of the oneness as a transcendental state involves a higher mystical conscious-ness often brought about only through meditation or spiritual reflection.

Personally, I do not like the waterfall image that Jung uses to describe the process wherein the opposites come together, as it implies a flow in one direction. He uses the image of the waterfall as a metaphor for the third thing connecting the above and below but in spite of the energy bound up in that flowing water the image has a frozen feel. (Jung, 1963: 495) What in fact needs to happen is a descent and return, a *circulatio*.

Especially when Jung is writing about the third stage in the *coniunctio*, he makes it sound as though it were a fixed goal, but actually none of the stages of the *coniunctio* are fixed. Rather, they are states that are fleetingly attained then lost. Hopefully, they are states that may be returned to time and again. Edinger writes of the greater and lesser conjunctions with the implication that the greater *coniunctio* is the ultimate goal, finally attained, whereas the lesser *coniunctio* is part of a *circulatio* process that also consists in *sublimatio* and *coagulatio*.

Active Imagination is a joint process that requires the interaction of the dynamic ego on the one side with the mass of the unconscious, with its "ancestral conservatism" (Jung, *CW 16*: para. 62, quoted in Cowan, 2002: 6) and innovative creativity, on the other. The main activity of the conscious ego is as an observer or witness who attempts to bring back to the upper world those insights gained within the lower. The patient's and her therapist's openness to the Nothing is the required attitude here—not telling the imagination what to think but letting it inform us. The Activity in Active Imagination is in the ego looking and seeing, asking the right questions, but letting go of the previously known answers. Active Imagination implies that consciousness is open to that which surfaces from below, from the unknown, the void; like the Atlantic salmon who migrate upstream to spawn, and will attempt to re-immerse themselves in the ocean once they have discharged their new life.

John Dourley's (2004) paper accentuates the idea that it is not the mystic's dissolution in the nothing so much as his return from that dissolution that is important. The young dope-head seeks dissolution as a thing in itself, a fuzzy union with the "mother". The mystic on the other hand seeks an identity or union with the divine and then necessarily undergoes an "othering" from that divine, and it is that process that leads to an ongoing renewal of life. The first part of the mystic's process implies a painful surrender of the ego, the I, whereas the second implies an even more painful awareness of one's "otherness" from God or the Self; there is first an immersion in, and then an emergence out of, or separation from.

Teilhard de Chardin says that "union differentiates. When I am most united with God I am most myself." (Quoted in Johnston, 1973: 15) This paradox is at first sight contradictory to what I have been saying. What does he mean? I wonder if he is not suggesting that through union with God we experience our God-likeness, our ambiguous natures, the *coniunctio oppositorum* that is as much part of human nature as it is of the divine. The Self has the qualities of God, the ego those of differentiated man. The ego is separate from the Self and from God and is far from the condition of "wholeness", the wholeness of the individuated self. That wholeness, the aim of the individuation process, the fullest embracing of "myself", is only possible through union with God. For, as quoted above, "the Self is the ground and origin of the individual personality past, present and future." The personal and the suprapersonal become one.

The coniunctio *in art*

Thinking about these terms in relation to art, I would say that the *unio naturalis*, which is equivalent to Soul in matter, is well-depicted in pre-classical art and in the classical art of the Greeks and Romans, and later in the art of the Renaissance, e.g. Michaelangelo's sculpture. Here, human forms in their natural perfection or idealization, if that is not a contradiction, are bound up with the spiritual. The works connect with the divine in a completely natural but unconscious way, although, of course, the forms have been generated with conscious intent. The human form contains and expresses the god.

The abstract works of a modern sculptor like Barbara Hepworth, in contrast, seem to be products of a search for pure form. They are distant from the body, soul has become embedded in mind, in a theoretical state of purity. Light as spirit or spirit as light bathes the outside and inside of her pierced forms but reveals no sign of the flesh. They are entirely sublimated works that suggest the *unio mentalis*.

Henry Moore's works demonstrate a return to the body, a reconnection that suggests the second stage of the *mysterium coniunctionis*. Still abstract, they are also full of substance, organic matter, the body. The *unio mentalis* has reunited with body, "the Word was made flesh, and dwelt among us, . . . full of grace and truth." (The Gospels John Chapter 1 verse 14) Moore sometimes seemed to be intent on seeing how much he could fracture or dispense with form and yet retain an essence of the whole.

Rothko, in his large colour field paintings, particularly the posthumously completed Rothko chapel in Houston, generates the experience of the final sinking of the individual into the ground of being. (Or is it an expansion into the fields of possibility?) I see this as the submersion in the *unus mundus*. He wanted people to view his large canvasses from a metre away. When this is done the colour fills the observer's field of vision, she is no longer looking at a picture or sculpture but is in that work, subsumed by it and her individuality is lost in it.

Regression or transcendence

I question whether the regressive and transcendent routes lead ultimately to the same place. Can drunkenness, the divine madness, lead to a more all-embracing consciousness? The same place that mysticism can reach? Are both routes "Witnesses to the Fire?" In Jung's diagrams from Aion, he suggests an enantiodromia that can take place between chthonic matter and elevated spirit. He draws it as a circulation suggesting a movement that is around a particular axis, but he does not make clear whether the whole wheel moves along, into new territory perhaps, or whether it expands or contracts, or simply spins on its axis. According to Murray Stein "regression serves and refreshes consciousness", and that is important for the integration by consciousness of numinous experience. (Personal communication) That regression would seem to lead to a *unio naturalis* but if some consciousness is brought to bear in this state, some awareness of the abandoned opposites, then this state would not be far from the third stage of the *coniunctio*.

Certainly, regression may lead to an *abaissement du niveau mental* or lowering of the level at which material becomes conscious. This suggests an immersion of the conscious ego in the unconscious with the possibility of discovering new territory within the watery depths of the imagination and bringing that discovery to the surface. For some enlargement or broadening of consciousness to occur implies also "being awake on the job", for something different has not only to be witnessed but that newness must then be integrated. Any integration of something new leads to the void but it also leads out of it. It implies a deintegration of that which is known so that the new-thing can be assimilated and a reintegration occur. Any change of our schemata is difficult and requires desperation, courage or both.

Drunkenness leads to a severing of the head, the "higher" functions, and this makes the "lower" ones more accessible to what consciousness remains at the time or is available afterwards for the process of assimilating "this too is me". And perhaps all excesses and addictions work in a similar way; they are ways of getting underneath, below the renunciations required by society and into the human aspects that the renunciations protect the society from. John Dourley makes clear from his reading of the mystics that to allow one's submersion in the "nothing" requires letting go of "virtue". Paradoxically, individuation does require virtuous effort; virtue is probably a pre-requisite in fact, but it is a pre-requisite for the first stage of the *mysterium coniunctionis* only, and it results in a sublimated state. Wilma's "doing the right thing", according to what books and groups instructed her, elevated her to a state above ordinary mortals and thus empty of her humanness. It took her long fall to reunite her with her humanity.

This getting below the head and below virtuousness may be the function of all the "usual" addictions and also those such as co-dependency and fixed-patterns of relationship. But at some point the addiction must be stood against if we are not simply to sink into matter. Consciousness must be brought to bear if we are to rescue ourselves from the less-than-human. But then too, its limits must be acknowledged if we are to aspire to the eternal, the more-than-human.

Perhaps this is how Active Imagination functions, it is a process that links two worlds. It connects the differentiating but limiting function of consciousness with the dark waters of the unconscious, allowing consciousness to expand and the unconscious to become known. In this sense the process is unidirectional, the river gets broader as it descends.

Some examples

I propose to round off this chapter with some examples of various sorts of Active Imagination that have been helpful in elucidating some of the void experiences. If a dream is a snapshot of the present situation, Active Imagination is a video that connects with a before and an after. Part of the analyst's role is to ask questions of the unconscious. I do not hold with the idea that "if you ask a question all you get is an answer" as some theoreticians would have it. Rather that the question is sometimes imperative.

In the story of the Fisher King, Percival misses his chance of seeing the Holy Grail by not asking what is being carried hidden to the king. If you do not ask you may miss that which you seek. But the therapist should not ask in order to elicit the answer he expects or that he feels the analysand should give, he should ask as a way of deepening the exploration of the void. He should not ask "Is that the grail?" But rather "I notice that you keep carrying that covered dish to the King, and I am intrigued about what it may contain." Questions should also be directed at attempting to elucidate the "what" of an experience rather than to ascertain its "why". As described above, "what" embodies the experience further, "why" takes it into the head.

Patience and courage are most required in the accompanying of a person in their Active Imagination; as the person falls ever further "out of the hands of the living God" it is tempting to halt their descent with some well-meaning interpretation or suggestion. Rather than do that, the analyst needs to face his own fears about how things might end, and suffer that silently. "Survivors" of the procedure often express having felt the presence of the analyst as a witness and that it was reassuring for them. Thus, I do allow myself the comfort that during this brief Active Imagination, in my presence, the analysand may, at the least, feel accompanied. Each descent and return, each survival of the fall, strengthens the ego/Self axis and makes it more feasible to do without the outside other in the future. But early on, the absence of an accompanying other may make the descent too frightening to contemplate doing again.

In the factually based film and book *Touching the Void*, two mountaineers survive unspeakable traumas and are separated from each other; each feels completely alone in the frigid mountains. In each of their accounts of this time, they describe the horror of that aloneness but how they then experienced, surrounded by a ring of mountains, a sense of an-other, but a malignant other, observing them. In the early stages of the exploration of the void within, the absence or inattention of the analyst may also be experienced as a malignant presence. (Bion describes that in the early stages of psychological development the "good breast" missing will be experienced as a "bad breast" present.) Once the analytic attitude has been internalized, absence is no longer of necessity experienced as malign. The "vast solitude" may become something sought, as Rilke did, rather than something to be avoided at all costs.

My most common vocalization during an Active Imagination in my consulting room would be "And then?" or simply a "Hmm? Hmm?" in a similar tone. I think that implies my belief that we are attempting to elucidate a process rather than a static position. I have noticed though that I tend to stop "Hmm, Hmming" after a descent has stopped or been reversed or when some connection has been made or danger apparently receded. This probably reflects my desire to end on solid ground, to find the order somewhere present within the chaos. It is in my awareness, though, that sooner or later the cracks will start to show, and spread, and the new but familiar abyss begin to open up.

Annette (see below), a post-middle-aged woman, dreamed of attempting to fumigate or disinfect the foundations of her house. Some rats came running out and a huge one stood facing her with its teeth bared: "We both screamed loudly and I woke up." In an Active Imagination, she was able to face the rat with more equanimity. She stood her ground and experienced both her own and the rat's terror and aloneness. The rat no longer wanted to attack her and she could feel some sympathy for it. Over time, she has learnt to use the rat's powerful-seeming aggression as a helpful antithesis to her more usual mousy resignation.

Annette's Active Imagination brought up many images for her. She remembered childhood episodes of being abandoned in a large house, her parents out and the maid not answering her, and she associated to the idea of rats eating kittens, and rats in the roof being poisoned. She also spoke of her previously distant brother who had communicated warmly with her son, and how this made her feel reassured. The dream had left her with a vague dread. The Active Imagination connected the above with the below, the past with the present, and the good with the bad. Filling what had been empty, it left her with feelings of empathy for aspects of herself that she had forgotten existed.

Timothy found himself shrivelling after an encounter with work colleagues where he had felt misunderstood. Instead of trying to "make it better" he went and sat in his car in the parking garage and allowed himself to experience how awful he really felt. He experienced a sense of falling into deeper and deeper blackness until, within that darkness, he saw an accompanying light as of gleaming brass or gold. When he surfaced, he felt more in contact with, and positive about, himself, and with a feeling that he would be able to tolerate those negative feelings much more ably in the future.

I am indebted to my colleague Peter Hodson for obtaining permission from his analysand to publish the following dream. A middle-aged woman dreamed of being surrounded by the dark and falling down through it. After a while she looked up (forward, I imagine) and saw dim light as though she were in a deep well. She realized she was moving upwards, and, at length, she was surrounded by light. (This is reminiscent of the pilgrim's journey through Dante's *Inferno*, he descends deeper and deeper down the torso of the giant Dis until he realizes that having reached a point in the region of Dis' groin he is now ascending into the light although still moving "down".)

In a later dream, the same woman is in the sea with divers who excavate one trunk and then another and then at her behest, yet another, even deeper one. The trunks are brought to the surface where three different men open them. The first two are scientists and the third a fool. During an Active Imagination, in the presence of her therapist, she looked into the boxes. The first contained old manuscripts, the second art works, and the third, that opened by the fool, contained nothing except some fragments of music.

The first dream suggests the Christian concept of kenosis, the descent and, changed, the return. And the second dream, the different ways of knowing about what is below the surface. In her Active Imagination this is elaborated so that the knowing is of three kinds. The first two suggest boundedness, first in the written word, then in the broader world of art, but the third opens up endless possibility. Words define and limit and may exclude, art demonstrates non-verbally but within a framework, but fragments of music suggest the idea of non-verbal structures of an infinite variability. These ways of knowing and expressing what is known are each of great value. It is only when one way becomes overvalued that it becomes negative, whether this reflects the rigidity of science or completely unstructured chaos.

Another patient of mine has modelled in plasticine, sketched, and painted, and used her computer to manipulate photographs from her childhood and other images. These processes, all Active Imaginations, have served to give more tangible shape and feeling to her different experiences in memory and always open up new territory. For some, music serves as the source of inspiration and connection with feelings, it seems to work in two directions, connecting soul with both spirit and body. For others, an enactment such as mimicking a posture or physical action unlocks a memory that seemed previously "trapped in the body". By seeing psychoanalysis as strictly a verbal interchange, the analyst turns his back on rich resources.

As Wilma found, the fall from the "hands of the living God" is a fearful thing but, by being accompanied in her fall, she learnt that she could endure it and in the process find herself; herself still within those all-cradling hands. The paradox is that in entering the void of emptiness, the void of infinite possibility surrounds you.

As D.H. Lawrence puts it, the plunge

goes further and further, and yet never finds an end
for there is no end,
it is the abyss of the immortality
of those that have fallen from God.
                    (From *Abysmal Immortality*, Lawrence, 1950: 124)

Lawrence's implication is that we need to break away from God in order to discover ourselves, we fall and fall, and yet that fall into the bottomless abyss is still within God. In her fall and rediscovered love, Wilma connected with the God image within.

Afterword

I realize that I have mainly focused in this chapter on Active Imagination as a process witnessed by an analyst in the therapeutic setting. However, I would stress that it is also something that can be performed, and mostly is, in the absence of the analyst and simply as part of the "getting to know yourself" that is the individuation process.

INDIVIDUAL EXPERIENCES

So I returned, and considered all the oppressions that are done under the sun: and behold the tears of such as were oppressed, and they had no comforter; and on the side of their oppressors there was power; but they had no comforter.

(Ecclesiastes)

Dreams, lies, lies dreams—nothing but emptiness.

(Euripedes, *Iphigenia in Tauris*)

CHAPTER EIGHTEEN

Void as a gender experience
Part I: Mostly masculine

Nothing is outside, nothing is inside; for what is outside is inside.
(Herman Hesse)

This section is in part a search for meaning but, in the spirit of the void as creative space, I do not want to choke this space by giving the impression that it is all understood. Instead, I have chosen a number of clinical examples to act as pathways through this broad landscape.

A question is whether men and women experience the void differently, or perhaps whether the void experience, which may be essentially similar in the two, has different origins in the two genders. I shall explore rather than answer these questions, and in so doing acknowledge my debt to Marilyn Charles (2000a; 2000b) whose two articles, *Convex and Concave, Parts I and II* with the subtitles *Images of Emptiness in Men* and *Images of Emptiness in Women*, I found stimulating.

Both men and women may have the negative-mother experience of feeling unheld within a universe that does not care for them. Acknowledging this "external void" affirms "one's inherent unlovability in the face of a disinterested or actively hostile universe" whereas to "admit internal emptiness is to acknowledge need." (Charles, 2000b: 119) Either I am unlovable or the universe is horrible; in either case, I need more than I am receiving. There are no gender boundaries when the void experience arises from hostility or lack of care from early caretakers.

To generalize, men must move into the world in order to create and feel effective whereas women can create from within the confines of their bodies. Men find it more difficult to be aware of their feelings, particularly the "weaker" feelings such as sadness or vulnerability, they build a defensive wall around themselves, and this attempt to defy need leads to an inner emptiness or state of feelinglessness. A natural development of this defensiveness, a sublimation of it, is the mystical journey or process in which the bounds of the flesh are transcended. (ibid.; and in *Psychotherapy and Spirituality*)

The infant's experience of the father is, in a very physical way, different from his or her experience of the mother. The father is physiologically separate, and may be emotionally more remote than the mother, and this remoteness may be experienced as void. The male child must identify with that remote (void) father so that for him the void may be more imminent.

I have noted that while women often speak of the remoteness of their fathers, they seldom use the word "void" to describe their experience of them. In my male patients this is very different. As mentioned above, one spoke of, in fantasy, approaching a door behind which he expected to see his father. When he opened the door there was simply an empty chasm. Or, when asked about his father, a man might say, "there is nothing there, it is like staring into the void." For women, the distant father may be experienced as simply that, "my father was distant or remote or absent", or, as one woman on the Oprah Winfrey show said, "there is an emptiness the shape of my father." For this woman, the father's absence was more personal and not felt as enormously as an unbounded or chasmic lack.

Children of both genders develop out of the physical substance of the mother and must move out of that early oneness with her. The father has a unique and important function in leading the growing child out of that oneness and into the world. His is the figure with which the boy-child must identify but he also has a crucial role in respect of the development of the animus in the girl-child. The father rescues or extracts the developing child from the constricting embrace of the mother, a function that is most critical when the mother is of the elementary type (Neumann, 1963) and he introduces her to the world outside the mother and outside of the home. Symbolically, the father as a masculine being stands for consciousness and the world of the spirit; he brings light into the darkness and aids differentiation from the *prima materia* or first matter.

The space that the father should fill may be filled by something else in a girl's or woman's experience of life, whereas, with a boy or man, the space that the father does not fill may just remain empty, a hole in the fabric of his being. The father should be helpful to his daughter in the process of finding out "you are different from your mother", but even in his absence the girl-child will have someone, her mother, to identify with, even though that one may be far from her own identity.

With a son, the father may indicate "you are like me" or at least "you are one of us", i.e. his presence can impart some sense of identity. That sense of identity is second-best compared to having "who you are", your true identity, recognized, but it does offer some protection against that feeling of being "nothing and nobody". If I am not like my mother and don't know my father, then emptiness with regard to who I am is likely.

In the sort of case that Balint describes (see *Empty of Oneself*), the child's identity is parasitized by the presence of the mother and this is more common in females. Being blind to the true identity of her child, the mother fills the internal space within the child with her own being or with her expectations, so that the child remains "empty of herself" but full of the mother. A boy-child in a similar situation, although he too may be intruded on by maternal projections, is likely to be empty of himself and anyone else.

A woman may feel that she must leave inside her, or even be, a space that can be filled by another, and she may fear that she will not be filled, or that the wrong thing will fill her. One young woman, asked to describe herself, said, "I am my boyfriend's girlfriend"; she was empty of her own identity. Women are containers for their children and often for their husbands as well. Charles suggests that a woman may create a state of aloneness as being preferable "to facing the terrible emptiness she experiences when she is with others." (2000a: 15) I'd put it like this; for some, being alone by their own choice is better than being alone in the presence of others over whom they have no control.

The anxious attachment style of compulsive self-reliance (Bowlby) gives one an illusion of competence but cuts one off from close feeling contact with another. It too is a void of one's own making. One compulsive caregiver wrote about the "vastness of (her) vulnerability" and compared her feelings with "The storm-tossed expanse of the sea—uncontrollable and unable to confine—raw and irrepressible." This is more chaotic than void-like but is on the same spectrum.

Women seem to be more competent at maintaining an affective attachment, both to their own inner cores and to those in the outside world, while men easily become estranged from their feeling centres. It is more "manly" to be need-less, empty, and with no need of being filled. (Charles, 2000b: 126) And this difference probably has biological as well as societal roots. Making contact with either internal or external objects and the feeling of need opens the door to the richness of feelings but also to the pain of vulnerability; it is often defended against. As discussed above (in *On the Territory of the Void*), this is the basis for the schizoid defence where feelings, particularly of need, are hidden beneath some defensive structure. There is a novel entitled *There is Nothing I Own That I Want*. The defended male's T-shirt might read *There is Nothing That I Cannot Have That I Need*.

I am intrigued that Erich Neumann's two "big" books were *The Great Mother* (1963) and *The History and Origins of Consciousness* (1954). There is no Great Father. The Great Mother is primary, and she contains both masculine and feminine elements; She encompasses both yin and yang, the Father only yang. This is not to say that human fathers may not have a feminine aspect but that the archetypal constellation of the masculine is more one-sided than the archetypal constellation of the feminine. The archetypal feminine is the ground out of which the masculine arises.

The father represents the "conventional forces of law and order as opposed to the . . . intuitive instinctual powers of the feminine." (Cooper, 1978: 65) The masculine is external, the feminine internal and yet all-encompassing. In *An Illustrated Encyclopaedia of Traditional Symbols* (1978), Cooper allocates ten column lines to "Father" and 115 to "Mother/Great Mother/Mother Goddess"! What this suggests is that there are many ways through which we may symbolically experience the feminine but a limited number of ways of experiencing the masculine. As a simple example, a containing place or home may take over the role of the mother and impart the sense of holding that is crucial to a coherent sense of oneself. And contrarily, multiple home changes can exacerbate feelings of emptiness engendered by an absent mother.

"Men and women each seem to entertain the fantasy that their emptiness should be filled by an other who becomes in fantasy a 'transformative object' (Bollas, 1987) who can save us from ourselves. Most often the other is of the opposite gender." (Charles, 2000b: 124) This idea coincides with the idea of the animus or anima as experienced by the woman and man respectively. We all contain these contra-sexual archetypes (and project them readily) but they may be particularly significant in those who have experienced a lack in relation to their same-sex parent, so that the humanizing and balancing out of the archetypal figures within their psyches has not adequately occurred.

Gert

One such man, Gert, was, as a child, kept away from his father in order not to tire him on his return from work. His father, a man distant from his own emotions, became experienced by Gert as highly remote and unattainable. Nevertheless, Gert identified with him, or rather, Gert identified with a sort of absence of the real. What was real, but confusing, was his mother; she was too present, in a way that demonstrated her identity and fears, but she failed to accurately mirror her son. This meant that although Gert emulated some of the external features of his distant father, such as his dedication to work and service, he was strongly drawn to the feminine, as though the emptiness that he suffered could only be filled by a feminine figure.

A woman he was attracted to would start off as a "transformative object", an anima figure, who brought with her the hope of a new sense of self, a completion through union. However, because of Gert's unresolved mother issues, this new woman would rapidly become contaminated with negative aspects such as a needy bossiness and he would subjugate himself to her. In this state he would take on the submissive role of suppliant to the goddess, losing his hard-won sense of identity and buying into her negative ideas of him. He later learnt to keep his distance from relationships with women, admiring from a distance their external forms and engaging on a professional level in the workplace, but dimly aware of the hovering spectre of "mother" waiting to take him over. At least part of Gert's emptiness is linked to his mother's invasion of him; she has filled the space where he, or his masculinity, ought to be.

Another aspect he demonstrated is similar to the pattern that seems to attract many therapists to their depressed female patients. The renaissance pictures of the *Mater Dolorosa* show her with huge blank eyes. These are eyes that are like black holes and they threaten to suck you in. (See above in *Another "Black Hole"*) The therapist, perhaps more often the male therapist, longs to bring light into those eyes and flirts with that danger. He desires to make better, to make some reparative gesture that will enliven his patient and make himself feel that there is a possibility of being "held" by this maternal substitute. By fixing the leak in the container the contained may not leak away, nor the container disappear through the rent in her own psychic fabric.

What kept the emptiness alive in Gert, was a deep sense that he was only valuable as a doer, the producer of special work for the team or his superiors in the workplace, the maker of fantastic soups for friends or family, a sensitive lover to his wife, and the doer of the worst chores around the home. These doings fostered a sense of purpose and a superficial identity. They were persona expressions but also partial expressions of his true self. To the extent that he identified with them as "me" rather than "what I do", they left a gap or hole in his experience of himself. In fact, one could say that they aggravated or enlarged that hole which for him was a more or less primary experience. The hole that is composed of denied pain or denied feeling, for "big boys don't cry", "real men" don't feel.

Other formulations

Hollis (1994) makes it abundantly clear that this situation is not peculiar to Gert, and that most men are burdened by the expectation that they should live up to roles that deny their individuality. "Work, war, and worry" are three of these roles which "do not support, confirm or resonate to the needs of men's souls." (Hollis, 1994: 21) He states further that for men "powerlessness in any of its forms, is worse than annihilation." (*ibid.*: 24)

Hollis quotes a passage from James Agee's book *A Death in the Family* that affirms the individual search for an identity and the yearning to be with those who know us; in this case figures from our dream landscape. "Sleep, soft smiling, draws me unto her: and those receive me, who quietly treat me, as one familiar and well-beloved in that home: but will not, oh, will not, not now, not ever; but will not ever tell me who I am." It seems to me that the positive maternal role is often like the dream world pictured here. Our mothers make us feel familiar and well-loved but not who we are. It is up to the father to tell "me who I am", and fathers often betray that trust by telling instead who we "should" be, what our roles should be in the external eyes of the world.

With my client Gert, there was an initial hole where the father ought to have been and another lacuna where the mother's idea of what the boy needed and who he was did not coincide with what he in fact needed or his true unfolding identity. Then, unreflected or unaccepted feelings about his experiences of life led to an expansion of the emptiness, and, finally, his own deliberate suppression of his feelings and thus himself, as part of "the male thing", resulted in a further dissociation from himself and an exacerbation of his experience of the void.

Charles suggests that the lack of acknowledgement of the actuality of a child's experience affects his capacity to perceive and sustain meaning (Charles, 2000b: 123) and this can give rise to a void experience. This is in part what Gert suffered. His own experiences went unseen by his parents; by his mother because she saw something different, and by his father because, being kept away, he could not see anything. Gert's early life was plagued by a sense of futility and meaninglessness.

Vagina dentata

The image of the *vagina dentata* is a particularly male way of expressing the terrible mother archetype. The image suggests the devouring mother who will castrate and render impotent any male figure who attempts to find refuge inside her. Charles feels that, for a woman, there is a comforting felt sense of the lack of teeth in her own interior, so the *vagina dentata* is not a female dread. But for the male, the mysterious interior of woman can be the home of terrifying phantasms, from devouring maw to complete emptiness, that can extract all meaning and reduce him to nothingness.

The problem is that one of the male roles is felt to be to fill the space within woman and risk being made into nothing. Spending himself within her he becomes consumed. There is a cartoon of a "just married" couple in their motel room. She is lying in the bed facing her husband who stands naked before her, his back toward the viewer. With shrivelling disdain she says, "You're going to make me the happiest woman in the world with *that*?" Man attempts to be effective and is easily shrunk into nothing. One of his dilemmas is how to be effective without being diminished.

Joyce McDougall (1986) writes of one man's void experience when early Oedipal fantasies came close to consciousness. His terror was of disappearing into the "chasm" that was the maternal interior and, within that dark emptiness, meeting persecuting figures. (Interestingly, her patient was comfortable sleeping with prostitutes because they were not empty, being filled by other men.)

The male can often be protected from these fears by a "good-enough" father who will extract him from the potentially lethal maternal embrace. But what if there are "no clothes on my father's side of the cupboard" as Gert once dreamed of it? Then another possibility is to find an alternative and safer space within the mother. Donald Meltzer writes of this space as being an anal masturbatory world, a "claustrum" within the maternal rectum as opposed to her womb. It is a form of "psychic retreat" (Steiner), another compartment of the void that leads nowhere.

In Gert's therapy we identified this place as a pink, chintzy world that surfaced in his dreams and carried the promise of good things happening. As in Meltzer's material, this world was entered through some dark back-way and entry was usually illicit. The anal masturbatory world is like the television world in the movie *Pleasantville*, (1995, director Gary Ross, USA) colourless but safe and going nowhere, for it evolves from the child's fantasy of an internal space where mother retains the "goodies" that she is not giving him. In it, he is safe from being ground by those vicious vaginal teeth or being birthed prematurely into the dangerous world outside.

This "claustrum", as Meltzer calls it, is a void space that is preferable to the more actively vicious aspects of the terrible mother and is used as a refuge from those. In other words, it is the use of the void as a defence against something worse. But it is an illusory world and ultimately he will have to leave it. The best way out of the claustrum is through disillusion, and this leads to one of the therapeutic challenges, how to disillusion without severing connection.

Another particularly male thing is the flight from the turmoil of feelings, that remind him of his subservience to matter, into abstract ideas. It is easy to disappear into the emptiness of outer space, unless one is grounded as well, brought back to mother earth. There is a common alchemical image of a soaring eagle chained to an earthbound animal, perhaps a dog, e.g. in Edinger's (1985) *The Anatomy of the Psyche*, Figure 4-2. This is a graphic depiction of a solution to the dangers inherent in the opposing alchemical processes of *sublimatio* and *coagulatio*, the one lifting up lightly as Mercury the god and the other bringing back to earth with all the Saturnine weight of lead. Or as a *coniunctio* image, spirit is to be connected to matter.

I like Jung's intuition of a "psychoid boundary" that surrounds the psyche, on one side psyche disappears into matter and on the other it blends into spirit, and it is in the intermediate realm that conscious man dwells. (Jung, 1969a) Whatever is on the other side of this barrier is beyond consciousness, "without form and void". And this is true whether we are rising too high on the wings of thought or sinking into the "waters of oblivion" (Bob Dylan) originating in physical surfeits of various kinds.

Omniscience (literally, all-knowing) is another aspect that is in the realm of the father. Charles writes of a young man who sought knowledge in an effort to appease his father. My analysand Gert experienced deep shame as he came to realize that his views were different from his father's and he initially took pains to deny those differences. This kept him superficially in a situation where he felt that he could be known and accepted by his father and yet he was estranged from himself.

In the early stages of therapy this was preferable to feeling alienated from the other but as time went on, and feeling supported by his therapist as a father figure, his need to be in agreement with his father became a need to be in disagreement with him. It was a way of separating from his father, and his father therapist, "I am different from my father", but not necessarily of reconnecting with himself as he was still defining himself in relation to his father rather than through self-knowledge and acceptance.

Sometimes men caught in this bind lose the capacity to think their own thoughts, really know what they believe in, or to feel that they can make a meaningful connection with another. One middle-aged man in this trap had been in analysis for some years, when, while reading a novel by an American feminist, he had the sudden experience of being able to differentiate his feelings and thoughts about what she had written. He could think his own thoughts and express them to himself.

In the past he had read in a doomed sort of way, usually in agreement with what the author was expressing, and swallowing any thoughts that ran counter to that general tone. This meant that if there was subtle argument in the narrative, with one character agreeing and another disagreeing with what he had supposed were the author's thoughts, he would become confused and not know what to think himself. Because there was no centre in him, his thoughts were always in reaction to another's. He had become a good listener because he was bent on really understanding other's thoughts or expressed ideas in order to fill the vacuum inside himself, but he was often in fear that his felt emptiness would be exposed; that the nothingness inside him would be seen.

The difference now amazed him, not only could he have different thoughts from the author, but he could have differentiated arguments in his head and even remember the plots and the train of ideas that he had read. He could then integrate them and retain them for use on other occasions. He was now a container for his own thoughts and instead of living on the edge of the frankly meaningless he felt a deepening connection with both himself and others.

Fear or desire re: the transformative feminine

As suggested above, in my experience women are more likely to hide their dreams than men are. Men seem to be attracted to the identity that dreams offer, whereas some women shy away from the knowledge that dreams seem to have of them. Because dreams can be interpreted in different ways and their meaning only becomes apparent over time, they can take the dreamer unawares, get behind her defences. The "aha" of a new insight is for them an "oh no".

For a woman who is "filled with the void in the presence of the mother" any hint by the Self that it "knows" the ego may constellate that void.

This can occur in men, such as described with Benny below, but this is a less usual constellation. If a man does not feel seen by the differentiating eyes of the father, then he may rely on acknowledgement from someone else, and this may be the "transformative other" who appears in dreams and fantasies. The longing to be known often translates into a desire to be reflected in the eyes of another, whether that be an enigmatic female or the dreaming self. It occurs to me that the function, if not the attributes, of the transformative feminine is similar to that of the heroic masculine. Both can deliver, or wrench if necessary, the individual from the embracing arms of "the mother" and start him, enlivened, on his way.

A middle-aged man had been plagued for years by an intense response to "the magical other". Sometimes the whole but often parts of a woman would release a physiological response that was not so much sexual as a yearning for recognition or connection. A curl of hair, the swoop of a neck, a downcast or piercing gaze could all release this response as long as the object was female. Sometimes he would be caught out by the long blonde tresses of a man and would laugh with wry amusement at this proof of the power of projection. What he seemed to be fantasizing was that here was someone who could see him, touch him, embrace him, and perhaps recognize him and his potential.

His mother had been a warm, loving woman but had suffered from depression during his early childhood and was somewhat unsure of herself as an adult. His father was a rather removed man who was intensely envious of the attention that his son received. He had been sent to a boarding school, his father's old school, a fate that none of his other siblings were subjected to, but his close relationships with men were few. He often felt empty and that life was essentially meaningless and he yearned for something more. He longed to be loved, but this seemed impossible by a male, and if by a female it would be a betrayal of something or someone. In his yearning for the "mysterious other" it did not seem as though he was trying to recreate the mother, as though the impulse was regressive, but as though he was trying to find some connection that would liberate him from her, as his father should have done.

Gert again

To return to Gert, one of the things that became clear to us as his analysis progressed was that there were often ideas or ways of seeing or relating to the world that seemed clearly to emanate from his father, that were like his father's. He would rapidly expel these "toxic" thoughts before shame overcame him, but, as his psychological separation from his father continued, he was able to accept that, as his father's son, it was reasonable for them to share similar impulses, and that having them did not mean he was identifying with his father or doing things to please him to his own detriment.

It became possible to notice, without shame, how his father, in spite of his distance to the growing boy, or perhaps because of it, had somehow been integrated into his personality. So where there had once been a felt emptiness was now a complex amalgam of self and internal father, external father, the desired father, the father needed for adequate growth, and the archetypal father. Most of these had been projected onto the analyst at one time or another and the teasing out of these transference projections formed an important part of the therapy.

One day, Gert's son said something to him that he experienced as a condemnation of his behaviour towards his wife. Gert became enraged, and, like Yahweh, "turned his face from him". After a while, he realized, in terror, that he had obliterated the image and the memory of his son from his mind. He realized how similar this was to his experience of his own parents who, if he showed who he really was or what he felt, would smack him or simply ignore him. Their love, he felt, had been conditional on his good behaviour and his very existence dependent on his ability to show them what he felt they wanted to see. Having his son "disappear" filled him with fear, remorse, and understanding; he now knew from both sides what it felt like; to obliterate what you love and be obliterated by those whose love you need. He felt a horror that he had allowed his son to witness his own absence from Gert's eyes.

Out of this experience, and also through the experience of other disparate parts of him, came a sense of "I exist". "That I am", but not yet "who I am". "That I exist" implies that "I exist for someone", i.e. "someone is aware of me," which is a mutual recognition of both self and other and opposite to the void experience wherein neither self nor other exist, or do not exist in a connected way.

Gert spent a week in a mountain retreat, alone except for his dogs, the mountains, and the sky. He found himself weeping often and wrote the following. (I quote it as written)

> Where does it all come from? It's like an endless sea. . . . I am just a body, a mouth to that sea. . . . I cry, but the impetus to howl, to sob comes from far away and finds its voice in me. It is me but it illustrates the endlessness of me. (The) 'me' is endless sorrow; a place with no walls, no boundaries; just trailing off into void . . .

> Why I think I cry is because I cannot believe I'm here (on this land). I don't want to move anything in this 'room' as it were in case I suddenly awaken to find that this is just a figment of my imagination. That I am not really here. That this place where I can be absolutely alone with my dogs, where I can cry and cry and cry, isn't here. That, instead, I am in a jagged place, cliffs, storms, me alone.

> Strange. "Here" I'm alone and feel protected. "There" (in the jagged place) I'm alone and alone. No one. This is aloneness with myself. "There" is aloneness without self. "There" is just shadow, non-being; unsubstantial. The deathness of the "me" there is what is scary. Because when the shadow ends, when it is snuffed out (and it is like a flickering, spluttering flame) then there is nothing but cold and endless emptiness. Here the "me" has substance. It's got body, it takes up space, it is present, it is benevolent, it nurtures. The "me" on the other side is at risk. When it snuffs out . . . then there can be nothing except the endless. Cold. Nothingness.

There are a few things that strike me about this man's powerful experience. The first is the sense that by experiencing aloneness in this way he reaches a space inside himself where he feels not-alone, in the sense of he is now "with myself". Being truly alone he becomes no longer alone. This ties in with Rilke's idea of the necessity to form a "vast solitude" around oneself in order to experience oneself fully.

Another is that the space in which he can cry is the containing feminine space which he writes of elsewhere as being "enfolding" and "nature still listening". This is in contrast to the "jagged" stormy cliff-edge that suggests the penetrating negative feminine or represents his experience of the masculine. The "enfolding" space is an unconditionally accepting space, and in being there he can be "alone in the presence of the mother". (Winnicott) In this state he can allow himself to feel impulses welling up from inside himself, carrying with them a feeling of "this is who I am". In the positive female world it is acceptable to cry and not to deny your feelings; in this open space feelings are simply contained, they can just be.

Gert described too a sense of being submerged. This was different from the dryness that he had experienced in the past and that had been so full of suffering. As Hollis pointed out, the male roles, while perhaps useful for society, are obstructive to man's individual experience of himself, they are counter to his soul. I think of them as being dry or desiccated.

In psychological terms this experience of Gert's represents a process whereby the ego separates from, and yet remains connected to, the Self. There is an acceptance of that connection but not an identification with it, and at this stage the "greater reality" feels nurturant, it seems to have him in mind. Can one accept that the "greater reality" is indifferent to you and has some other purpose afoot? That you as an individual may be part of some Grand Plan but that you are neither the subject nor the object of it? This would prove difficult for Gert. He no longer denies the connection to a greater reality but neither does he fully accept that that greater reality is ultimately what continues when the "me" is no more.

John

Another man whom I saw for a very short time, worked for a multinational company based in London but with tentacles in developing nations in Africa. From his position at the Southern tip of this dark continent, he ran a "virtual operation" dealing with electronic media in those countries. He made infrequent visits to them "in-the-flesh" and still more infrequent visits to the UK, where the company, whose directors he experienced as distant and unsupportive, was based.

John described both of his parents as being insular and undemonstrative and his father as being often physically absent from home, working. When my patient was 21, his father died, having suffered for two years with a wasting disease. He thought of his father as being "like an absentee landlord", which described vividly his absence from John's psychic economy. Thinking about his father, and his own bosses, was "like delving into a void"; as with Gert, there was emptiness where the father should have been. At work he felt he was on the positive edge of controlling the chaos, perhaps aided by the sense in his mind of the distant fathers in the UK, but at home he felt "like a stranger amongst strangers" and felt completely fatherless, here the chaos seemed uncontrollable.

The powerful effect of the absence of the father was brought home to me by another middle-aged man who found himself weeping uncontrollably on reading Arthur Ransome's novel *We Didn't Mean to go to Sea* to his children. The weeping was not precipitated by the adventure, where four young children are swept out of a river mouth and into the English Channel in deep fog and make their way across the sea to Holland; perhaps their self-reliance seemed as it should be to him. What caused his tears was that the children's father was on the Holland dock, by some chain of coincidence, and could both acknowledge and contain the children. He suddenly realized how much of a void he felt in relation to his own father.

Lysander

In the case of another analysand, who I'll call Lysander, the father was the hen-pecked husband of a very destructive woman who successfully emasculated both him and their first-born son, Lysander's brother. Lysander was an intelligent and physically talented child who rapidly learnt what to do to gain mother's approval. He despised his father and sought in vain for some support from his two-year-older brother and then became mother's "little" helper. He took it upon himself to make sure that the lights were off to save electricity, his little sister was behaving well, and above all, that there were no more fights between his parents, an impossible task. In addition, he performed stunningly on the sports field, captaining most teams that he played in, and he regularly came top of his class. All this was to maintain the precarious love of his mother. He was the golden boy with all shadow elements repressed, but living a dread-filled life with only the thinness of a mask between him and the exposure that he felt would lead to nothingness.

When he was twelve, his maternal grandfather had used to lie with him in the afternoons and touch his genitals. He had been unable to tell anyone or ask his grandfather to stop doing this, as he felt this would have shamed his grandfather. At the age of fourteen, when the family emigrated to South Africa, he simply stopped trying at school. He bunked classes, drank and smoked, and would attempt only those things he knew he could achieve. He hated to be looked at and judged, would compete in sport only "if I knew we would win" but would not "perform", for example sit a music exam or play in an eisteddfod. He remembered how, when he first came to South Africa, he had been cajoled into competing but when he did compete he felt an increase in his sense of nothingness. Smoking marijuana temporarily filled that emptiness.

He existed somewhere between feeling like nothing in nowhere, and feeling "like a lump of shit in a cesspool". His mother saw only the good in him, and as a small child this had been very important to him. As an adult, however, it increased his sense of alienation and precipitated a feeling of falling into an abyss. When he was eighteen he told her how bad he felt inside, dirty and hopeless. She responded simply, "Rubbish!"

He did want people to see the good, and this was especially true in relation to women, but when they did he felt the abyss looming and protected himself by being offensive towards them. This increased his sense of alienation.

Having initially terminated his therapy with me after only a year, he reappeared one day clutching a mountaineering book entitled *Touching the Void*, an apt title for his further work. He complained that he was unable to bring things together in relation to work plans, that he had recurrent dreams of interrupted intercourse and that he was suffering from an unremitting sense of emptiness within. Even though he was a strong, 190cm adult, he felt insubstantial, a fraud waiting to be unmasked, for unless he was top at everything he felt an utter failure and he could not maintain top position for ever. As the gunfighters in the old Western novels would have it: "There's always someone out there trying to prove that they are faster than you."

He told me one day of a friend who was talented, sporty, and good-looking, was liked by many people and was never without a girlfriend. And yet this man shot and killed himself. "In spite of all those people mirroring him," he said. I responded that perhaps what was being mirrored was not what he felt he was, as in the case of Lysander himself.

One of the main foci of our work together was Lysander's desire to smear himself with his own faeces. This had a sexual connotation but was also associated with considerable shame. In trying to understand the phenomenon we came up with different formulations which were that:

1) the smearing was associated with Eriksen's phase "autonomy versus shame and doubt". It seemed to be linked to a sort of petulant two year old who would fluctuate wildly between what a narcissistic patient has called "delusions of adequacy" and acute feelings of uselessness and shame. Smearing was a rebellious act under his autonomous control, his mother may think he was good-and-clean-and-fresh but he could prove to himself something different.

2) The smearing was an unconscious expression of shame about himself and of an identification with shadow aspects. As such it was an act that ran counter to the deeper sense of his wholeness, i.e. counter to the Self.

3) It was an expression of his true nature, it highlighted his sense of identity and the shame was because of his realization that smearing was not acceptable in the public domain.

Wrestling with these formulations but not coming to a hard conclusion, Lysander noted one day that his desire to smear had simply ceased. He also felt more empowered and less empty and as though he could contain some of the emotion that previously had simply spilled out. He was becoming filled with himself and that feeling presaged a reduction in his sense of alienation from others.

What had been valuable was the act of wondering about his behaviour in a thoughtful yet non-judgmental way. This enabled him to remember without shame, to know himself more clearly. The literary image of this is when Dante is plunged into the river Eunous at the end of his journey through *Purgatorio*; he remembers his life but without negative judgments.

Having had no effective father figure with whom to identify, Lysander still struggled with being a father to his son and step-daughter, and parented them using his intellect more than his feeling.

His new-found sense of himself meant that he was more able to be a container for his feelings and those of his children, and thus be guided by them. He also felt that he could demand from his mother something different on behalf of his children; this was not coming from a position of compliance nor opposition to her but from his own sense of what was right. The void where his father should have been was becoming filled with the presence of himself.

He has become, he articulated, like the catcher in J.D. Salinger's book *The Catcher in the Rye*, whose job it was to catch the children who would otherwise have fallen over the edge. He protects them from the void and is himself protected.

Benny

Another man, who I will call Benny, presented himself at the age of 39. He was severely depressed and suffered from an Obsessive Compulsive disorder or OCD. The OCD served as a shell or external carapace that effectively walled off the emptiness within. This was, again, an emptiness where his father should have been but also where he himself should have been. He scarcely knew what he desired, but was extremely sensitive to the desires of others, a state that consistently led him into difficult situations. For example, should he play golf? His friend wants him to, but he thinks his wife wants him at home; he will have to lie to one or other, or both of them.

He demonstrates what I think of as the void of non-differentiation as well as the void of absence, absence of his own identity. The void of non-differentiation is the condition that obtains when there is no sense of separateness from another object, i.e. person or thing. For him, all things seemed to have feelings, the toy left in the rain felt abandoned, "it is so cold outside". The broken golf tee would feel useless if thrown away, the leftover food feel rejected if not kept until rotten in the fridge, the tie feel hurt if not worn. He was not owned by himself as a separate being but by anyone who had need of him, whether they were work colleagues, members of the public or his own family. He would often be late for work because his three-year-old daughter wanted to dress him or order him around as though he were a toy and he "had" to submit to her.

As he put it, "I will do anything for recognition or to be accepted"; but to be "accepted" meant sacrificing his identity or sense of self so that he continued to remain "empty of himself". He was driven to a life of perpetual appeasement of others and I came to think of him as a new species, *Homo capitulatus*.

He was the youngest of three boys who, for his mother's sake, "should" have been a girl. His experience of his childhood was of being sacrificed to a highly intrusive mother while his father was absent. His father "tried so hard to make a living that we never saw him" and when he was about he was no match for Benny's stridently demanding mother. Silent evidence of the father's presence would appear in regimented stacks of shirts or a pile of socks rolled up in cubes in Benny's cupboard, for his father gave expression to his own OCD by tidying cupboards late at night. Otherwise, he was an unemotional man showing little warmth or closeness to his wife or sons and unable to demonstrate a capacity to parent through setting firm limits.

When Benny was thirteen and enuretic, he was taken to a psychiatrist who rightly identified anxiety due to an absent father as a causative feature. The father was given a lecture by the psychiatrist and, on the family's return home, he took Benny aside and, for the first time ever, hugged him and said "I love you—whatever happens I'll always love you." Benny did not wet the bed again until nearly 30 years later when he faced severe midlife uncertainties.

Neither of his parents recognized his positive qualities. Even when he passed his university examinations and became a member of one of the professions, they assumed it was because his intelligent wife had helped him. And that he held down a job for many years was, in their eyes, through the generosity of his employers and not because of his own actions.

He had felt "owned" by his mother who required him to be her constant companion and plaything. He used to sit with her and visit her friends with her, deep into his teen years. Should he express a desire of his own that was different from what she required, she would accuse him of "ungratefully preferring" his bike, friends, ball or whatever it was, to her. Thus, he grew up with an intolerable sense of dutiful responsibility towards others and a deep loathing for, and tendency to deny or abuse, himself. Born on his brother's birthday he felt "I don't even have my own birthday."

It seemed to me that his mother had performed an act of filicide on the deeper psychological parts of her son; she had forced a dissociation from the Self and encouraged an identification with bits of his persona. His father had allowed this to happen and had not been supportive of his individuality.

Benny collected negative anecdotes about himself in the same way as he collected other junk: broken golf tees, ruined model aeroplanes, outdated raffle tickets, etc. It was as though he constructed a skin around himself from all these items or ideas or the stories that he told about himself. When I once suggested that inside that skin was an emptiness, he replied with feeling, "Yes—a void!" And later, as though reciting a creed, "I am empty, I am void, I am lonely of myself."

As he began to recognize some aspects of his own individuality, he started playfully trying out different accents and allowing himself more conscious fantasies of achievement at work or on the golf course. As he was starting to wean himself from his old way of being, these tricksterish games became more threatening to him and then he would pretend to his mother that he was ill, for example, with hepatitis. Perhaps then she would treat him as an incompetent ill infant again.

For the first time in years he attended Synagogue again on *Yom Kippur* and spent that afternoon with friends. He started contemplating a change in career. He had discovered a part of himself that wanted to do those things, but that night he had a dream. In it, he was being held hostage in his home and his two-year-old daughter came into the room. He shot her repeatedly, killing her, and then quite dispassionately placed her body in a large shoebox, which he left next to the rubbish bin.

Both he and his daughter had been born six weeks prematurely. History tells him that he was placed in a shoebox when he came home from the hospital. This particular daughter is high-spirited and demanding. It seemed to us that she represented the possibility of a new development within himself but one that he felt terrified of and needed to eradicate. This is a good example of the Self-care system in operation. (Kalsched)

A few months later, he reported that he felt as though he was falling into nothingness. He had been offered a wonderful job opportunity but could think of nothing but his fear of losing the security of his present employment. He felt disengaged, hopeless, and indifferent to his fate, as though passively awaiting a benefactor whose arms he could lie in. He became ever more aware that his life was one of emptiness and loneliness with no sense of his own desires. He felt that others could be effective in the world and had busy social lives that they appeared to want.

The main subjective features of Benny's void state are emptiness, loneliness, and a disconnection from his desires and passions, and from his will, drive, and sense of effectiveness. He had little sense of "You will be okay in the world, even without your mother," which is one of the gifts of a good-enough father, and no sense of separateness or differentiation from the surrounding chaos or undifferentiated oneness; put simply, he was in a mess. He had become disengaged from, or perhaps had never been engaged with, himself.

His defences against the threat of losing the love of his mother and of feeling invisible to his father were to suppress his own desires, pretend to be what he thought they thought he was (stupid, helpless, etc.), and to do what others seemed to want him to do, i.e. be a compliant son, colleague, and father. This last required him to be like a stuffed toy, which his children could pull around. These defences furthered his alienation from himself and the Self, and thus extended his experience of the void. As with Balint's patients, he felt himself to be full of rubbish—he could say that word with a heart-rending resonance—"Rrubbbisshh!"

What was the difference between Benny, and my patient Clint mentioned below, and Balint's patient Sarah? I think age and the fact that Benny was never confronted by his aloneness in another country. From school he went to university near his hometown and early in his university career he connected with the woman who later became his wife. So he always had someone who filled him with their projections, and he did not realize that he was "empty of himself" until the birth of his first child when he was in his late-thirties. Then his wife became intimately involved with that child as well as suffering from postnatal depression.

It was then that he started to flounder. The fragile shell that he had constructed around himself with his fantasies and his OCD symptoms served to shore up some sense of identity but this was an identity that was an amalgam of ego and persona rather than based on his wholeness. It needed to be bolstered by the feeling that he was loveable in the eyes of his wife and employers, even the general public, in fact everyone; a position that was just not sustainable.

He could not allow himself to know what his own desires really were, in case they contradicted what others wanted, so he remained out of touch with his own interior. He had been "stolen from himself" by his mother, for her own purposes, and his father had been powerless to prevent that happening.

One of the tools that Benny used to try and save himself was lying. As a child he did not lie, because he did not feel powerful enough or individual enough to lie and would feel that his mother could anyway see right inside him; he could not hide from her because of her omniscience and his transparency. Later on he would lie to help make himself feel more than he was in the eyes of others. He would lie about whom he knew and what deals he had managed to swing, what he had been doing or was going to do, even about how he felt. As mentioned above, he told his mother that he had hepatitis in order to gain her sympathy and I was never sure whether an excuse as to why he had missed a session was true or not. He would exaggerate both his achievements and his failures.

The lying was double-edged. On the positive side, it enabled him to find a secluded space in which to start experimenting with "Is this me?" This was a shell within his shell, in which the emptiness could feel encapsulated and start to be filled with the laying down of the rudiments of his chosen identity. With a healthy lie he could stand against "the mother", start to differentiate between "what she thinks of me" and "what I really am". It became a form of opposition where he could start by saying, "This is what I am not," and finally reach a point where he might say, "This is what I am." For this to work though, he did need to have some consciousness about what he was doing. Without this consciousness, his lies and fantasies simply constructed a bubble and added to his sense of alienation.

At the time of writing, Benny has resigned from his job, changed his hair colour, even, on occasion, disciplined his children, and left his therapy with me. He has heroically entered the dark labyrinth that is his life.

Clint

When Clint first stepped into my room, he was 36 years old and had become painfully conscious of his own aloneness for the first time in his adult life. As part of his job, he had been forced to spend a few months in a foreign country away from his wife and children and he had become "petrified". "I had this empty, hollow feeling, and realized I needed my family around to keep me normal." On his return, his wife took up employment outside of the home, and this made him feel anxious and envious. "They get the pleasure of her," he said, "usually I can compartmentalize things but this is invading my brain." In a graphic description of one of the void experiences, where a defence against the void aggravates the void feeling, he said, "I feel like a balloon inside covered over with a thick crust."

Clint had been brought up by an elderly maternal aunt and her husband. They had four children of their own whom Clint always felt less-than. His biological father was unknown to him and his mother lived a few kilometres away with her husband and their three younger children. Although materially not wanting, he was rarely hugged or encouraged and developed a style of "compulsive self reliance", parenting himself to deal with the anxiety of being parentless.

He was acutely sensitive to any unfairness in the world, and to others being bullied or deprived, and was himself unable to receive gifts, which made him feel "like a charity case" and not in control. Others' needs were more important than his own were and he had great difficulty in accepting what we came to call "the dark side of God". It was important to him that institutions like the church or his employers, and also people like his wife or his mother, behaved well.

He became involved in a protracted case against his employer, a massive state enterprise, his superiors in which, he felt, had unfairly promoted some individuals and not others; "jobs for pals" is how he saw it. Although the individuals had now moved on, as it was years after the event, he wanted the organizational hierarchy to admit that wrongdoing had occurred. That would somehow redeem the organization in his eyes.

He finally dropped the charges after we had done much work linking his childhood experiences and his need to have a good mother with his present reactions. As he realized how rejected he felt by her abandonment, he felt that it would be tolerable if only she would admit that she had made mistakes, or that she had been pressured to do things in the way she had. He could not bear to think of her as bad. By admitting wrongdoing she, and, later, the organization, would be showing that they were actually not bad or immoral. He found it difficult too to acknowledge his wife's shortcomings to himself and he repeatedly felt betrayed when she failed to live up to his expectations.

While being sympathetic towards others in a general way, he did lack empathy, as his rationalistic, logical style of thinking resulted in a lack of acceptance of their feelings. His rigidity extended into living his life within the boundaries of a strict timetable and regular habits. One of his comments about the effects of therapy was that he had used to see the world in black and white "but now I notice there are shades of grey."

When he realized that his wife had been having an affair with another man, his sense of certainty, meaning, and purpose evaporated. His sense of identity was shattered and he described the feeling like this: "It is like my soul has been wrenched out leaving a small void inside." Before this happened, he had felt "enfolded" in his usual way of thinking but now the loss of certainty left him feeling totally exposed.

I understood his experience something like this: instead of allowing his early feelings of abandonment and lostness to rise into consciousness, he developed a strong sense of responsibility. This sense of responsibility had twin aspects of "I can do something about things," but also, "I am to blame." He thus lived a life of repressed feeling and heightened rationality in an effort to cover over the emptiness where his mother's presence as an internal object, or his feelings about her absence, should have been. This worked quite well, except that by not knowing his own feelings, other than in projection, the void not only remained but slowly extended, although still "under cover". His wife having an affair shattered that "cover" and the void feelings, now released, swamped him.

The rage he experienced against his wife carried the weight of his archaic anger towards his mother and the institution that had betrayed him. He felt murderous and suicidal, and, in his fantasies about his bereft children, torn between a horror for their looming state "who will take care of them without responsible me?" and thoughts of filicide "for their own good." The crust that surrounded the emptiness of his existence had cracked apart and he was filled with terror.

The emptiness here is the space that should have been filled with the sort of primitive or infantile emotions that he projected onto those around him, in this case his children, and taking back what was projected was the most important part of our work at that stage. Of course, it could only happen within the supportive frame that had developed over the months of analysis.

One day he fainted at home, and, feeling shaky and hopeless thereafter, he went to curl up in a corner; he was now forced to acknowledge his fragility and impotence. As he lay there, he began to experience a feeling of being like a grain of sand that had been lifted up out of a hill and set apart; he was being taken notice of as an individual, had noticed himself. This is similar to an experience of Gert's of feeling like being "held between the thumb and forefinger of God", and is striking in that it contains the double idea of being minutely small in the grand scheme of things and yet held in the mind of God. As I have quoted D.H. Lawrence above:

> It is a fearful thing to fall into the hands of the Living God,
> But it is a much more fearful thing to fall out of them.
>
> (Lawrence, 1950)

Sammy

I always think of Sammy as a "young" man in spite of his being in his mid-fifties. He lived in a state of continually re-shattered perfection. In spite of the constant betrayals that his life brought him, he retained the illusion that he should be, and was in fact, well looked after by "invisible hands". This term came from his reading of Apuleius' version of the Eros and Psyche myth where Psyche, having been whisked down to Eros' castle, is tended by invisible hands. All her needs are taken care of in this magical way and she waits only for the nocturnal attentions of her lover.

For Sammy, the "invisible hands" could be conjured by seeing his salary appear in his bank account each month without him having to deposit a cheque, seeing his clothes laid out for him on the bed ready to be put on after his shower, or finding the light on in his room. He would have had to engineer these events but their appearance still gave him the feeling that he was the recipient of caring attention, he was being looked after. Yet that "being looked after" was only permissible in his fantasy world. In real life, he needed to be in charge of any giving, otherwise he would feel fragile and vulnerable. He wanted to receive too much to risk not getting.

Sammy was brought up in a comfortable Jewish home until his father was jailed for a white-collar crime when he was about ten years old. The family went to stay with relatives and he was told that he was now the young man of the family and should protect his mother. This was a role that he felt completely inadequate to fill. His betrayal by his father had begun a few years before this event when, in a concretization of the Jewish story that Hillman recounts in his chapter on *Betrayal*, his father had called up to Sammy, standing on a balcony about three metres up, "Jump I'll catch you." As Sammy jumped, his father stepped back. "Never trust anybody, not even your own father."

Betrayed by his father, the threat of falling forever was never far away. When his first son died of a congenital disease at the age of fifteen months, he could not cry. "It was as though there was gossamer covering over a deep well of sadness. I could fall forever into it." At times, he would have fantasies of rising weightlessly into the air, what would stop him? At others, he would imagine falling down and down. One fantasy was of being in a comfortable bed that started tumbling through the air adjacent to a mountain pass.

Peter Pan and the Lost Boys, "the motherless boys" I reminded him, was an image that resonated with him, as was the story of *The Earl King*, that haunting song by Schubert. In this song, a father is galloping homeward through the snow with his young son perched on the horse ahead of him. The three voices heard are the desperately encouraging voice of the father, the weakening voice of the son, and the seductive sound of the Earl King calling to the boy. The father is impotent to save his son and the son feels he cannot reach his father. Both are aware of his slipping into death, they can feel him falling. The Earl King betrays by offering a crown to the boy and yet giving a shroud. Both father and son enter different voids.

Sammy had studied and performed much music. For him it represented the possibility of perfection and a connection with the universe. It was linked to "the oneness" and also to a deep sense of coming home. As he put it, when listening to music "it is like being inside the still eye of a tornado, it is quiet like the womb." Even in the stillness or calm there is a feeling that turmoil is not far off. Usually, he could stop himself from crying, but music would get beneath his defences and "connect with the source" and "the lake of tears" that was always somewhere, just out of reach.

Music connected too to what we called the "white wall", the state of perfection that he aspired to. This expression arose one day from his admission that he preferred a perfectly painted blank wall to one ornamented with pictures. There was something about a blemish-free area that would ever and again create the illusion of perfection. But "perfection" could never in reality be a lasting state. Once he had tidied his space or was up to date with his work or had finished a project, he would feel a sudden anxiety as the "void" or "the vastness of self" as he called it, returned. It was as though, in completing his task, he had reached the end of bounded space. It was like climbing a hill and seeing a vista of possibility unfold. This was the void as an openness of choice, and possibilities of self-expression, and it was frightening. If "shoulds" and "oughts", a code-of-behaviour, did not contain him, he would experience a fearful emptiness.

The artist, Kandinsky (1955), writes about white as being active nothingness, but a nothingness that contains everything or contains the potential for everything, that extends like a wall into infinity. His concept does not encourage the questions of what is behind that wall nor whether it is effectible or not.

Sammy's "white wall" was shattered in small ways when he was let down in a variety of situations by family members and friends, and then in a big way when his 82-year-old neighbour was raped and bludgeoned to death. Once the "wall" was down, he started to acknowledge his own shadow aspects, how manipulative and selfish he could be for example, and also to become more aware of his own limitations. His fragility and inability to trust that others could hold him also came into consciousness. He was not always able to keep those he loved safe and alive, he could not ward off danger by being a "good boy". With his growing awareness of his own imperfection, or badness even, came an increased awareness of the "dark side of God" and he was able to talk about his feelings about the Holocaust for the first time in his years of therapy.

He had always had difficulty driving over mountain passes, particularly in the daytime when he could see the drop, i.e. was not enclosed by the darkness. He had rarely spoken to his wife about this fear but drove more and more slowly as the "danger" increased. Now he made himself acknowledge to her what he was going through and how bad he felt. He could in this way receive support and understanding from both himself and her and he managed the passes without much difficulty.

He also noticed that putting a blanket over his duvet gave him a feeling of containment. He could feel his mattress supporting him and his bedding containing him, and in that "warm holding space" drift off easily into sleep.

For Sammy the void was constellated by his anxiety about experiencing life as it was, "the real" as Lacan called it. Perhaps his father's early betrayal of him and subsequent disappearance into jail created a lack of trust that things would generally work out in the end. He defended against his own feeling of inadequacy by arranging that the "invisible hands" should care for him, always under his own control. But it was the stillness within the mother that he achieved rather than being effective within the stormy world. Filling the emptiness within, with his more consciously experienced fears and other emotions, enabled him to live in a more related way without having to wall himself off from the real world. At the same time, he developed a sense of solidity and capacity to peer into the darkness rather than hide the unconsciously presumed worst behind the fantasized "white wall".

Eric

Now a middle-aged professional, Eric, as a child, had needed his over-involved yet often distant mother to protect him from an, at times, brutal father. In adulthood he was plagued by a sense of inner emptiness and a difficulty in finding the right distance from women with whom he was in a relationship. During his marriage and in a later long-term relationship, he experienced an intense loneliness and ennui from which he could rouse himself only through excessive masturbation and porn-surfing on the internet. He experienced those activities as "filling the void". But they interfered with his professional life.

When his relationship ended he was deeply upset, but it slowly dawned on him that he now felt energized, stimulated, and connected with himself. He no longer felt lonely, his obsessional masturbation diminished, and he felt creative stirrings within himself; he wrote poetry and began a long-dreamed of novel. Somehow, when in a relationship with a woman, he lost his sense of identity; his connection with the self became submerged by his drowning in "the mother". In fact, when he was not losing himself in a woman and what she desired of him, he immersed himself in drink or drugs. This seems to be the negative anima experience elucidated by Neumann and suggested above in the section on Active Imagination.

Again, here is a man who suffered from the lack of a father by whom he could feel known, valued, and supported. His father was either away from home furthering his career, or he was too present in a rigidly autocratic way that left Eric feeling misunderstood. His mother offered her ample bosom as a refuge from the violence of the father and as a place of mutual comfort when he abandoned them. But she too could turn away and be too involved in her own work for him to feel held.

So Eric experienced the void constellated by a lack of holding, being alone in space, the void constellated by negative mirroring, "you are not who you think you are", and the void caused by sequestration within the soft maternal embrace which was constantly being reconstituted in his relation to women and to soothing substances. Those soothers, in the shape of alcohol, sex, and drugs, like the soft autistic shapes delineated by Tustin and discussed above, keep the real world at bay but at the price of a felt connection with both oneself and the other.

Behind the veil

I felt a particular warmth and sympathy for a young man who described himself as feeling overcome by a leaden numbness when talking about himself or else as feeling as though he were wrapped in cling-film. His thought was, "If I was someone else I would be OK." Although a successful businessman, in a job that stimulated and challenged him, he always felt "less-than" because he did not feel "beautiful", and the message in his head was, "If you are not beautiful you are not OK." He felt that in just being who he was he was not acceptable and thus he must always be doing for others. In fact, he found it difficult to see the faults in others, particularly women, but would see them in himself.

He was lucky enough to have a mother who was able to articulate to him, as a young man, how depressed and empty she had felt when he was a toddler. She told him how powerless she had felt to reflect back to that toddler the love that she saw streaming out of him and how she had just stared blankly at him.

His father expected him to "do it yourself" but was always critical of the result; "Why didn't you do it the way I would have done it?" He described his experience of a "black hole" which was a cold hard darkness associated with his father. He needed to be open in relation to his mother, so that he could attempt to enliven her and receive any light that might find its way out of her, and yet be closed to his father's destructiveness. Cling-film suggests the thinness of his defences but also the claustrophobia engendered by them.

Timothy

Another image of disconnection came from a post-middle-aged man, "Timothy", who had always felt that he did not really fit in. As a child he had watched others' reactions to find out how he should react, and he had never felt good enough in the eyes of his father or illuminated by the gleam in his mother's eye. He described it like this: "Life is like negotiating a dark inner-city area with tall buildings and not much light but many roads to choose from. I am afraid to make choices and so keep going straight. Others seem to know where they are going and sometimes shine a light for me, a torch in the darkness. But I have always felt that I am not who they think I am and that I must stumble on in my own darkness."

Good feelings had to be suppressed because they may be taken away or not re-conjured and bad feelings suppressed because he might not be able to circumvent them. Desires had to be stifled because they were sinful. He loved thinking-subjects such as mathematics or computer science, within which he felt he could construct a universe that could not be challenged; he could construct the truth. He was attracted to but felt confused by the religious world that offered "revealed" truths, God's truths. His difficulty in a religious context was to differentiate between "truths" that had been constructed by the church, dogmatic truths, and those that were revealing God's will. His quest was for "meaning"; that made him feel solid.

An early thought of his was, "Daddy, I don't need you." To be seen by his father was to be unseen, as he felt that he existed only as an image in his father's eyes rather than that his father's looking at him solidified his own sense of identity. One can have no sense of identity without relationship, but in relationship with his father his identity was false. The seemingly insoluble problem was how to feel related to himself and others at the same time.

An image from his therapy that proved useful over time was that of feeling that he was immersed in the sand of a desert; a dry emptiness in which he was disconnected from both himself and others. When he did something "meaningful" such as become involved in solving a work problem, he would feel relieved, as though he was standing with his head in the fresh air, but yet not fully satisfied. There was another part to the desert image and that was that there was an underground stream or river beneath him that was just out of his reach. The challenge was to discover a way to reach down into that "water of life", for that is what it symbolized, the water of his life.

We came to realize that feelings were the link, not only "good" feelings but the "bad" ones too and as he learnt to immerse himself in those, he felt as though he was rooting himself in the water, the source. The sand then came to symbolize the void of his disconnection, the air above related to church and societal expectations, and the river below to the soul, God, the Self, himself. In a leap of understanding, he realized that thinking had been separating him from himself and the feeling of being connected. In another leap, he realized that even a lowly act such as masturbation could be a link to God. He could link body and spirit.

Another image connects with the Active Imagination mentioned in relation to Wilma. (In *On Active Imagination*) He imaged himself as being imprisoned in a tower, trapped by a black magician. The tower was in a deep forest filled with dangerous beasts and, like Rapunzel's tower, had only a high-up window in it. He felt that, to be freed, he had to convince the magician that he had a plan to deal with the beasts.

A wistful idea was that he could be whisked away by a helpful bird, but otherwise he seemed to have three options: 1) Don a heavy suit of armour and essay forth. 2) Serve the wizard. Or, 3), leap naked from the window into the darkness. The first option seemed like another trap, walling himself off from danger but rendering himself almost immobile. The second, a well-tried fairy-tale solution, he was averse to. So he chose the third and leapt into the unknown, feeling that even though he was falling it was by his own choice. He fell into blackness, silence, emptiness, and yet he felt energized as though this place where nothing was defined, contained the possibility for anything; all *in potentia*.

At his next session he expressed a feeling of no longer knowing "who I am or who God is." He felt reborn and renewed but not in a Christian sense where he "knew" how it would all turn out, instead he was filled with wonder and expectancy. This is the void of creative possibility.

As Timothy surfaced from the depression that he had been in for some long time, he realized that he had become accustomed to dwelling in the dark. He described the state he was now in as being "white" although he felt that the true antithesis of darkness was light. He put it this way, "White has connotations of a wall, it is closed and one can't see into it. It is not generative. Light has depth and movement. Darkness has energy and things happen in it. Even if it is filled with grief and woe it is alive. Black is dead, closed and flat." He valued the darkness that he had been through, and the fact that he had had to wrestle with not knowing. What became clear to him was that he had worked hard to understand both God and himself and understood that what he thought of as God's voice rather than the Church's voice emanated from himself.

Many years ago, Rolf Harris ran a television programme during which he told a story and at the same time drew a picture. The picture made no sense until Harris applied the last stroke of the brush; abruptly its meaning became clear. Timothy felt that his working in the dark was like that, he could not know the outcome of the work until the end but he knew it would not be what he had initially envisaged. You can't find "it" by looking for "it" but its coming into being is connected with the searching.

The discovery will be serendipitous and it will never occur if you are not working at something. (Serendipity has been defined as "searching for a needle in a haystack and finding the farmer's daughter.") (Ashley Robbins, anecdotal communication) God lies behind the "clouds of unknowing" but God will not be discovered should God's identity be "known" with certainty by the searcher. One must work towards something but be open to whatever one might discover, in this way what is *in potentia* might become realized.

Void as a gender experience
Part II: Female encounters

> The breath of life is in the sharp winds of change
> mingled with the breath of destruction.
> But if you want to breathe deep sumptuous life
> Breathe it all alone, in silence, in the dark,
> And see nothing.

> (D.H. Lawrence)

Wilma

ilma, a woman in her mid-fifties, was not empty of herself because she was full of her mother, she was empty of herself because she was empty both of her mother and of any sense of being a loveable person in the world. She had, by this age, a tenuous sense of identity, which would disintegrate when she felt excluded, particularly by one of her children.

Her father had died when she was two months old, a maternal aunt when she was one, and her maternal grandfather when she was aged four. In addition to these catastrophes, which had plunged her mother into depression, Wilma had had to deal with a new stepfather when she was two and a new sibling when she was three. Her mother became an alcoholic and her stepfather was prone to aggressive, even violent, outbursts. Sustained to a certain extent by the house in which she had lived until the age of eleven, when the family moved to another town she expressed her worry that she might now die.

Her lack of mirroring must have been extreme and she can remember how her mother "used to put on a blank face, turn away from me, and sit drunkenly in a dark room." She sometimes thought that her mother was poisoning her food. So Wilma felt that she was nothing, or, later, that she had only a dim outline, like the sort of sign found on the door of a public toilet, but was empty inside. She gained some feeling of substance from the reflected glory of her successful husband and children, and from their loving glances.

Because she only existed in reflection, when the reflecting object reflected a negative image of her or, as happened when her husband became unemployed and her daughter was admitted to a psychiatric clinic, the reflecting object was tarnished, she shrank to a shameful nothingness.

She attempted to flesh herself out by reading "self-help" books on a wide range of subjects such as co-dependency or spirituality or how to deal with a husband or children, etc., but she eventually found that more successful ways were to write poetry and journal her feelings and experiences. Just before entering analysis, she wrote a poem about a tree under its "gay entourage" of leaves. She felt that she focused on those leaves, the outside show, and she had the fear that nothing else existed except for that flimsy exterior. As her therapy progressed, she was amazed to feel the solid substance of the trunk and branches inside her.

I came to feel that the self-help books increased her sense of the "gay entourage", bolstering a surface identity but denying the validity of her own experience, and, in suggesting "this is what you should do", subverting her own creativity. On the other hand, her own poetry, being an expression of her own interior, added to her substantiality.

Wilma demonstrated an aspect of the void experience that is particularly known to women, and that was the feeling of having dropped one of her babies into the void. This was her middle, "easy" child, who fell through the cracks in her attention because of the urgent demands made on Wilma by her other two children.

When crossing an ocean in a small boat, I had a personal experience that let me experience something of the desperation of that feeling. A somewhat deaf man was helming the boat when I went for a "surf"; this meant being pulled behind the yacht holding a rope. My daughter, aged eight at the time, decided to come and join me but found that the speed of the boat was too great and she could not hold on to the rope fixedly enough to prevent herself sliding backwards. I was the backstop but with only one hand to help her and one to keep us connected to the rope. My imagination "saw" her let go and recede behind us. For a few stretched minutes I could not attract the attention of the helmsman or crew. The fantasy of being adrift in mid-ocean while the boat steams away from you is a frightening enough void image, but this other, which is like the snapping of the umbilical cord leaving your baby adrift in space, is absolutely terrifying for a parent.

On South African television was an advertisement for a cellphone network company that showed a newborn baby, still attached to its mother by its umbilical cord, standing teetering on the end of its birth bed. Suddenly it launches itself into space using the cord as a bungee-rope. The punch-line was "seize the minute". This advertisement filled Wilma with anxiety; an anxiety she linked to the feeling of seeing one of her children fall.

In *The Inner World of Trauma*, Donald Kalsched mentions the following dream of a middle-aged single woman: "I see a little girl floating away from a space ship without an umbilical cord, arms outstretched in terror, eyes and mouth distorted as if by a silent scream for her mother." (Kalsched, 1996: 30) The patient's inner-child had long since been abandoned, through her need to care for a large sib-ship, as well as her alcoholic, phobic mother. Both Wilma and this woman had early on slipped from the minds of their mothers and they had allowed each of their own inner-children to slip away from them.

Wilma knew what it was to drop and be dropped, to feel the free fall into space, and to witness her child receding from her irretrievably. For this reason, she tended to cling on to her family and hated the anger that bubbled just below the surface, for she felt that that anger could push her children away from her and they would all be lost. In the dream of leaping from the building that I have mentioned in the section on Active Imagination, she associated the falling with letting go, and felt that that was to do with "giving up control of the family and their interactions." For her, admitting that things were outside of her control was initially worse than owning that she had done something wrong, taking the blame maintained some sense of omnipotence. Landing on her hands and knees in the Active Imagination felt like a submission and realization of her powerlessness, and it was then that she felt the welcoming presence of the women around her.

Shortly before she ended her therapy, she had the following dream: "I am cleaning up a very dingy coffee shop, lining the shelves with clean newspaper and throwing out an old chip-fryer. ("Old fat is damaging to your health" she associated.) I am poor and doing it cheaply but there is a very nice feeling as of "Home". I feel connected with a wide range of people on the street or from the neighbourhood, this feels meaningful and will sustain me."

What initially felt like a dangerous fall turned out to be a descent from too high and disconnected a place, a coming down to earth. In this dream, there is a realization of the dismal and potentially damaging place that she originated from but also that by working at it in a realistic uninflated way, she can come back into her own (home). Hence her statement "I feel I have fallen in love with myself."

Sarah

Sarah's void originated in the experience of a depressed mother and a muddled relationship with a father who was remembered as having been warmly present during her childhood and yet who became progressively more distant, alternating with periods of sudden intrusion, as she grew older. Sarah dwelt behind schizoid defences that she used to shut out the other, seemingly they were a defence against connection with others but we came to understand that actually they protected her from a felt disconnection or non-connection. The mother who turns her back on you creates a chasm between you and her, better to turn your back on her and the emptiness is no longer apparent. As she put it: "If I can't feel seen by others, or taken notice of, then I fall into the void."

This experience surfaced in her therapy where she expressed feeling that she should break the silence to ensure that her therapist was awake and thus alive and present. If he were asleep it would be as if he were dead and then she, being alone, would die too.

At times she felt that life and her work as a lecturer were essentially meaningless but at other times she created what meaning she could as a bridge across the void. Intuition was her dominant function but she used thinking as a way of creating meaning, "I think therefore I am." Another way of attaching meaning and a sense of "going on being" is through connections via memory. Her disabled daughter had a large collection of comforters and she and Sarah would reminisce about when and where they came from, making links across the emptiness.

How this emptiness had arisen, was a question we asked ourselves often. Initially, it seemed as though it arose from her need to shut people out. She experienced contact with "the other" as an unbearable intrusion. The sound of their eating or walking, snoring or even breathing, was an intolerable reminder of their otherness, their not-me-ness. And the fear that came with that was threefold: first, that her aloneness or separateness from them came into consciousness, her need for the other felt again. Second, that she could be invaded by the other, engulfed or colonized (cf. her relation to her mother); and third, that she may lose that which she now consciously desired, contact with this other.

When her brother and father died soon after each other, during her early twenties, she felt that she was now entirely responsible for keeping her mother alive. She had similar feelings about her therapist and about students she taught; she must enliven them. If she could not, she ran the risk of dying herself, falling into nothingness. She would fix her therapist with her gaze that was sometimes desperately quizzical. She felt that if she did not look at him, he may not be there and then she would become too terrified to look, as it was his presence that ensured her "going on being".

Her previous therapist, who left South Africa and therefore terminated with her, had at times felt that the therapy was either disappearing into a hole or was sitting on the surface. In a classical example of Kalsched's ideas on the self-care system, she noted that, whenever she felt that she had made meaningful contact with Sarah during a session, Sarah would miss the next few sessions due to illness. A breakthrough came when she interpreted to Sarah that she felt she was hiding her competence rather than her incompetence from the world. This connected Sarah with memories of her childhood when, as a verbally precocious child, she had deliberately toned down her language so that her father could tell her things and she could feel connected to him. She might, for example, tell him of "the man making sparks" at the garage so that he could tell her "that was a welder".

Her mother had had preconceived (literally) ideas of who Sarah was. Before she was married even, she had told her own mother that she was going to have a girl-child who would be called Sarah. Sarah had had to fight to free herself from the "we-ness" that threatened to immerse her in a oneness with grandmother, mother, and herself. Her mother could not see her as an individual, nor could her father see her as herself. She was void of herself and longed for a reflective identical twin who would know "what is inside my head without my having to communicate."

Presenting as compulsively self-reliant, in Bowlby's sense, she walled herself off from her need for others, taking refuge in ideas or sleep, and yet took on the care of desperately needy individuals, and was clearly in dire need herself. But she only became aware of that need once her defences had been breached.

It was a dream, in which she was giving a lecture to a group of people who paid no attention to her, leaving her feeling devastated and alone, that alerted us to this idea that her way of keeping aloof from others was both a defence against connection and a defence against non- or dis-connection.

Some years into the therapy, she was able to articulate how her therapist's apparent exhaustion upset her: "Your mind may simply slip away through a crack in the fence and leave me alone not seeing my desperate need." Strangely, to be wrongly mirrored by another was in a way reassuring although also distancing. "My analyst (or mother or boss) is alive, but he (she) does not see me; perhaps I am dead." Perhaps it was tolerable because through that she finds a safe distance, somewhere between being engulfed by the other's knowing and being totally but consciously alone. Rilke, in a story of the Prodigal Son, expresses something similar. Here, it is the father's love that the returned son finds intolerable, until he realizes that his father does not know him at all.

The one source of unconditional warmth that Sarah had experienced as a child came from her maternal grandparents, but she had a memory of a conscious decision that she made after a warm holiday with them, aged about seven, to not miss them. To cry about that loss in the present would feel like falling into the void, being "more lonely" in the presence of her analyst, and could, she felt, result in collapse, fragmentation, and admission to hospital. And yet, by cutting herself off from her feelings, she felt alienated from those feelings and from other people.

She also felt cut off from a sensory experience of the world. Having intuition as her dominant function this was not surprising, except in the degree to which it obtained. She could not easily find her way from one place to another unless she followed the exact route that she had pursued for years, and to get to an old place from a new one required careful planning that would take her via a previously travelled route. She could follow verbal instructions and her glove box was filled with scraps of written-down directions kept for future reference.

This difficulty became clear to me one day as she described how she visualized her fifteen-kilometre journey to my rooms as a straight line, in spite of its obvious curves and right-angled turns through the suburbs and along six-lane highways. She thought of her route as being like a seamless tunnel that was enclosed or encapsulated. She doubted whether she would notice even "if someone rubbed out Table Mountain or built a few factories next to the road."

Sarah had been an infant who spoke very early, barking out an instruction to some children when only nine months old and making full sentences before one year. I think she is an example of someone who has become separated from herself by language.

We worked, initially, on the assumption that sensory stimuli did not reach a sufficient intensity to impinge on her, but it later became clear that as a child she had felt intruded on and was easily overcome by such stimuli. They filled her consciousness, leaving little room for thought, so she learnt to block them out. Her choice was chaos or emptiness, and she chose emptiness.

This situation was clearly visible in the first sand-tray that Sarah constructed, trying to get away from words. She placed four small items only; a rabbit and a tortoise at the left rear of the sand-tray, a sewing machine at the right rear and a bridge slightly forward of the centre. Rabbit and tortoise were friends and were going to go over the bridge together, the sewing machine reminded her of her beloved grandmother who had enjoyed sewing; on it clothes could be made for rabbit. I sat on the right side of the sand-tray and I silently felt that the sewing machine referred to her hope that the therapy could indeed clothe her frightened flightiness so that she did not have to go through her empty life encased in a shell. The bridge suggested to me a capacity to connect the opposites together, the transcendent function perhaps.

Two years later, she made another sand-tray; this was after we had been working on aspects of her "compulsive self reliance" and difficulty with taking things in. This was an enormous contrast to the previous one, full of houses, trees, and other vegetation, including vineyards. "My" house, primitively painted, stood where the tortoise-rabbit combination had stood previously and the therapist's "witch-house" was on the right. Both had fruit-bearing trees adjacent to them. Behind was a church and, in front, were two rows of small houses. In her imagination, the left side of the sand-tray, which contained some stones and the bridge from before, extended onto a beach and thence to the sea, while the right side gave onto a farm landscape. There were still no people but a rich feeling of connection and creative possibility had now developed.

Deliberately working on her inferior function, by drawing maps and house plans for example, opened up the outside world to her. She started noticing and enjoying paintings, and the Cape's beautiful scenery, and she found herself able to experiment with different routes, to find her way in the world.

Surgery necessitated her being bedridden for a few weeks during which time she had to receive care from others. In contrast to a previous admission where she had felt that no one could keep her in mind or care for her, now, although initially frightened, she developed a sense of trust in the containing aspects of her world and the people in it, even of her own skin. She realized that "you don't need a wall, a skin will do," and that without a wall you can be more receptive to people. Her void started to shrink; she could accept the love of a man and his presence in her home and life and consider having other children. Now married and living in a dream-house of her own choosing, she remains amazed that life can offer so much that is new and fulfilling and may be chosen. Like a fruit plucked from one of the trees in her sand-tray.

Annette

Annette was another woman, now in her mid-fifties, who felt that no-one could understand or accept her feelings, which were often of intense anxiety and insecurity. Her mother had been the passive recipient of verbal abuse from a "charming" man, Annette's father, and his demands kept her mother away from her. An early memory of hers is of being in her mother's room suffering from severe earache; her mother was present but quite unavailable to her. She felt abandoned to her pain and unable to reach into the empty shell that was her mother.

This is different from Winnicott's aforementioned "being alone in the presence of the mother", a reassuring space that allows the child to discover her own inner impulses. It is different too from Balint's "void in the presence of the mother" where the emptiness is internal, resulting from one's identity being displaced by another. In Annette the emptiness is of the mother and what she stands for, e.g. nurturance, warmth, and acceptance, and results from there not having been a good-enough object to internalize. There has been a severance of connection with the other and a suppression of those of her feelings that could not be contained, also resulting in an internal emptiness.

For her, almost any emotion led to a feeling of vulnerability and an expectation and fear of being alone. She would sleep or take tranquillizers to help her feel more secure, and she binged at times, because any trace of hunger made her worry "where will the next meal come from?" She had no sense that she could understand or accept her feelings and she initially needed her therapist to simply describe to her what she seemed to feel rather than try and interpret why she felt it. In this way she slowly came to be able to identify her feelings and express them to others, thus partially filling the emptiness.

A cycle in the present day went something like this: she felt unable to express to her husband her wishes about a planned holiday with him. This resulted in her feeling empty, so she phoned a friend to commiserate with her, but the friend was unavailable, there was no one to mirror or echo her, and her loneliness expanded. She started to binge, hating herself and feeling an increase in her sense of disconnection and emptiness, and thus experienced an escalating craving.

My sense is that the emptiness could not at that stage have been filled with anything pleasant. After all, there was nothing pleasant in her welter of feelings to fill it with; but it might have been filled with an acknowledgement and acceptance of the awful feelings that were there. And these were the feelings of emptiness and abandonment.

Annette had spent twenty years of her adult life looking after a son who was intelligent but dyslexic and disorganized. She had dedicated her life to helping him succeed and when he left home to live in a flat closer to the university, she experienced a feeling of something being torn away from her chest. She feared that "I will feel that I don't exist anymore. Like entering the void . . . flying through empty space." It was as though she was losing her identity as a mother but had not yet regained her identity as a woman.

After her initial sadness, Annette started doing things for herself and not her son. She noticed the sunset from her balcony, submerged herself in her music, and chose food that she wanted to eat. She began to realize the extent of the self-suppression that being a mother to this needy boy had required of her.

Two episodes of Active-Imagination helped her enormously. The first followed a nightmare in which she had been travelling through the darkness of space with only occasional lights flashing past her. She woke terrified. Re-imagining the dream in her next session she felt alone, abandoned, and not wanting to be there. She then imagined her therapist on the same journey, seeing herself ahead of him and rocketing through empty blackness. As she continued with the Active Imagination, more light infiltrated the scene, and she felt herself slowing down; she felt she was being witnessed by her therapist, there was more sense of connection, and she was less alone. Finally, she landed on grass in the soft dawn light. She was quite alone now but felt at peace with that.

Speaking about her feelings afterwards, she related the sense of connection that she had experienced to her years of psychotherapy and the attention of her analyst. But I felt it was also to do with the witnessing of herself that had recently been taking place, in that she had begun to allow herself to revisit her childhood and find it imperfect. On her arrival back on earth in her active imagination she felt embraced by her own acceptance.

The second Active Imagination was more of an enactment; it started with an image of having a small child on her lap. She followed my suggestion of holding her arms in the position she would have if she were comforting the child. In this posture she experienced a profound two-way connection; she could nurture the child and feel loved by her. At home she found a quiet corner where she sobbed out her relief, and later she could articulate: "I do not feel alone any more—even when I am alone I am with myself."

This episode crystallized for me the idea that one of the ways to the Self is via painful repressed emotion. When we are able to uncover that emotion, we connect with the Self, or the objective psyche, and we feel "in the presence of an-other", no longer in a void. (There is a striking similarity to Gert's observation of feeling alone but with himself. See above.)

Sophia

A Jewish woman who I will call Sophia brought home to me another way that the void can present. For her the void lurked behind the truth about her origins, which she attempted to keep hidden.

Her father had been an unreliable man, not a good breadwinner, and frequently absent from the family. Jewish by birth but not by practice, it was his Jewishness that resulted in the family's small-town business being destroyed by right-wing agitators at the start of the Second World War. Her mother, a non-practising Christian, was a weak woman, not someone whom Sophia felt she could burden with her problems. When Sophia went to a Catholic school, she was treated abusively by the Mother Superior who labelled her a Jew and yet she had no contact with other Jews until one day she stumbled onto a Jewish youth group in her home city. Here she found a sort of home for herself and yet still did not identify herself as being Jewish.

It was some years later that she fell in love with an orthodox young man who made it clear that their marriage depended on her converting to Judaism. She was not Jewish enough. She took this challenge very seriously, moving in with his family and studying dutifully, converting and marrying and keeping a committedly religious home throughout her married life. She celebrated her golden wedding anniversary during her therapy and was mother to four daughters. In spite of being an active member of the Jewish community all her married life, she never felt that this was her rightful "inheritance" and she lived in dread that people would discover that she wasn't "really" Jewish.

She was in her seventies before she could admit to herself how different her likes and dislikes were from those of her husband. She felt that she would be nothing without him and without her children and was always fearful of losing them; "If I lose them, then what am I?" Judaism had become something that identified her and she felt that questioning it threatened her with a loss of identity. Yet she was beginning to realize that there were definite aspects of Judaism of which she disapproved.

In living her life so dutifully, she had amassed an internal library of supportive phrases that people had said to her over the years and she could bring out these sayings to counter her experience of shame. They covered the pit of her shame and thus precluded a full experience of herself. She had lived her life in a "second-skin" way, energetically pursuing sport, business, bridge, and roles in many voluntary organizations, but nothing dislodged the core of emptiness inside.

While in therapy, she dreamed that she was an infant inside a womb. There was an obstructing partition that prevented her taking up the whole space. This was a powerful metaphor for the way she could not grasp the fullness of her own identity. Because of shame she partitioned herself off from her self and felt an emptiness where she could have been full.

Slowly, in her therapy, she learnt to listen to the voice that expressed her own desires, even though expressing that voice out loud brought her into conflict with her husband and children. An image, which presented itself in a dream, was that, she could now stop being sweetly "pink" and become more stridently "orange". This was not a colour that she liked to associate with herself but it was closer to what was often unconsciously expressed in her relationships.

Mary

The patient who has perhaps taught me most about the void I have been seeing for more than ten years, mostly twice a week. I have called her Mary, which may have a connection in my mind to the profaned Magdalene but the name also relates to the idea of Mary as the mother of Christ, the bearer of the possibility of the incarnation of the God image, the Self. As was the Mary portrayed in many of the Renaissance paintings of the Annunciation, Mary has been ambivalent about taking on the full responsibility of that incarnation.

Mary's wounding comes from incest in many of its forms. The family belonged to a fundamentalist religious sect and believed that even thoughts could be known and therefore judged by God, and a spoken "bad" thought heard by the ever-vigilant devil, who could thus gain a foothold in you. There was no sense of an inviolable boundary between the individual and those around her. Her parents attempted to suppress any instinctual connection within Mary by labelling it "sinful". And by insisting that any "sin" performed by even so small a child was another nail into the feet or hands of Jesus, they fostered the development of deep shame and a sense of being responsible for others' suffering.

Incest "ran" in the family, in the sense that Mary's mother was a product of brother–sister incest, there was some form of incest in her father's first-wife's family, and father's family was a secret-filled emptiness. (Who could tell what went on in that dark space?) The many houses that she lived in seemed also to harbour dark secrets, and her early memories have an unreal, nightmarish quality about them, full of painful affect but not of clear pictures. I sometimes feel that she has been penetrated by the darkness.

Her father is a compulsive gambler who aggrandizes himself and his life, paying attention to his daughter for his own needs only, calling her "princess", usually in a bitter way, or else by a boy's name, for he expressed wanting another son. He abused her physically and sexually as a young child. When Mary let out the secret of the incest to her therapist and a close friend, it felt as though she was breaking down the wall that separated the family mush from others and it resulted in her feeling emptier. The emptiness inside had been contained to some extent by the wall of secrecy.

Her mother is also a self-obsessed woman who uses Mary for her own gain and feels that she owns her, "I am your mother after all". As a child Mary was disciplined by her in a sexualized way, shamed by her, and intruded on, and yet abandoned and unprotected by her.

Mary was brought up with a number of foster siblings, a few years older than her, and a half-brother and sister several years older than her, her father's children from a previous marriage. In their adult life this brother has been emotionally abusive and sexually suggestive towards her and Mary has felt that she is powerless to withstand him.

I first met Mary when she was a student, after a suicide attempt that she had made. This followed the ending of an initially loving but finally highly abusive sadomasochistic relationship with the pastor of her church. This had left her confused, distressed, and full of shame. Our journey together has been fraught with difficulties, not least in the transference and countertransference where intimacy seemed to threaten intrusion; to be a loving object was to be an abuser, and to be removed was to seem to abandon.

Mary has always tended to somatize and also dissociate, sometimes "sitting in the corner of the ceiling" of the room, watching the two of us having a session, or sometimes "losing time" particularly after a traumatic session. She had a fear of being alone and a horror of being filled by another. Sometimes it seemed to me that emptiness was her worst fear and at other times she seemed to deliberately court emptiness rather than discover the reality about herself and her family. She could shred or obliterate meaning, experience, and memory in the way that Bion characterizes as minus-K. (Bion, 1967) She could throw aspects of her life into the abyss. During the early years of her therapy, in her avoidance of intimacy, insight, awareness of loss, or self-knowledge, she would choose nothingness rather than facing what was.

On the other hand, she has been absolutely consistent in her involvement in her therapy, fighting Medical Aid companies and employers for her right to continue with it, and delving deeply, fighting the "abyss seeking" aspects of herself. She has returned time and again to the therapeutic encounter, braving what she has felt as my anger or distaste and enduring both her destructive and loving feelings toward me. She has moved out of her parents' apartment, where she had been unable to close the door of her room or lock the bathroom door, to an apartment of her own whose position she kept secret from her parents until it felt truly hers. She now owns her own home.

Hardly letting up on her for a moment, her psyche has thrown up many dreams that have felt both destructive and instructive, and she has engaged with it through painting, drawing, photography, and writing. Some images from her photographs: deserted beaches, one set of footsteps in the sand, green shoots peeping through the snow, dawn over Table Mountain after a storm, a swooping gull over a storm-tossed sea.

Working with computer-distorted photographs of herself, she generated powerful images of failures in mirroring that have led to void experiences. In one set, a group of three mirrors reflected views of herself so distorted that the subject cannot recognize herself. She looks down to see herself, only to see an empty pair of shoes; no one where she should be standing. This work brought the insight that for Mary even inadequate mirroring is better than no mirroring because without some sort of reflection she ceases to exist. She is thus in a continual search for a mirroring object with whom to connect and she feels that she would sell her soul, or body, to effect connection with that new object.

In relation to her mother, who was a teacher at the primary school Mary attended, Mary felt wrongly seen and, further, that her mother would force her view of Mary into the other teachers; there was no place for Mary to hide. In trying to be appreciated she would be super-good, repressing her childish desires, thus severing the connection with her Self, but then she felt like an ornament in the house that was more or less unnoticed. Being "bad", of course, resulted in severe retribution.

Her lack of a sense of self showed itself in undifferentiated feelings characterized by the colours red and black rather than being describable in words; in fact, in our early sessions she was often wordless. She was initially unable to separate hunger from thirst in her mind, or know when or how much to eat. She was able to say what food her mother liked but not the same for herself. Any feelings, positive or negative, towards another were potentially sexualized and therefore dangerous.

As a self-comforting procedure she used to rock and I once asked her what she thought it would feel like if she were to stop rocking. She replied: "As though I would leak away. I feel like a container that is a reject from a factory. I am lonely and small and alone." Other fears of hers were like Winnicott's "primitive agonies"; that she was falling or slipping off the edge of the known world, adrift in deep space, crashing into "the other side", going mad, or was being compressed by something.

She was also scared of knowing the truth, e.g. about having been abused, or of really knowing the person she was relating to. When I suggested one day that looking into the eye of the other meant that one could see one's reflection and also see the other, she retorted, "But I'm too scared to look." This was one of the reasons that Mary was unable to make eye contact with me during sessions.

Looking into a mirror and seeing no reflection of oneself there is terrifying. If you know you exist then the lack of reflection says something about the reflector, but if you do not know that you exist then the lack of reflection confirms your non-existence. Mary portrayed this situation in another image. She photographed her reflection standing in front of a mirror and then, on her computer, extracted the colour from the image so that emptiness took the place of the person. A group of Teddy Bears sit dispassionately by and are reflected in the mirror. They link the real and reflected worlds and seem more filled with life than does her empty shell.

When friends, or someone she had formed a close connection with, left the country, she relegated them to the void, leaving emptiness where they once had been. She was initially unable to stay with the love and the loss, the grief. Loved objects had been gathered into the area of infantile omnipotence and rather than confront her lack of omnipotence, she made the loved objects into nothing. Her ego was not capable of enduring the torment that would otherwise ensue.

In relation to her primary objects it is different, here, to avoid intimacy or else the loss of connection that might result from insight and self-knowledge, she chooses nothingness for herself. For her, to be as nothing is preferable to knowing the truth about her father, the abuser, and the mother who has never "seen" her, and to her being aware of her own weakness and reliance on these essentially unreliable objects. To know them as they truly are would be to demolish the fantasy that she has built up around them. In fact, it would be to deliver them over to the void, leaving her, a vulnerable infant, adrift in space.

A vivid dream of playing on a multicoloured carpet highlighted the fact that her contact with her therapist opened up a world of colour, light, and life. Leaving the therapeutic space, on the other hand, felt at times like being swirled about into a grey world, the ground tilting under her feet. Often, connection with her therapist would be followed by the sort of attack by the self-care-system that Kalsched describes; this was traumatizing at first but later healing as she began to be able to remember both the closeness and the resultant attack. In that way she could start mapping the void.

She described an image of a neglected kitten or infant inside her that I wondered how she could care for. "What if there is nothing inside?" she asked. When I asked which would be worse, the neglected infant or nothingness, she responded, "I feel I should say that it is better to care for the infant than to let it die ... but perhaps emptiness is better." Aliveness penetrates to the quick; if the infant died she would no longer feel its pain.

To obtain nurture from the outside world seemed hopeless and to nurture herself was problematic. Her reaction to a picture of the uroborus was that for a snake to eat itself would be painful and also it may poison itself. (In *Another "Black Hole"*) She had no feeling that it could also represent something generative.

One of her poems "I stretch forth" I quote in full as it captures so much of the void experience and how that experience can be secondary to something else, a defence.

I stretch forth, but pull back in repulsion
For the known touch of coldness
Of emptiness full of doubts and confusion
For glass that bounces secrets within itself
A Johari's window of the unknown
A cube crying to be solved, but not broken
A university of needs with a primary school of answers.

I stretch forth, but pull back at the fear
The fear of the unknown becoming an unacceptable known.
The glass of emptiness becoming the vastness of vulnerability
And the saucer of unfeeling becoming
The storm tossed expanse of the sea—uncontrollable
And unable to confine—raw and irrepressible.

I look forth and shrink back in repulsion
At the shadow image I confront before me
To avoid is to remain uncertain
But to remain uncertain provides safety
Safety from the madness I may be.

I pray and cry a tearless plea
That what I think and believe **is** a dream of nothingness
For then at least I can wake up to more
More life, more known
More me.

It may be preferable to live in a void because there is something more fearful out there. It is as though she has tried to encapsulate her life and its experiences to prevent them expanding into something outside of her control. But it is already outside of her control and what she is repelled by and fearful of become the walls of the prison in which she is alone, void of contact with another and with the other within.

Coldness, emptiness, confusion, doubting, i.e. not knowing, are all attributes of the void, and the glass, "that bounces secrets within itself", a vivid symbol of that which is hidden in what appears to be clear. Alongside her fear is her terror of that "university of needs"; needs that have little chance of being met and may simply overwhelm. (Mary described her mother as being like a vortex of need that threatens to suck her in, and her own needs are similarly threatening.) It is better to keep the feelings "unfelt", then, one can believe, they won't take you over.

She makes that seem possible—the emptiness contained in a glass, the "unfeeling" in a saucer—and alluring; better that containment, or imprisonment even, than the irrepressible unconfinable needs that might express themselves as feelings and submerge her in an ocean of madness.

She begs for the solution that she thinks will free her, which is to discover that what she deeply believes, but cannot fully allow herself to believe, is <u>not</u> true. That it was just an insubstantial dream. She wishes beyond anything to "know" that her father did not sexually abuse her, that her parents did not physically and emotionally misuse her, that her mother did not turn a blind eye. It is a wan hope, given the amount of felt evidence that she has amassed, but one that she cannot let go of, and, paradoxically, it is that hope that keeps her from experiencing what she most desires, herself. If she could join with those other wayfarers journeying into Hell, and, as Dante's gateway instructs "Abandon all hope, ye who enter here", she may come to accept her knowledge of her past and her own life might begin.

Mary heard the song *Let Me Fall* sung by Josh Groban on the radio one day; it struck a deep chord. The song, written by Linda Thompson, begins by capturing the ambivalence of the state before the fall.

Let me fall
Let me climb
There is a moment when fear
And dreams must collide.

The dreams take you up and the fall takes you down and at some time there must be a collision between the two. What Mary has begged for is that her stretching, looking forth, will find the answer that she longs to find and not the answer that she dreads she is falling towards. Yet to fall is precisely what Mary has to do, As the song continues:

. . . fall
Away from all these
Useless fears and chains.

Someone I am
Is waiting for courage
The one I want
The one I will become
Will catch me.

"The one I will become" must surely refer to the Self, her wholeness as an individual, and it is that wholeness that can accept and contain her, all parts of her.

It is Mary's defences against the void that keep her in the void. It will be at the moment (or those repeated, many moments) when she acknowledges to herself that her fears are deeply founded and not a "dream of nothingness", that moment of falling and of the death of what she wishes were true, that she can wake up to more—"more life, more known, more me."'

From the therapist's point of view there is little to be done except to be there as a supportive witness. He cannot know the outcome of her fall before it happens and, as the song points out, "The phoenix may or may not rise". Glib assurances are not helpful. We do not know beforehand whether the work will end in destruction, death without resurrection, or a miraculous birth.

Will Mary be submerged under the enormity of her emotions, "the vastness of her vulnerability"? In spite of not knowing the outcome and fearing the worst, she follows her impulse to stretch forth. That push comes from deep within her and has led to a journey, full of anxiety and self-doubt. Yet, I think it is a journey that will save her eventually, once she is able to relinquish her need to be good and to have good parents, and instead embrace the protean manifestations of herself; that self that is good and bad, wise and idiotic, playful and serious, childlike and aged, supportive and destructive.

Mary had often spoken about the many voices within and it seemed to me that part of the emptiness of her experience was that she refused to accept many of the parts that gave rise to these voices and would act in a way that was contrary to the impulses they articulated. If she felt angry and rebellious, she would appear softly contrite, if fragile, she would seem darkly brooding and self-attacking. It took years before she could accept, let alone feed, a need rather than beat herself up for having it.

Having read *The Obsidian Mirror* by Louisa Wisechild (1988), she started naming and cataloguing the different manifestations of herself. Initially horrified, as she felt this "naming of parts" indicated how sick she was, she slowly put more energy into it and, in the course of a few weeks, identified more than 30 splinter parts. These she put together in a sort of mind-map and was able to see how each had some sort of role within her. Some worked together, some individually, and some were divisive or plainly destructive.

Part of her fear was that where there had been a big emptiness inside, there were now "a thousand small emptinesses". Over time, and through the careful work of definition, the emptinesses seemed to take in substance and then she became frightened of being over-whelmed by them. Haltingly, she came to imagine that the paper on which she drew this mind-map was like her whole psyche and that none of the parts was as powerful as that "bigness". Her ego was doing the work of looking and identifying and bringing together the disparate parts and became stronger and more coherent each time it did so.

Each part may become filled by a differentiating knowledge and, with a little help, can lead to variety and vitality. Since my first draft of this paper, Mary has explored, in increasing depth and by using artistic techniques, multiple aspects of these fragments of herself. As she has done so, they have taken on more and more three-dimensionality and become increasingly incorporated into her being-in-the-world. Consequently, her experience of the void, while not absent, is more tolerable and her experience of her own life increasingly richly differentiated.

Comparing the genders

Looking for the common threads in the stories of the nine men for whom the void has been an issue, we find that their fathers are mostly described as being weak, absent, or over-critical, or even moderately abusive. The father's weakness was mostly in relation to the mother, who was described by the men as being emasculating and/or penetrating. The father's absence was portrayed in terms such as "absentee landlord", "void where my father should have been", "no clothes on his side of the cupboard", "a black hole" or "a cold hard darkness". In some cases, there was a feeling that the father could not value the child for whom he was, although that sometimes changed in adulthood so that the admired adult son had difficulty remembering his negatively viewed child predecessor.

Being let down by a respected father, being betrayed by the father that you trusted, is another theme in some of these men. That betrayal is on a spectrum from complete abandonment, through "not seeing", to physical abuse; although gross physical abuse was not part of the histories of these void dwellers. Perhaps being abused is to be taken notice of and it also hardens the child's view of the sort of man his father is. The father's absence seems to be the most void-generating trauma. Looked at from the child's perspective "not being recognized by my father" is what he suffers.

In relation to their mothers, the commonalities are that the mother is often emasculating in her relationship with the father and that she sees the child in a one-sided way. One man complained of his mother not seeing his bad side and another that she could not ever see the good in him. In this one-sided way of being seen one's identity is lost. In two of these cases the mother thrust her views of how or even whom the child should be into them. Only one man expressed that his mother had been depressed when he was a child and that she was thus unable to reflect him.

Two of the men showed a sort of compulsive self reliance that left them empty of feelings for themselves, especially with regard to knowledge about their frail sides, coupled with a need to succour those in their surroundings. Many felt cut off from others and from themselves and yearned for an uncomplicated connection; for connection, when it came, often felt engulfing.

Clearly, it is impossible to say whether these parental factors are causative or a result of looking back through the tinted lenses of their pathology. But looked at symbolically, the primary defect is one of not finding a structure that is containing in the face of "the real" chaos that is life. Imposed structure often comes from the masculine side as opposed to the gift of the sort of felt rhythmic structure that comes from the feminine. A lack of any early felt structure will lead to a search and reliance on externally imposed structures. These may be supportive and yet constricting for the rest of a man's life, giving rise to the commonly seen combination of extroverted thinking and sensation that link a man to the ideas of other men and to concrete reality, but these may separate him from himself and a comfortable intuition of the great unknown.

With my female patients, the pattern has been different, here the presence of a depressed mother is much more commonly articulated and if the mother was not depressed, she is likely to have been ineffectual, passive or masochistic. All these ways of being a mother are likely to leave the child feeling un-mirrored and not acceptable to anyone.

The absence of the father seems to have had a more secondary role in these women, perhaps in not having been there to "rescue" the child from the maternal embrace, from the "we-ness" of mother and child. However, the combination of a sexually intruding father and an emotionally intrusive mother who yet "does not see" is particularly damaging to the sense of being a separate and valuable individual.

The constellation of the compulsively self-reliant person is common in these women, presumably because it results in a loss of connection to one's wholeness. One cannot easily succour someone in the outside world without sacrificing that inner connection. As Bowlby described, this constellation is one of the products of anxious attachment in infancy and there will also have been societal role expectations at play that push the female child into a caring role and away from herself.

Summary

In these chapters, I have given many clinical examples of the void experience as described by my patients, in order to flesh out the felt nature of the void and to suggest the wide variety of causative features. Mostly these cases describe the sorts of trauma that have given rise to the pathological feeling of being in a void but I would stress again that dealing with that primary experience leads to a strengthening of the individual's capacity to more willingly enter the "clouds of unknowing" that are appropriately encountered in and post mid-life.

For some, the void experience has been central to the work, whereas for others it seems to have been of little significance. Again, for some the void is to be shied away from and for others it is at least tolerated if not deliberately sought and embraced. I have no doubt that the capacity to tolerate and accept the void is of great importance in psychological health and that the psychotherapist has a significant role to play in helping to foster the right attitude towards it.

Rilke reminds us that:

All of us are falling. See this hand now fall.
And now see the others; it is part of all.
And still there is one who in his hands gently
Holds this falling endlessly.

And Winnicott wrote:

On the seashore of endless worlds
Children play.

May we learn to live, work, and play alongside the great emptiness and find that it does contain us and everything else imaginable.

NOTES

1. When I use the word mother, it frequently has connotations far wider than that of the personal mother. As *The Great Mother* (Neumann, 1963) she carries both negative and positive traits, masculine and feminine aspects, traits of The Good Mother and of The Terrible Mother. The mother who helps one grow within her embrace as well as the mother who prevents that growth by squeezing too hard. The life-giving as well as the death-bringing mother. She is symbolized by anything that contains, from the uterus or a vessel of some sort, to a coffin or grave. She is symbolized too by matter of any sort and by anything that grows or fosters growth, i.e. the animal and vegetable kingdoms. One can imagine ever-widening circles of "containment", as within a Russian doll. A child in a family, in a cave, in a mountain, on the earth, in a galaxy, in the cosmos, within the void, these are all maternal images.

    The actual human mother is, in general, an attenuated, humanized version of this great archetype but she too can move towards the extremes of hostile rejection or benevolent acceptance. Mother substitutes may be as varied as the pleasant nursery-school teacher, the authoritarian army, whose structures make it unnecessary for you to thinkingly care for yourself, or an overzealous keep-you-safe-at-all-costs government

2. I describe many different void words or conditions that for some may be experienced as states of emptiness. I do not mean to imply that all individuals will always have the void constellated for them by these states, rather that these are states that have been brought to my attention by a wide range of individuals over time. Not everyone

will find not-knowing to be a frightening experience, for example, some will find it comforting. Nevertheless, where we defend against knowing, there will be an area of emptiness within that could be called void. Meaninglessness is another example of an experience that may be felt as threatening or as comforting. Perhaps this highlights my thesis that the void is not necessarily something negative.

3. Fordham.

4. What is meant by the self or one's self or the Self is a potentially fuzzy area in Jungian psychology. When I use Self with a capital S, I mean the purely Jungian idea of the wholeness of the individual, containing both conscious and unconscious aspects, but also the central ordering principle behind that wholeness. I think of the Self as being virtually limitless shading away at its periphery into what it is simply to be human. This implies a downward connection to the animal world as well as an upward expansion into the world of the gods. Wilber calls the Self the only Jungian archetype that is truly transpersonal and it has been called the God image within the psyche.

   The sense of self is closer to a sense of identity, the conscious feeling of "who I am". When I use self without a capital, it is that sense that I am writing about. This is closer to a sort of amalgam between ego-identity and persona (the external or social mask that we wear).

5. Meltzer coined the term *claustrum*, which comes from the Latin word meaning cloister or an enclosed space. The implication is that an individual retreats into a fantasized space of this type, as a defence against the openness of reality.

6. A thorn-kraal is a South African term for an enclosure for livestock constructed from branches of thorn trees.

7. God or gods. I use these words in a psychological rather than a metaphysical context and I use them because they have a meaningful resonance within most of us whether religious or not. I do not wish to enter the debate about whether God exists as an external-to-the-individual being and I have been careful to speak about God in terms that do not define or limit God. I like Bion's formulation of "O" as being "ultimately unknowable reality" and the Jungian idea of the Self being the God image within the psyche. They both give one the sense of the felt reality of the concept of God but also of its ineffable nature. In this sense God, the pleroma and the void are not far apart.

The word god is more strictly defined as a superhuman being or object of worship and I use that more as a word that expresses the feeling of an archetype or a complex that seems to have an origin outside of what is felt as "me". In this sense the gods seem to thwart the individual often and do require an attitude of reverence. Whether we stand against them or let them guide us they do need to be taken seriously.

8. The Other, other or object. Again, these are words that I use because of their deep resonance and multiplicity of meanings. The word "other" means something or someone that is different from the subject, from the sense of being "me". Thus, it can refer to another person (often called "object" to differentiate it from the "subject") or, as a plural, to a group who are different. Or it may refer to an interior figure that feels foreign, like one of the "gods" or complexes. The first "other" that a developing consciousness becomes aware of is the breast or the mother, and this suggests that "the other" can refer to a part- as well as a whole object. When I use a capital O I mean the word to carry more significance or weight and it is then closer to the idea of the Self or God.

9. Uroboric or ouroboric. The (o)uroborus is depicted as a dragon or snake with its tail in its mouth and it is symbolic of both consumption and renewal, life and death, movement and stillness. In Jungian literature it has come to represent both the Eternal Round, with all *in potentia*, and the primitive state of non-differentiation. It is often given a negative connotation as symbolic of the regressive impulse to return to paradise before the fall, a pre-conscious state, but it may also refer to a transcendental state.

BIBLIOGRAPHY

Adler, G. (1979). *Dynamics of the Self.* London: Coventure.

Adler, G. & Buie, D.H. (1979). Aloneness and borderline psycho-pathology: the possible relevance of child development issues. *International Journal of Psychoanalysis, 60*: 83–95.

Alighieri, D. (translated by C.H. Sisson, 1980). *The Divine Comedy.* Oxford: Oxford University Press.

Ashton, P.W. (2002). Review of "The Jewel in the Wound". *Mantis, 14/1.*

Baal-Teshuva, J. (2003). *Mark Rothko: Pictures as Drama.* Köln: Taschen.

Bailey, J. et al. (1981). *Gods and Men: Myths and Legends from the World's Religions.* Oxford: Oxford University Press.

Balint, E. (1993). *Before I was I: Psychoanalysis and the Imagination.* London: Free Association Books.

Ballou, R.O., Spiegelberg, F., & Friess, H.L. (Eds.) (1939). *The Bible of the World.* London: Kegan Paul.

Beckett, S. (1956). *Waiting for Godot.* London: Faber and Faber.

Beckett, S. (1979). *The Trilogy.* London: Picador.

Beckett, W. (1999). *Sister Wendy's 1000 Masterpieces.* London: Dorling Kindersley.

Berg, A. (2002). Ancestor reverence. *Mantis, 14/1.*

Bick, E. (1968). The experience of the skin in early object relations. *International Journal of Psychoanalysis, 49*: 484–486.

Bion, W.R. (1967). *Second Thoughts.* London: Karnac Books.

Boe, A. (1989). *Edvard Munch.* Barcelona: Ediciones Poligrafa.

Buckley, J.H. (1958). *Poems of Tennyson.* Boston: Houghton Mifflin Company.

Carim, E. (1969). *The Golden City.* New York: Grove Press.

de Chardin, P. (1955). *The Phenomenon of Man.* London: Collins.

Charles, M. (2000a). Convex and concave, part I: images of emptiness in women. *American Journal of Psychoanalysis, 60/1.*

Charles, M. (2000b). Convex and concave, part II: images of emptiness in men. *American Journal of Psychoanalysis, 60/2.*

Cooper, J.C. (1978). *An Illustrated Encyclopaedia of Traditional Symbols.* London: Thames and Hudson.

Cowan, L. (2002). *Tracking the White Rabbit: A Subversive View of Modern Culture.* Hove: Brunner-Routledge.

Cowan, L. (2004). *Portrait of the Blue Lady: The Character of Melancholy.* New Orleans: Spring Journal Books.

Dante Alighieri (translated by C.H. Sisson, 1998). *The Divine Comedy.* Oxford: Oxford University Press.

Davis, M. & Wallbridge, D. (1990). *Boundary and Space: An Introduction to the Work of Winnicott.* London: Karnac.

Desteian, J.A. (1989). *Coming Together—Coming Apart.* Boston: Sigo Press.

Dike, F. (1976). *The Sacrifice of Kreli.* In Johannesberg: Theatre 1 Domker, A.D. Premiered at the Space Theatre, Cape Town on 16th July 1976.

Doidge, N. (2001). Diagnosing the English Patient: schizoid fantasies of being skinless and of being buried alive. *Journal of the American Psychoanalytic Association, 49/1*: 280sq.

Dourley, J.P. (2004). Memory and emergence: Jung and the mystical anamnesis of the nothing. In: *Proceedings of the 17th International Congress for Analytical Psychology.*

Edinger, E.F. (1972). *Ego and Archetype.* New York: Putnam.

Edinger, E.F. (1985). *Anatomy of the Psyche.* La Salle, Illinois: Open Court.

Edinger, E.F. (1995). *The Mysterium Lectures.* Toronto: Inner City Books.

Eliot, T.S. (1950). *The Cocktail Party.* London: Faber and Faber.

Eliot, T.S. (1974). *Collected Poems 1909–1962.* London: Faber and Faber.

Emanuel, R. (2001). A-void—an exploration of the nature and defences against nothingness. *International Journal of Psychoanalysis, 82/6*: 1069.

Eve, N. (2001). *The Family Orchard.* London: Little, Brown and Co.

Fox, M. (1980). *Breakthrough: Meister Eckhart's Creation Spirituality in New Translation.* New York: Doubleday.

Freud, S. (1960). *Totem and Taboo.* London: Routledge and Kegan Paul.

Gardner, W.H. (1953). *Poems and Prose of Gerald Manley Hopkins.* Harmondsworth: Penguin Books.

Gibson, M. (1999). *Symbolism.* Köln: Taschen.

Giegerich, W. (2004). The death of meaning and the birth of man: an essay about the state reached in the history of consciousness and an analysis of C.G. Jung's psychology project. *Journal of Jungian Theory and Practice*, 6/1: 1–66.

Graves, R. (1955). *The Greek Myths: Volumes 1 & 2*. Middlesex, England: Penguin Books.

Grimm, Brothers (1975). *The Complete Grimm's Fairy Tales*. London: Routledge.

Grotstein, J.S. (1997). *Bion's "Transformation in 'O'" and the Concept of the "Transcendent position"*. (Obtained from the Internet.)

Henderson, H. (1995). Sound and symbols in childhood pathologies. In: *Proceedings of the Congress on Infant Mental Health*. Cape Town: University of Cape Town.

Hill, S. (1989). *The Accumulation of Small Acts of Kindness*. London: Chatto and Windus.

Hollis, J. (1994). *Under Saturn's Shadow*. Toronto: Inner City Books.

Hooke, S.H. (1963). *Middle Eastern Mythology*. Middlesex, England: Penguin Books.

James, W. (1960). *The Varieties of Religious Experience*. London: The Fontana Library.

Johnston, W. (1973). *The Cloud of Unknowing*. New York: Doubleday.

Johnston, W. (1993). *The Mystical Way*. London: HarperCollins.

Jung, C.G. (1959). *Collected Works 9, Part ii*.

Jung, C.G. (1963). *Collected Works 14*.

Jung, C.G. (1966a). *Collected Works 15*.

Jung, C.G. (1966). *Collected Works 16*.

Jung, C.G. (1967). *Memories, Dreams, Reflections*. London: Fontana Press.

Jung, C.G. (1968). *Seminar on Nietsche's* Zarathustra. Princeton, NJ: Princeton University Press.

Jung, C.G. (1969a). *Collected Works 8* (Second Edition).

Jung, C.G. (1969). *Collected Works 11* (Second Edition).

Jung, C.G. & Basilides (1916). *Septem Sermones ad Mortuos*. (Translated by H.G. Baynes.)

Kalsched, D. (1996). *The Inner World of Trauma: Archetypal Defences of the Personal Spirit*. London: Routledge.

Kandinsky, W. (1955). *Concerning the Spiritual in Art*. New York: George Wittenborn, Inc.

Klonsky, M. (1980). *Blake's Dante*. London: Sidgwick and Jackson Ltd.

Kundera, M. (1980). *The Book of Laughter and Forgetting*. Bungay: Penguin.

Lahr, J. (2003). Men behaving badly. *The New Yorker*, Jan. 27th.

Laing, R.D. (1965). *The Divided Self.* London: Pelican.

Lawrence, D.H. (1950). *Selected Poems.* Middlesex, England: Penguin.

Macdonald, A.M. (1967). *Chambers Etymological Dictionary.* London: W & R Chambers.

McDougall, J. (1986). *Theatres of the Mind.* London: Free Association Books.

Manguel, A. (1993). *The Gates of Paradise: The Anthology of Erotic Short Fiction.* New York: Three Rivers Press.

Mann, T. (1951). *The Holy Sinner.* London: Penguin.

Meier, C.A. (Ed.) (2001). *Atom and Archetype: The Pauli/Jung Letters.* Princeton: Princeton University Press.

Meltzer, D. (1965). The relationship of anal masturbation to projective identification. *International Journal of Psychoanalysis, 47.*

Meltzer, D. (1967). *The Psycho-Analytical Process.* Perthshire: Clunie Press.

Milner, F. (1995). *Frida Kahlo.* London: PRC Publishing.

Moore, T. (2003). *The Soul's Religion.* London: Bantam Books.

Neumann, E. (1954). *The Origins and History of Consciousness.* New York: Pantheon.

Neumann, E. (1959). *The Archetypal World of Henry Moore.* London: Routledge and Kegan Paul.

Neumann, E. (1963). *The Great Mother.* New Jersey: Princeton University Press.

Owen, M. (2002). *Jung and the Native American Moon Cycles.* San Francisco: Red Wheel/Weiser.

Pecotic, B. (2002). The "black hole" in the inner universe. *Journal of Child Psychotherapy, 28:* 41–52.

Piontelli, A. (1989). A study on twins before and after birth. *International Review of Psycho-Analysis, 16:* 413–25.

Piontelli, A. (1992). *From Foetus to Child: An Observational and Psychoanalytic Study.* London: Routledge.

Rilke, R.M. (1967). *Sonnets to Orpheus.* (Translated by J.B. Leishman.) London: Hogarth Press.

Rilke, R.M. (1986). *Letters to a Young Poet.* (Translated by S. Mitchell.) New York: Vintage Books.

Rilke, R.M. (1987). *The Selected Poetry of Rainer Maria Rilke.* (Translated by S. Mitchell.) London: Pan Books.

Robinson, H.S. & Wilson, K. (1962). *The Encyclopaedia of Myths and Legends of all Nations.* London: Kaye and Ward Ltd.

Rustin, M. (2001). The therapist with her back against the wall. *Journal of Child Psychotherapy, 27/3:* 273–84.

Salinger, J.D. ( ). *The Catcher in the Rye.*

Samuels, A., Shorter, B., & Plaut, F. (1986). *A Critical Dictionary of Jungian Analysis.* London: Routledge.

Satinover, J. (1980). Puer aeternus: the narcissistic relation to the self. *Quadrant.*

Schellinski, K. (2004). *Life after Death: The Replacement Child's Search for Self.* Paper at the 16th Congress of the IAAP, Barcelona.

Schindler, M. (1964). *Goethe's Theory of Colour.* Sussex: New Knowledge Books.

Schonstein Pinnock, P. (2000). *Skyline.* Cape Town: David Philip Publishers.

Schopenhauer, A. (1970). *Essays and Aphorisms.* London: Penguin Books.

Schore, A.N. (2004). Commentary. *South African Psychiatry Review, 7/3:* 16–17.

Schwartz-Salant, N. & Stein, M. (1988). *The Borderline Personality in Analysis.* Wilmette, IL: Chiron Publications.

Smith, D.N. (Ed.) (1921). *Wordsworth: Poetry and Prose.* Oxford: Oxford University Press.

Solomon, H. (2004). Self creation and the limitless void of dissociation: the "as if" personality. *Journal of Analytical Psychology, 49:* 635–656.

Stein, M. (1998). *Jung's Map of the Soul: An Introduction.* Chicago: Open Court.

Stern, D.N. (1985). *The Interpersonal World of the Infant.* USA: Basic Books.

Stevens Sullivan, B. (1989). *Psychotherapy Grounded in the Feminine Principle.* Illinois: Chiron Publications.

Taylor, C.H. & Finley, P. (1997). *Images of the Journey in Dante's Divine Comedy.* New Haven: Yale University Press.

Tembo, M. (1996). *Legends of Africa.* New York: Metro Books.

Tustin, F. (1988). Psychotherapy with children who cannot play. *International Review of Psycho-Analysis, 15:* 93–106.

Valman, H.B. & Pearson, J.F. (1980). What the fetus feels. *British Medical Journal,* Jan. 26th: 233–234.

Von Franz, M.-L. (1972). *Creation Myths.* Dallas: Spring Publications.

Von Franz, M.-L. (1990). *Individuation in Fairy Tales.* Boston: Shambhala.

Waddell, M. (1998). *Inside Lives.* London: Duckworth.

Weinberg, S. (1983). *The First Three Minutes. A Modern View of the Origin of the Universe.* London: Fontana Paperbacks.

White, P. (1966). *The Solid Mandala.* Middlesex: Penguin Books.

Wilber, K. (1991). *Grace and Grit.* Boston: Shambhala.

Wilkinson, P. (1998). *Illustrated Dictionary of Mythology*. London: Dorling Kindersley.

Williams, G. et al. (Eds.) (2003). *Exploring Feeding Difficulties in Children: The Generosity of Acceptance. Volume 1*. London: Karnac.

Winnicott, D. (1947). Hate in the countertransference. In: *Collected Papers: Through Paediatrics to Psycho-Analysis*. London: Hogarth, 1958.

Winnicott, D. (1963). Fear of breakdown. In: *Psycho-Analytic Explorations*. London: Karnac Books, 1969.

Winnicott, D. (1965). *The Maturational Processes and the Facilitating Environment*. London: Hogarth.

Wisechild, L.M. (1988). *The Obsidian Mirror*. Washington: Seal Press.

Wright, K. (1991). *Vision and Separation—Between Mother and Baby*. London: Free Association Books.

INDEX

abandonment:
  by God, 115–116
  as void experience, 67
absence: as void experience,
  215
absence of proof: as void
  experience, 69
abusiveness, 108–109, 110–112
abyss: and void, 9
acceptance, 206
Ackermann, D., 176
active attitude, 164–165
active imagination, 185–186
  clinical vignettes:
    Annette, 241–242, 287–290
    anonymous, 242–243
    Timothy, 242
    Wilma, 227–229, 233–234,
      239, 243
  function, 240
  Jung on, 232–233, 236–237
Adam, *see* Dimitri
addiction, 166–167, 212–213, 239
Adler, G., 101
Alan: psychic retreats (clinical
  vignette), 22
albedo, 232

alexithymia, 106, 194
Alighieri, D.:
  Divine Comedy, 142
    Inferno, 105, 201–202, 212,
      263
    Purgatorio, 211–212
All, the, 8, 11
aloneness:
  and memory loss as void
    experience, 102–103
  as void experience, 221–223
Amity: empty of oneself (clinical
  vignette), 74–76
anaesthesia: and void, 39–40
Anderson, H., 220
Angier, C., 111
anima, 163
Annette: active imagination
  (clinical vignette), 241–242,
  287–290
annunciation, the: depictions of,
  146
anomie: and void, 16–17
antinomies, 225–226
archetypes, 53–54, 66
Aron: void as disconnection
  (clinical vignette), 136–137

art:
    coniunctio in, 237–238
    symbolist, 131
    unio naturalis in, 237
Ashton, P.W., 40
Asper, K., 67
atonement, 150
autism, *see* psychogenic autism
autistic objects: as defences, 82–83,
    88
autistic shapes, 167, 217–218
    as defences, 83–84, 88
awe, 50, 51

Babylon: creation myths, 128–129
Bailey, J., 128
Balint, E., 72–74, 75, 76, 155, 225
    Empty of Oneself, 18, 200
    Before I was I, 72–74
    on mirroring, 94–95
Balint, M., 106
Balou, R.O., 128
Bantu: in creation myths, 126
Barrie, J.M., 92
Basilides & Jung, C.G.: *Seven
    Sermons to the Dead*, 30, 55–56,
    59, 188, 235
Beatles, The, 38, 65
Beckett, Samuel: *Waiting for Godot*,
    7
Beckett, Wendy, 11, 131
behaviour: incorrect, 114
Benny: fathers and the void
    (clinical vignette), 264–268
Bible:
    New Testament:
        1 Corinthians 13, 47
        John 1.1, 125, 205, 238
    Old Testament:
        Ecclesiastes 4.1, 245
        Job 38, 175
        Proverbs 8.22, 130

Proverbs 8.23, 130
Psalms 22.1–2, 171
Psalms 22.6, 171
Psalms 22.14–15, 171
Psalms 23.1–6, 173
Psalms 139.1–2, 173–174
Bick, E., 23–24
Big Bang: and void, 17–18
Bion, W.R., 40, 41, 87, 119, 153, 241
    letter "O", 113
    memory, 143
    minus-K, 137, 293
    reverie, 207
Bipolar disorder, 20
black hole:
    Mary (clinical vignette), 95–96
    psychogenic autism described as,
        84–87, 89, 91
    void experience, 91, 145–150,
        152–153
blackness: and void, 11–12
Blake, W., 26, 45, 140
    The Ancient of Days, 11, 130
Blum, D.: *Conversations with the
    Wise Old Dog*, 156
Bly, R.: The Sibling Society, 163
Boe, A., 158
Bollas, C., 251
Borderline condition:
    anonymous clinical vignette,
        105–106
    as void experience, 101–102
Buckley, J.H.: *The Ancient Sage*, 131,
    144
Buie, D.H., 101

calcinatio, 230
Calvino, *If on a Winter's Night a
    Traveller*, 46
Central America: creation myths,
    126
certainty: and the void, 71

chaos, 166
  and void, 9
Chardin, Teilhard de, 237
Charles, M., 26, 27, 136–137
  Convex and Concave:
    Part I, 247, 249
    Part II, 247, 248, 250, 251, 253
  Images of Emptiness in Men, 247
  Images of Emptiness in Women, 247
  on vagina dentata, 253–254
chasm: and void, 10
Christ: as the Word, 59
Christianity: mystical, 176
circulatio, 236
claustrum, 21, 254–255
Clint: fathers and the void (clinical
  vignette), 268–271
coagulatio, 230, 232, 236
complexes, 204
coniunctio, 230, 232, 234, 236
  in art, 237–238
consciousness, 38–39, 188–189
  changing states of, as the void,
    61–62
  collective, 60
  ego: and filling the void, 199
  Jung on, 55
  mystical, 190
  Wilber on, 54–55, 212
Cooper, J.C.: *An Encyclopaedia of
  Traditional Symbols*, 180, 250
cosmos: and void, 8–9
covering, 36–37
Cowan, L., 181
creation myths, 13, 129–132
  Babylon, 128–129
  Bantu in, 126
  Central America, 126
  the East, 126–127
  Egypt, 122–123
  Greece, 124–125
  Hindu, 128

modern West, 129
Norse, 125
Polynesia, 126–127
Rig-Veda, 127–128
creatura, 8, 59, 60, 125, 175, 188, 235

darkness:
  and light, 177–178
  and void, 10–11
David, J, 33
death: and void, 11–12, 13
defence(s):
  desire, 143
  memory, 143
  psychogenic autism
    autistic objects, 82–83, 88
    autistic shapes, 83–84, 88, 167,
      217–218
    nothingness as, 85–87
  and void, 16
  Second Skin, 23–25
deintegrates, 41
denial: and emptiness, 68
desire:
  as defence, 143
  exploring, 211–213
desolation, 210
Desteian, J.A., 19, 36
differentiation:
act of, 59–60
  as ego activity, 235–236
Dike, F.: *The Sacrifice of Kreli*,
  145–150, 159
Dimitri: void as disconnection
  (clinical vignette), 133–144
disconnection:
  clinical vignettes:
    Sarah, 283–287
    Sophia, 290–291
    Timothy, 276–279
  fathers and the void, 275–276
  void as, 133–144, 197

divine madness, *see* drunkenness
divine, the:
    connection to, 48–51
Doidge, Norman: on the Schizoid
        patient, 20–21
doodles: cases expressed as, 95–100
Dorn, 184, 185, 234
Dostoyevsky, F.M.: *Brothers
        Karamazov, The*, 114
Dourley, J.P., 40, 62, 185, 237, 239
Dream Matrix, 31
dreams, 200
drunkenness, 238–240
Dylan, B., 89, 163, 255
    Ballad of the Thin Man, 160, 171

East, the: creation myths, 127–128
*Edges of Experience: Memory and
        Emergence*
    IAAP congress, Barcelona, 30–31
Edinger, E.F., 55, 123, 171, 188
    The Anatomy of the Psyche, 255
    The Mysterium Lectures, 232
Edwards, B., 218–219
ego:
    conscious: and filling the void,
        199
    differentiation an activity of,
        235–236
    Jung on, 53
    and music, 220–221
ego-Self axis, 149–150, 153, 175
    and mother-child interaction,
        151–152
Egypt: creation myths, 122–123
Elliott, T.S., 176
Emanuel, R., 22
empirical reality: transcendental
        background, 184–185
emptiness, 63
    and denial, 68
    desire to fill, 76–77

grades of, 198
Mary (clinical vignette), 291–300
and void, 8, 18–19, 26–31, 181,
    197
see also empty of oneself
empty of oneself, 139
    clinical vignettes:
        Amity, 74–76
        Robyn, 76–77
        replacement child, 79–80
        void as being, 73–74
    see also emptiness
enantiodromia, 162, 182, 194, 238
enclosures: and knowlegde,
    223–224
English Mystic, The, 178–179, 180
    on meditation, 204
English Patient, The (film), 20–21
Erebus experience, 200–203
    Megan (clinical vignette),
        202–203
Eric: fathers and the void (clinical
    vignette), 274–275
Eros, 108
Euripides, 112
    The Bacchae, 34–36
    Iphigenia in Taurus, 245
eurythmy, 216
Eve, N.: *The Family Orchard*, 28–30
evil: God as, 180
exploration: as defence against the
    void, 113, 240–241

fall from the grace of certainty:
    void as, 71
false self: Sarah (clinical vignette),
    73–74
father, 300, 301
    symbolism, 250
fathers and the void, 258–260
    clinical vignettes:
        anonymous, 275–276

Benny, 264–268
Clint, 268–271
Eric, 274–275
Gert, 260
John 260–261
Lysander, 261–264
Sammy, 271–274
finitude, 40–42
foetus, the: and rhythm, 214–215
Fordham, M., 41
Fox, M., 185, 188
Freeth, J., 37, 182
Freud, S., 9, 55
    Id, 205
    Totem and Taboo, 111

gender *see* void, as gender
    experience
Gert: void as gender experience,
    251–252, 253, 254, 255–256,
    258–260
    fathers and the void, 260
God, 8, 304–305
    abandonment by, 115–116
    acknowledgement of, 202
    as evil, 180
    and Job, 174–176
    need for, 171–174
    rejection of, 114
    relationship with, 208, 210–211
    separation from, 178–180
    and void, 186–189
Godhead, 8, 59, 60
Good Girl (film), 15
gorge: and void, 9
Graves, R., 9, 13, 36, 124–125,
    200–201
Great Mother, 164, 250
Greece: creation myths, 124–125
grievance: as a psychic retreat,
    22
Grimm: *The Robber Bridegroom*, 69

hatred, 109–110
Hel: and void, 10
Henderson, H., 220
Hepworth, B., 238
Hesse, H., 247
Hildegard of Bingen: *A Feather on
    the Breath of God*, 221
Hill, S., 151
Hillman, J., 139
Hinduism: creation myths, 128
Hinton, Ladson, 39
Hollis, J., 252–253
Hopkins, S.M., 177
Hughes, T., 63

imagination:
    void reached through, 45–47
    see also active imagination
individuation, 231, 234, 239
infant development, 85–86
infinitude, 40–42
insight, 229–230

Jacobi, M., 86
James, W., 37, 39, 116
    *The Varieties of Religious
        Experience*, 51
Job: and God, 174–176
John: absent father (clinical
    vignette), 260–261
Johnston, W., 177, 179, 180, 210
    The Mystical Way, 36–37
    on the void, 186–187
Jung, C.G., 52, 53, 77, 108, 132, 166,
    209–210
    & Basilides: *Seven Sermons to the
        Dead*, 30, 59, 188, 235
    on active imagination, 232–233,
        236–237
    Aion, 56, 59, 238
    Answer to Job, 175
    on archetypes, 53

on being seen, 206–208
on chasm, 10
Collected Works 14, 234, 235, 236–237
on consciousness, 55
on darkness, 10
on the ego, 53
on incorrect behaviour, 114
Mysterium Coniunctionis, 57, 182–183, 185, 199–200, 230–233
on Philo Judaeus, 184
on the pleroma, 8, 60
on the Self, 182
Typology, 86

Kali, 112
Kalsched, D., 32
The Inner World of Trauma, 282
Kandinsky, W., 12, 13, 273
kenosis, 175
Khalo, F., 167
Kindalini, 212
Klein, M., 109–110
Klonsky, M., 105
knowledge, 41–42
and enclosures, 223–224
known-ness, 199–200
Kohut, H., 66
Kundera, M.: *The Book of Laughter and Forgetting*, 28

Lacan, J., 40
Lahr, J., 197
language, 70–71, 218–219
of the void, 14–15
Larkin, P., 191
Lawrence, D.H., 36, 227
Abysmal Immortality, 243–244
Basta!, 142
Lederer, W.: *Man's Fear of Women*, 163
left-brain, 205

Let Me Fall (song), 297–298
letter "O" (Bion), 113
levels: Wilber on, 56–57, 61
Lewis, C.S., 197
light: and darkness, 177–178
"lilt", 216–217
linking: and Moore, 224–225
Logos *see* Word, the
Lost Boys, the, 92
love: unifying nature of, 47–48
Lucifer, 60
Lysander: fathers and the void (clinical vignette), 261–264

Macdonald, A.M., 7, 10, 153
Macho Man, 163
Mann, T.: *The Holy Sinner*, 219
Mary:
    black hole (clinical vignette), 95–96
    emptiness (clinical vignette), 291–300
    sacrifice (clinical vignette), 154–158, 159
massa confusa, 9, 231
Mater Dolorosa, 92
maw: and void, 9
McCallum, I., 46
McCormack, E.: *Birthday Present*, 160–162, 164
McDougall, J., 194, 254
    recognition, 106
meaninglessness:
    loss of, 180
    and void, 12
Medea, 112
meditation, 180–181, 184
    English Mystic on, 204
Megan: Erebus experience (clinical vignette), 202–203
Meister Eckhart, 59, 187–189, 210
Meltzer, D., 21, 254, 304

memory:
    and aloneness, 102–103
    as defence, 143
    evocative:
        loss of and void, 102–104
        recovery of, 104
    loss of:
        and rage, 103–105
    recognition memory rage
        and void, 103
metamorphosis, 33–36
    see also skins
Milner, F., 26
    The Tree of Hope, 167
mirroring, 73, 74, 75, 77, 93–95,
    281
misattunement, 18
Mitchell, S.: introduction to Rilke's
    The Letters to a Young Poet, 79
Monster's Ball (film), 34
Moore, H., 198, 238
    Figures in a Setting, 168–169
    and linking, 224–225
Moore, T., 52, 133, 193, 210–211
mortificatio, 233–234
mother, 300, 301, 303
    dead, 92–93
    good mothering, 104
    withdrawal of, 84–85
        expressed as doodle, 98–100
    see also Great Mother
mother-child interaction: and ego-
    Self axis, 151–152
Multiple Personality Disorder,
    69
Munch, E.: Metabolism, 158
music, 47, 218–219, 272–273
    and ego, 220–221
    see also rhythm
mysticism, 54, 211
    Christian, 176
    mystical consciousness, 190

mystical experience, 58
    Wilber on, 54, 185–186
myth, 52–53

narcissism, 20
Neumann, E., 55, 174, 188, 248
    Great Mother, 9, 10, 12, 162, 250
    The History of the Origins of
        Consciousness, 250
    on Moore, 198
Nietzsche, F., 131, 166
nigredo, 231–232
Norse creation myths, 125
not-knowing: and void, 11
nothingness:
    and psychogenic autism, 85–87,
        122
    and the pleroma, 121–122, 235

Obsessive Compulsive Disorder,
    32, 264
one-sidedness: and void, 108–117
One Thing, 11
Other, 305
ouroboric, 305
Ovid: The Metamorphoses, 34
Owen, M.: Jung and the Native
    American Moon Cycles, 139

PA, 197, 214
pain: as void experience, 167
Papadopoulos, R., 112–113
passive attitude, 164–165
Pearson, J.F., 215
Pecotic, B.: The "black hole" in the
    inner universe, 89–91
penumbra, 39
Peter Pan, 92
peur aeternus, 14, 92
Piaget, J., 16, 41
Piontelli, A., 39
Piotelli, A., 215

Pleasantville (film), 254
pleroma, the, 8, 13, 55–56, 60–61, 87,
    125, 175, 184
  connection to, 48–51
  and nothingness, 121–122, 235
poetry, 219
Polynesia: creation myths, 126–127
pop culture: and void, 16
Post Natal Depression, 151
Post Traumatic Stress Disorder,
    115, 152, 230
potjie-kos, 189–190
Prince Lindworm, fairy story, 32–33
Prodigal Son, 79–80
psychic retreats, 21–22, 254
  Alan (clinical vignette), 22
psychogenic autism, 18
  autistic objects, 82–83, 88
  autistic shapes, 83–84, 88, 167,
    217–218
  as black hole, 84–87, 89, 91
  and nothingness, 85–87, 122
  skins, 88
  treatment, 87–88
psychoid boundary, 255

rage: and memory loss, 103–105
Ranson, A.: *We Didn't Mean to go to
    Sea*, 261
rebirth, 142–143
regression, 238–239
rejection: of God, 114
rejection sensitive dysphoric:
    diagnosis category, 168
religion, 52–53, 208
renewal, 162
replacement child: and being
    empty of oneself, 79–80
Representations of Interactions that
    have become Generalized
    (RIGs), 41
repression, 67

return to the womb, 169–170
reverie, 207
rhythm:
  and the foetus, 214–215
  as therapy, 214–219
  see also music
Rig-Veda, 10–11
  creation myths, 127–128
right brain, 204–205
Rilke, R.M., 5, 71, 72, 108, 121, 227,
    241, 259, 285, 302
  The Letters to a Young Poet, 23, 79
  *The Notebooks of Malte Laurids
    Brigge*, 79–80
  Sonnets to Orpheus, 126
Robbins, A., 279
Robinson, H.S., 122, 124, 125, 127
Robyn: empty of oneself (clinical
    vignette), 78–79
Rothko, M., 238
  "Seagram murals", 209
Rustin, M.: *The Therapist with her
    Back against the Wall*, 70

sacrifice, 152–154
  Mary (clinical vignette), 154–158,
    159
Sammy: fathers and the void
    (clinical vignette), 271–274
Samuels, A., 60
Sarah:
  disconnection (clinical vignette),
    283–287
  false self (clinical vignette), 73–74
Satan, 60
Satinover, J.: *The Puer Aeturus: The
    Narcissistic Relation to the Self*,
    58
Schizoid patient: Doidge on, 20–21
Schonstein Pinnock, P., 145
Schore, A.N., 204–205
Schubert, F.: *The Earl King*, 272

science: and spirituality, 58–59
Second Skin: defence against the
    void, 23–25
Self, the, 54, 58, 205, 211, 228, 237,
    304
    connection to, 48–51
    Jung on, 182
    and sound, 220
    see also ego-Self axis
Serendipity, 278–279
Sinason, V., 36
skins:
    as defence, 31–33, 88
    see also metamorphosis
Solomon, Hester, 18
Sophia: disconnection (clinical
    vignette), 290–291
sorceresses, 9
sound: and the Self, 220
spirituality: and science, 58–59
Stein, M.: Jung's Map of the Soul, 59
    regression, 238–239
Steiner, J.: Psychic Retreats:
    Pathological Organisations in
    Psychotic, Neurotic and
    Borderline Patients, 21
Steiner, R., 215–216, 254
Stern, D.N., 32, 41, 70–71, 110, 205,
    216
    The Interpersonal World of the
    Infant, 85–86
Stevens Sullivan, B., 77:
    Psychotherapy Grounded in the
    Feminine Principle, 109–110
story telling, 68–69
sublimatio, 236
symbolism:
    father, 250
    tree, 35

Tamos, R., 133
Tennyson, Alfred Lord, 153

Thanatos, 108
therapy:
    complementary therapies, 205
    rhythm as, 214–219
Thérèse of Lisieux, 178–179, 180,
    181
Thompson, J.W.M., 112
thorn-kraal, 304
Thousand Nights and One Night, 45
Three Colours Blue (film): void
    explored in, 42–45
Timothy:
    active imagination (clinical
    vignette), 242
    disconnection (clinical vignette),
    276–279
torture, 68
Touching the Void (book/film), 241
transcendental, the: background to
    empirical reality, 184–185
transformation, 230
transformative feminine, 162–165,
    256–257
transition : and void, 16
trauma, 68, 230
    effects of, 115–117
    as void experience, 152–153
treatment:
    aspects of, 195–196, 197–213
    see also therapy
tree: symbolism, 35
Trudeau, Gary, 52
Truth and Reconciliation
    Commission, 117
    on perpetrators of violence,
    113–114
Tustin, F., 43
    psychogenic autism:
        autistic object, 82–83, 88
        autistic shapes, 83–84, 88, 167,
        217–218
        black hole, 84–85, 89, 91

nothingness as defence, 85–87
  skin, 88
  treatment, 87–88
Typology, 86

unio mentalis, 183, 230–231, 231
unio mystica, 57
unio naturalis, 231
  in art, 237–238
unus mundus, 183, 184
uroboric, 305

"vacant": as void, 27
vagina dentata: void and gender,
    253–256
Valman, H.B., 215
Vaughan, Stevie Ray, 101
Viola, B., 211
violence, 111, 117, 113–114
virtuousness, 239
void, the, 7–13, 16, 303–304
  and abandonment, 67
  and absence, 215
  and absence of proof, 69
  abyss as 9
  active imagination, 227–229,
      233–234, 239, 241–243, 287–290
  and aloneness, 102–103, 221–223
  and anaesthesia, 39–40
  and anomie, 16–17
  as being empty of oneself, 73–74,
      139
  and Big Bang, 17–18
  as black hole, 91, 145–150,
      152–153
  and blackness 11–12
  Borderline condition as, 101–102,
      105–106
  and certainty, 71
  and changing states of
      consciousness, 61–62
  and chaos, 9

  and chasm, 10
  and cosmos, 8–9
  and death, 11–12, 13
  and darkness and light, 177–178
  and differentiating, 235–236
  as disconnection, 133–144, 197
  as distance from God, 58
  as empty of oneself, 73–74
  and emptiness, 8, 18–19, 26–31,
      181, 197
  and Erebus experience, 200–203
  experiencing, 203–204
  exploration as defence against,
      113, 240–241
  as fall from the grace of certainty,
      71
  and fathers, 258–260, 260–261,
      264–268
  filling: conscious ego, 199
  as a gender experience, 300–302
      feminine, 280–283
      masculine, 247–251, 251–252,
          255–256, 260–261
      vagina dentata, 253–256
  God and, 186–189
  as gorge, 9
  as the great unknown, 60–61
  and Hel, 10
  and imagination, 45–47
  Johnston on, 186–187
  language of, 14–15
  and light and darkness, 177–178
  as maw, 9
  and meaninglessness, 12
  and memory loss, 102–104
  music, 220–221and not-knowing,
      11
  and one-sidedness, 108–117
  pain as, 167
  and pop culture, 17
  in practice, 13–14
  as primary experience, 40–42

as psychogenic autism, 82–88
reached through imagination,
    45–47
and Second Skin, 23–25
as secondary experience, 38–40
in *Three Colours Blue*, 42–45
and transition, 16
as trauma, 152–153
and 'vacant', 27
and whiteness, 13
volvas, 9

war, 111–112
Watson, S., 219
Weinberg, S., 123
West, the: creation myths, 129
White, P.: *The Solid Mandala*,
    141
whiteness: and void, 13
wholeness, 205
Why, the: quest for, 208–210
Wilber, K.:
    on archetypes, 54
    consciousness, 54–55, 212
    on the Godhead, 60
    Grace and Grit, 180, 183
    levels, 56–57, 61
    on mysticism, 54, 185–186
Wilkinson, P., 121, 123
Williams, G., 27

Wilma:
    active imagination (clinical
        vignette), 227–229, 233–234,
        239, 243
    void and gender (clinical
        vignette, 280–283
Wilson, K., 122, 124, 125, 127
Winnicott, D., 65, 84, 88, 115, 205,
    260, 302
    The Capacity to be Alone, 221–222
    Hate in the Countertransference,
        109
    infant in need, 138
Wisechild, L.: *The Obsidian Mirror*,
    299
Witness, the, 57, 90–91
womb: return to, 169–170
Word, the: 123, 205
    Christ as, 59
Wordsworth, W.:
    *Composed upon an Evening of
        Extraordinary Splendour and
        Beauty*, 49–51, 179
    *Ode on Intimations of Immortality
        from Recollections of early
        Childhood*, 48–49, 55
Wright, K.: *Vision and Separation*,
    174, 189

Xhosa tradition: diviners in, 146